THE CLINICAL CHILD INTERVIEW

The Guilford School Practitioner Series

EDITORS

STEPHEN N. ELLIOTT, Ph.D.
University of Wisconsin—Madison

JOSEPH C. WITT, Ph.D.
Louisiana State University, Baton Rouge

THE CLINICAL
CHILD INTERVIEW

JAN N. HUGHES, Ph.D.
Texas A&M University

DAVID B. BAKER, Ph.D.
University of North Texas

THE GUILFORD PRESS
New York   London

© 1990 The Guilford Press
A Division of Guilford Publications, Inc.
72 Spring Street, New York, NY 10012

Printed in the United States of America

This book is printed on acid-free paper.

Last digit is print number: 9 8 7 6 5 4 3

Library of Congress Cataloging-in-Publication Data

Hughes, Jan N., 1949–
    The clinical child interview / Jan N. Hughes, David B. Baker.
        p.   cm.–(The Guilford school practitioner series)
    Includes bibliographical references and index.
    ISBN 0-89862-361-8 (hardcover). – ISBN 0-89862-240-9 (pbk.)
    1. Interviewing in child psychiatry.   I. Baker, David B.
II. Series.
    [DNLM: 1. Child Behavior Disorders–diagnosis.   2. Interview,
Psychological–in infancy & childhood.   3. Interview, Psycho-
logical–methods.   4. Mental Disorders–diagnosis.   5. Mental
Disorders–in infancy & childhood.
WS 350 H893c]
RJ503.6.H84 1991
618.92′89075–dc20
DNLM/DLC
for Library of Congress   91-6501
                                                                   CIP

To Beeman Phillips for his mentorship
—JNH—

To my family
—DBB—

About the Authors

JAN N. HUGHES directs the doctoral program in school psychology at Texas A&M University, where she is an associate professor in the Department of Educational Psychology. She is author of *Cognitive Behavior Therapy with Children in the Schools,* coeditor of *Cognitive–Behavioral Psychology in the Schools,* and author of numerous articles on child and school psychology published in scholarly journals. A licensed psychologist since 1978, she maintains a private practice in affiliation with a pediatric clinic.

DAVID B. BAKER obtained his doctorate in counseling psychology from Texas A&M University in 1988. He is an assistant professor of psychology at the University of North Texas. His teaching and research activities are in the areas of child psychopathology, child assessment, and child psychotherapy. His practice in clinical child and family psychology is in Denton, Texas.

Contents

I

THEORETICAL AND DEVELOPMENTAL FOUNDATION

1

The Child Interview: Rationale, Purposes, and Evidence of Utility

Interest in child interviewing has increased dramatically in recent years. This increased interest is a result, primarily, of two developments. First, considerable evidence has accumulated to contradict the assumption that children are inaccurate reporters of their behaviors and internal states. Indeed, children provide more accurate and clinically meaningful information concerning some aspects of their functioning than do parents or teachers (Edelbrock, Costello, Dulcan, Kalas, & Conover, 1985; Garber, 1984). Second, the view that affective and cognitive variables mediate behavioral difficulties has gained preeminence in American psychology (Bandura, 1989; Mahoney, 1974). If internal events mediate behavior, assessment of these processes is warranted.

If one wants to understand a child's beliefs, perceptions, reasoning ability, attitudes, and affective experiences that have relevance to the child's current difficulties, it is logical to ask the child to report on these self-processes. The ways of asking children to report on these processes, however, must differ from the ways of asking adults, because children possess different communicative abilities. The child interviewer must learn interview strategies that enable children to communicate competently and to share with others their rich and complex subjective experiences. The following quotation emphasizes the fact that the value of information derived from a child interview depends on both the child *and* the interviewer:

> Young children are able to describe their thoughts and feelings, but they require specialized interview techniques to do so. Moreover, characteristics

1

of conceptual organization and information processing associated with cognitive and linguistic development result in a phenomenological world for the young child that is qualitatively different from the adults' world. Clinicians who are unfamiliar with the thought processes associated with various developmental levels are likely to find children's reasoning exceedingly difficult to follow or comprehend. To conduct effective child interviews, clinicians must both acquire an understanding of the characteristics of developing social cognitive processes and ... must make some major adjustments in their interviewing techniques and strategies. (Bierman, 1983, pp. 218–219)

A similar sentiment is expressed by McNamee (1989, p. 90): "What adults learn from talking with young children has as much to do with the adult's competency, sensitivity, and knowledge about the child and his way of thinking and speaking as it does with the child's linguistic competencies."

CHILD INTERVIEWING
AND RECIPROCAL DETERMINISM

Behavioral approaches to child assessment and therapy have dominated child clinical and school psychology during the past two decades. Whereas contemporary behavioral theory incorporates cognitive constructs into assessment and intervention methods, traditional behavioral assessment and intervention practices have focused almost exclusively on observable behaviors and the functional relationships between behavior and environmental factors. Thus, such assessment efforts are focused on identifying appropriate target behaviors and determining the antecedent and consequent conditions in the environment that elicit and maintain these behaviors. The assessment is followed by strategies to modify target behaviors through the systematic alteration of antecedent conditions and of reinforcement and punishment contingencies. Because the individual's self-processes (e.g., beliefs, attitudes, interpretations) are not incorporated into behavioral change strategies, they receive little or no attention in the assessment of behavioral difficulties. According to the strict behavioral view, "internal events are epiphenomenal by-products of conditioned responses that do not enter into the determination of action" (Bandura, 1989, p. 1175). In this view, child self-report data have little relevance to the assessment, because adults' reports yield more accurate factual information, and because naturalistic observations provide information on the functional relationships between target behaviors and environmental conditions.

When child self-report data are obtained in traditional behavioral assessment, the type of information that children are asked to provide is restricted to reinforcement preferences and factual information about the functional relationship between the environment and behavior. Children younger than 5 years of age are viewed as unable to provide any useful information, whereas older children may be asked to report on "various situations at home and/or at school in an attempt to obtain the child's perception about what is happening in these problem situations. Sometimes such questioning is fruitless; other times the child's understanding of the situation and the role he or she plays is quite accurate" (Atkeson & Forehand, 1981, p. 196). This view of the child's communicative inadequacies ignores the fact that "communicative skill is an attribute of speaker–listener pairs, not just the speaker" (Melton & Thompson, 1987, p. 216).

The well-chronicled cognitive revolution in psychology, which began in the 1960s and achieved maturity in the 1980s, has brought with it an appreciation for the role of self-processes in mediating the influence of the environment on behavior. Eschewing a unidirectional model of causation, social-cognitive theory postulates a triadic, reciprocally deterministic model of causality. According to this view, behavior, self-referent processes (both affective and cognitive), and environmental events operate as interacting determinants (Bandura, 1969, 1977, 1989). Reciprocal determinism is central to cognitive–behavioral therapy, which attempts to modify problematic behavior by focusing on cognitive processes assumed to be proximal determinants of behavior.

Although reciprocal determinism has gained broad support in American psychology, the development of methods of assessing self-processes has lagged behind both theoretical advances and advances in the development of effective cognitive–behavioral therapies. Thus, child clinicians continue to rely primarily on behavioral assessment strategies and assessment strategies based on trait theories of personality. The purpose of this book is to present guidelines for interviewing children that permit children to report on their beliefs, perceptions, expectancies, and interpretations of experience, which in turn inform decisions about treatment planning, execution, and evaluation.

This chapter presents the general advantages of the child interview, reviews research on the reliability and validity of the child interview, and delineates dimensions on which child interviews differ. Chapter 2 reviews developmental changes in children's social-cognitive processes and memory. Implications of these developmental issues for interviewing are stated as practice guidelines.

Part II of the book discusses interviewing within the context of three theoretical orientations, or traditions, in child assessment: psychodynamic, psychometric, and behavioral. Interview approaches consistent with each tradition are reviewed and evaluated, and interview excerpts illustrate each approach.

Part III discusses disorder-specific interview strategies and pragmatic considerations in interviewing children who present with one of the two major classifications of childhood psychopathology: internalizing and externalizing disorders. The two chapters in this section illustrate how information from the interview is integrated with other assessment information to increase the completeness and treatment utility of the assessment.

INTERVIEWING AS DIFFERENT FROM THERAPY

The clinical interview is a venerable tradition in adult clinical psychology (Benjamin, 1969; Wiens, 1983). Not surprisingly, definitions of interviewing are more appropriate to interviewing adults than to interviewing children. For example, the interview is described as a primarily verbal process in which the interviewer exerts control, in the sense that he or she initiates and terminates the verbal exchanges (Martin, 1988). The child interview, however, may be more nonverbal than verbal, and the child may be given considerable freedom to initiate topics and to select the format for the interaction (e.g., to choose to communicate through drawings, toys, or words). Providing the child with a relatively large degree of control in the interview is supported by research documenting that young children's memories are best for those events for which the children initiate the discussion and are allowed to report on events with minimal interference from the interviewer (Todd & Perlmutter, 1980).

Although a given interview may both yield assessment information and promote therapeutic change, an interview is typically undertaken primarily for assessment or therapeutic purposes. The following definition of the child interview has guided the selection of content and emphasis in this book: The child interview is a face-to-face interaction of bidirectional influence, entered into for the purpose of assessing aspects of the child's functioning that have relevance to planning, implementing, or evaluating treatment. Interviewing that is the method of therapeutic intervention, as in some types of therapy, is not the focus of this book.

BENEFITS OF THE CHILD INTERVIEW

Knowledge of the Child's Subjective Experience

Individuals actively construe meaning from their experiences. Rather than being passive recipients of environmental influences, they selectively perceive and respond to certain aspects of their experiences, interpret experiences in light of what they know about themselves and the world, distort experiences according to their beliefs, formulate expectations about their ability to perform responses, anticipate outcomes associated with different responses, attach values to these outcomes, select goals, and generate plans to achieve goals. These cognitive processes regulate their interactions with their environment. Thus, a focus on assessing and changing these processes is both reasonable and practical, as attested by a growing body of literature (see Kistner & Torgesen, 1987; Hughes, 1988; Hughes & Hall, 1989). The interview is uniquely suited to collecting information on these covert processes and events, collectively referred to as one's "subjective experience." Consider the following children.

Case 1

Cheryl, 9 years old, was an attractive Hispanic girl with long dark hair. Cheryl and her twin sister, Beth, were both in the second grade; however, Beth attended a class for pupils classified as educable mentally retarded, whereas Cheryl attended a regular second-grade class. Cheryl had a 3-year-old brother, Ben, who was developing normally in all areas. Both Cheryl and Beth had been adopted at 1 year of age, when their biological mother lost parental rights because of her severe neglect of the girls. At the time of adoption, both girls had significant developmental delays. Whereas Beth continued to have general cognitive delays and delays in adaptive behavior, Cheryl performed within the average range on tests of intelligence. Cheryl, however, was socially withdrawn, especially at school. At home, she complained if she was asked to do any chores, and she showed little interest in such independence-seeking behaviors as riding her bike around the neighborhood or visiting at friends' houses. Since the beginning of school 5 months earlier, she had often failed to complete her classwork and homework, and her teacher described her as "sad-looking" and "low on energy." On both the teacher and parent forms of the Child Behavior Checklist (Achenbach & Edelbrock, 1983), Cheryl was described as uncommunicative, depressed, and anxious.

During the first interview, Cheryl reported that she had no friends at school and that she did not think anyone would want to be her friend. The interviewer presented a drawing depicting two girls playing a game of jacks and a third girl standing off to the side. The interviewer asked Cheryl what the third girl might be feeling and thinking. Cheryl said that the third girl was thinking she would like to play, but that the other girls would probably not want her to play. If she asked to play, she would probably do something silly and the girls would laugh. Cheryl reported using recess time to work on class assignments she did not have time to finish. She also stated that she would like to be 3 years old because she would not be expected to do chores and would get more attention and help, like her brother. She wanted to be a mommy when she grew up so she could stay at home. She talked a great deal about Ben, with whom she reported spending most of her play time. In the initial unstructured part of the interview, Cheryl made frequent references to Ben in her play, and her play themes were similar to those of a preschool or kindergarten child. When asked to draw a picture of her family, she drew herself the same size as Ben.

The interview provided information about Cheryl's subjective experience that would be important in selecting treatment goals and methods. Cheryl believed that she was not capable of interacting successfully with her same-age peers, and she avoids interaction by working on assignments at recess. The prospect of growing up threatened her relationships with Beth and Ben, and she believed that growing up would mean less nurturance and more responsibility. The recommended treatment included social skills training that emphasizes the behavioral skills of joining in, participating, and making conversation, as well as coping self-talk. Cheryl's parents were encouraged to treat their children differently and to emphasize the positive aspects of increased independence (e.g., shopping trips with a parent to select own clothes, books, and school supplies; cooking lessons with the mother; piano lessons). Cheryl's teacher was advised to provide social reinforcement for Cheryl's interactions with peers and to pair Cheryl with other girls for classroom projects.

Case 2

Chris was a 10-year-old boy referred for counseling because of his aggressiveness and defiance at school and at home. As part of the assessment of Chris's behavioral difficulties, the interviewer used a semi-structured interview patterned on Selman's (Selman, Jacquette, & Bruss-Saunders, 1979) social reasoning interview (Hughes, 1989). The interview revealed that Chris's reasoning about friendships was immature, as he defined friends in terms of physical possessions (e.g., "He has a trampoline") and proximity instead of personal characteristics. In addition, Chris tended to infer aggressive intent to peers' actions. For example, he recounted an incident in which the joystick to his computer broke while a friend was playing with it, and he thought the friend broke it on purpose because he was jealous. He did not seem to understand the importance of collecting information upon which to base one's decisions about another's motives (e.g., ask the friend how it happened).

His solutions to social problems were almost exclusively aggressive rather than prosocial.

The information yielded by the interview suggested that Chris was unable to perceive social situations accurately and was deficient in generating nonaggressive solutions to conflict. A social skills remediation program recommended for Chris included training in attending to more social cues (instead of only those cues consistent with hostile intent) and in evaluating social cues. The interviewer suggested that playing detective games in which the task was to find out why a protagonist acted as he or she did, and memory games in which the task was to remember as many "cues" as possible, might improve Chris's ability to interpret social situations. Role plays might be effective in helping Chris to take the perspective of another person and in improving Chris's social problem-solving skills.

Case 3

The third case study provides the most dramatic evidence of the value of the child interview. Carrie, age 4, was referred for counseling by her father and preschool teacher because Carrie had become socially withdrawn at school and overly fearful at home following the accidental death of her mother 6 months ago. Carrie had been in the truck when her mother stepped out of the car to check her rural mail box. The truck had slipped gears and backed over the mother, killing her. The father had not been able to discuss the mother's death with Carrie at the time because of his own emotional anguish, and now Carrie refused to talk about her mother or the accident.

During the second diagnostic play session, Carrie continued with a game begun in the first session, playing with the toy cars. When she had something to say to the interviewer, she used the toy phone and insisted that the interviewer use the other phone. In this manner, she maintained control over the conversation, and she hung up whenever she wanted to. She enacted a car wreck, with police cars and ambulances screeching, which she reported from her phone. Frequently, she would hang up the phone because she needed to turn the pancakes or whatever. The interviewer made empathic comments such as "That sounds scary," and asked about the events depicted in Carrie's play (e.g., "Is anybody hurt?"). Carrie described the scene (blood all over the ground, the mommy's head turned around), and then said that the little girl had been "bad" and had gotten out of her car seat. At this point, she began to cry, and the interviewer was able to comfort her: "It is very scary. The little girl thinks she was bad, but it is not her fault—she is just a little girl and did not know better."

The play interview revealed both Carrie's struggle to resolve her feelings concerning a traumatic event and her feelings of guilt. In subsequent play therapy sessions, Carrie continued to reenact the trauma until she resolved her feelings of loss and guilt. The therapist's acceptance of her feelings and reassurances were important to Carrie's progress.

Observational Opportunities

An important advantage of the child interview is the opportunity it affords for direct observation of important aspects of the child's functioning, including behavioral, cognitive, and emotional functioning. The nature of the observations made will depend on the type and purpose of the interview. Table 1.1 lists behaviors that may be observed during the interview. Some of these behaviors can be observed in the child's play in natural settings or in direct testing of the child. Those aspects of the child's functioning that can be best observed in a clinical interview include social reasoning, interpersonal behaviors, and emotional expression.

TABLE 1.1. Child Characteristics to Observe in Interview

Responsiveness to limit setting
Impulsivity
Distractibility
Reaction to frustration
Reactance to praise
Level of organization in play
Communicative competence
Responsiveness to interviewer (human relationship capacity)
Emotional reactions to different topics
Recurring themes in play and conversation
Social reasoning
Nervous mannerisms
Range, degree, and appropriateness of affect expressed
Physical and neurological development
Mood
Use of environment
Motor coordination
Attention span
Activity level
Logic of thought

Social Reasoning

Knowing how children organize their experiences and how they reason about themselves and others has important implications for diagnosing and treating emotional and behavioral disturbances. The interview provides excellent opportunities to observe a child's reasoning about social relationships. Children typically develop the ability to reason about interpersonal relationships (i.e., social reasoning) and to reason about inanimate relationships (i.e., logico-physical reasoning) concurrently. Thus, one can usually predict a child's level of social reasoning from knowledge of that child's level of logico-physical reasoning. Some children reason in the social sphere at a level significantly below their logico-physical reasoning level. Such discrepancies between logico-physical reasoning and social reasoning are more common in emotionally disturbed children than in normal children (Selman, 1976). Specifically, these children tend to lag behind their peers in social reasoning, and these differences presumably contribute to their difficulties relating to peers (Selman, 1976).

Although social reasoning abilities can be assessed with formal, semi-structured interview procedures (Selman, 1980), these interview procedures require extensive training and are time-consuming to administer and to score. Thus, they are used primarily in research endeavors. Equipped with knowledge of the stages of social reasoning, the interviewer knows what is expected of a child of a given age and can detect immature or advanced social reasoning. Chapter 2 discusses developmental progressions in children's social reasoning and implications of these developmental changes for the child interview. Two aspects of social reasoning are discussed next in order to illustrate opportunities within the interview to assess such reasoning.

Multiple Feelings. Several researchers (Donaldson & Westerman, 1986; Harter, 1982; Harter & Buddin, 1983) have investigated children's ability to coordinate contradictory feelings toward the same person or event at the same time. This capacity represents an important developmental achievement, as it enables children to maintain stable relationships with others, despite conflicts, and to integrate their emotional experiences without reliance on denial of negative feelings or behaviors. Young children find it difficult to integrate information with opposite valences, such as "happy–sad" or "mad–loving." For example, when 5- and 8-year-olds are told a story in which a doctor (positive valence) becomes a thief (negative valence), they deny that the story character is still a doctor. However, these children are able to accept that a daddy becomes a doctor (same valence) (Saltz & Medow, 1971).

Donaldson and Westerman (1986) have provided evidence that young children's difficulty with coordinating conflicting feelings may be based on their reasoning about the causes of feelings. Under 6 years of age, children seem to believe that feelings are directly evoked by events. They do not act as though internal states, including thoughts and memories of events or persons, mediate emotions. Rather, feelings are momentary experiences evoked by events. When Daddy punishes, the child believes Daddy is "bad." The child's momentary feelings toward his or her daddy is unaffected by positive memories. Children 7 to 8 years old are in transition between locating feelings in events that give rise to them and relating them to internal events, including stable perceptions of the qualities of the person or events and memories. They recognize that contradictory feelings can coexist toward the same object, but they explain feelings in terms of a temporal or spatial dimension. Thus, a child reports that a story child would feel sad about losing his or her dog and happy about getting a new puppy. The child does not understand that the conflicting feelings interact with each other and modify each other. The 10-year-old recognizes that two contradictory feelings can coexist at the same time toward the same object. Furthermore, the contradictory feelings modulate each other. Thus, older children report true ambivalence in the sense of mixed feelings, and they know that feelings are elicited and mediated by inner processes.

In an interview, children may deny their misbehaviors, even in the face of clear evidence that they engaged in the "bad" behavior. A child's denial may be a result of his or her inability to integrate contradictory feelings. For a child to admit to "bad" behavior or feelings, the child would have to see himself or herself as "all bad." The young child's inability to integrate contradictory feelings leads to all-or-none expressions of feelings that are temporary. For example, a young boy may report, "I hate my daddy" because his daddy has punished him. When his daddy gives him a treat, he loves his daddy again. Such a child lacks even a rudimentary ability to coordinate conflicting feelings, and the child's relationships with others are likely to fluctuate.

Person Perception. Several studies have documented a shift in how children think about others. The direction of change is from focusing on overt characteristics of persons to focusing on persons' stable traits and dispositions (e.g., Livesley & Bromley, 1973; Rholes & Ruble, 1984). This shift is similar to the shift in reasoning about feelings from focusing on external events to focusing on internal processes. Preschool children's descriptions of people are limited in number, undifferentiated, and concrete (Livesely & Bromley, 1973). They focus on a few physical and behavior characteristics ("He is big with dark hair," " He walks funny") and on characteristics that have high personal salience to them ("She gives me candy"). Their perceptions of others exist on two global dimensions, "good–bad" and "strong–weak" (Saltz, Dumin-Markiewicz, & Rourke, 1975). By middle childhood, children use more constructs, and their conceptions are more complex and differentiated (Livesley & Bromley, 1973). They make comparisons, such as "Jane draws better than Sally" or "Joe throws the ball the best in the class," but comparisons are based on overt behaviors as opposed to psychological traits (Barenboim, 1977). Children under 10 years old are limited in making inferences about individuals' traits and dispositions. After age 11, children can reason inductively about persons; for example, they can conclude that a person is shy after multiple observations of the person (Barenboim, 1977).

In a typical child interview, the child is asked to describe their relationships with others and to describe others. Thus, the interviewer has an opportunity to observe the complexity and distinctiveness of the child's personal constructs.

Interpersonal Behaviors

The clinical child interview provides an excellent opportunity to observe a child's capacity to relate to others and characteristic relational approaches. Although the child's responsiveness to the interviewer should not be expected to generalize to all interpersonal relationships, it does provide diagnostic information regarding the child's way of relating to people. Rutter and Graham (1968) found that interviewers' ratings of children's emotional responsiveness and relationship with the interviewers correlated better than their other ratings did with children's level of psychiatric impairment.

The interview offers the opportunity to observe a child's use of eye contact, sense of humor, appropriateness of conversation, use of polite language, and other social skills. Does the child express an interest in the interviewer as a person (e.g., by asking whether the children in the pictures on the desk are the interviewer's children)? Does the child seem apprehensive about the interviewer, keeping at some distance physically and disclosing very little information? Some children are overly accepting of the interviewer, asking a string of nonstop questions, inviting the interviewer to play too, and demanding the interviewer's constant involvement with them. These children are often emotionally needy and are nondiscriminatory in their acceptance of adults. Some children share control in the interview, whereas others try to control the interviewer by making numerous demands and resisting the interviewer's efforts to structure the interaction. Conversely, some children respond passively in the interview, showing reluctance to make any decisions on their own or to express their preferences or opinions. The following two children expressed very different relationship capacities.

Relationship Capacities. Larry, age 7, was referred for fighting and stealing in his first-grade classroom. He ran into the play room, glancing at the interviewer. He then went to the corner with the cars and began crashing them together, with his back to the interviewer. When the interviewer responded nondirectively with statements such as "You like the cars I have," Larry did not respond. Larry next began to play in the sand box, building tunnels and bridges. The interviewer handed Larry a Lincoln Log for a bridge, but Larry reached for his own log. Larry continued to explore the toys in the play room while rejecting the interviewer's attempts to establish some reciprocity. When the interviewer said that their time was over for the day, Larry bounded out of the room without acknowledging the interviewer's "good-bye." Larry was aloof and detached with adults, and he did not view adults as sources of help or support. The interviewer felt no sense of connectedness with him.

Larry was very different from Gregory, age 8, who was referred for a "nervous stomach." He frequently felt nauseated at school and had to go home. Gregory walked beside the interviewer on the way to the play room. He also selected the cars to play with, but he turned toward the interviewer and directed comments and questions to her ("My best friend had a car like this. He moved away"). He talked about the model car his father had given him, and stated that his father did not have time to play with him since he had taken a new job that required evening hours. The new baby in the family was sick, and his daddy needed to make more money. He asked whether it would be okay for him to bring his model car next time so that he and the interviewer could work on it together. Gregory was lonely and felt sad about his father's lack of involvement in his life. The interviewer felt connected with Gregory and believed that Gregory would respond positively to short-term counseling, to help him recognize and cope with his feelings of loss and to establish new social support systems.

Control. In standardized testing situations, the examiner imposes a high level of structure and control, so that the child's test results can be compared with those of the standardization sample. Although some types of interviews, especially the diagnostic interviews reviewed in Chapter 3, offer limited opportunity for the child to exert control in the interview, semistructured and unstructured interviews involve more shared control over the content, pace, and form of communication.

Some children share this control well, whereas other children either dominate or wait for the interviewer to offer structure and control. Mary, 7 years old, refused to go to school and complained of headaches and tummyaches on school mornings. After explainingthe purpose of the interview, the interviewer asked Mary whether she would like to begin getting acquainted by drawing together. Mary said she did not want to draw but would like to paint with the water colors. She began to issue directives to the interviewer, telling her what to paint and where to sit, and directing her to go get clean water and to put the lids back on the paints. She was meticulous in her painting, counting the petals on each flower to assure sameness and using a ruler to make the grass level. After painting, the interviewer said it was time to do some different kinds of work. Mary began to clean her brush and instructed the interviewer to wipe the smeared paint and not to let anyone else use the paints until she came back. Mary's need for control over the situation and the interviewer reflected her insecurities and coping strategies. At school, she wss not able to exert that level of control over her environment and felt threatened.

Range and Degree of Emotional Expression

During the interview, the interviewer is able to observe the child's range and intensity of emotional expression, as well as the child's predominant mood and differential responsiveness to different topics. Cory, age 10, was referred for rapidly falling grades and difficulty concentrating in class. During a semistructured interview, Cory was asked about his friends, family relationships, schoolwork, hobbies, and sports. Although Cory was generally calm during the interview, when he was asked questions about his music lessons he began shifting in his seat, his voice faltered, and his face flushed. Rather than pursuing this topic further in the intake interview, the interviewer brought it up again during the second interview, when Cory revealed that his music teacher had sexually molested him. He felt terribly guilty about the incident and frightened that it would happen again. He had told his parents he wanted to quit violin lessons, but they thought he was just trying to get out of the work of practicing.

Loretta, age 13, was referred for falling grades, lack of energy, and social withdrawal. During the interview, she spoke slowly and in a flat, monotone voice; she rarely made eye contact with the examiner; and she did not smile in response to the interviewer's attempts at humor. Even when describing things she reported enjoying doing, her affect remained depressed. When asked to draw a picture, she drew a landscape with little detail and dark colors, and made self-disparaging comments about her drawing ability. She expressed a sense of hopelessness about the future and a low self-concept. When asked to tell what she liked about herself, she was unable to name anything at first. With prodding, she stated that she did not pick on her little sister as much as she used to. Loretta's emotional expression in the interview, combined with questionnaire and history data, contributed to the diagnosis of a major depressive episode.

Flexibility and Breadth of Interview

Additional advantages of the child interview are the flexibility and breadth of coverage that the interview format makes possible. The flexible approach permits the interviewer to cover a wide range of behavioral and emotional functioning while obtaining more detailed information concerning problem areas. These dual purposes, breadth and depth, are accomplished by interview formats that permit the interviewer to make general inquiries regarding a child's functioning in a particular content area, followed by more specific questions when the child's response to the general inquiry suggests problems in that area. For example, the Child Assessment Schedule (CAS; Hodges, Kline, Stern, Cytryn, & McKnew, 1982) consists of 75 questions in 11 content areas. The child obtains a score for each of the content areas and each of nine symptom complexes (Table 1.2). If a child reports problems in a content area or symptom complex, the interviewer asks more detailed questions in that area. Following the interview, the psychologist can administer narrow-band, high-fidelity instruments relevant to problem areas or symptom complexes identified in the interview. For example, if the child reports problems with impulsivity and concentration in school work, the psychologist can follow the interview with task performance measures of impulsivity (e.g., Matching Familiar Figures Test; Kagan, 1966), as well as teacher- and parent-completed measures of impulsivity and inattentiveness (e.g., Conners Teacher Rating Scale; Conners, 1969). Contributing to the flexibility of some interviews is a built-in "skip" structure. For example, the Schedule for Affective Disorders and Schizophrenic for School-Age Children (Kiddie-SADS; Puig-Antich & Chambers, 1978), a diagnostic interview schedule, permits the interviewer to skip questions in a section when the child's response to an initial question indicates that a particular symptom is not present. Both the CAS and the Kiddie-SADS are discussed in greater detail in Chapter 3.

Breadth is an important asset in initial assessment procedures because a child may be referred for one problem but the interview may uncover a more fundamental problem, as occurred in the case of Cory,

TABLE 1.2. Content Areas and Symptoms Compexes Scored from the Child Assessment Schedule (CAS)

Content areas	Symptom Complexes
School	Attention Deficit Disorder with Hyperactivity
Friends	Attention Deficit Disorder without Hyperactivity
Activities	Undersocialized Conduct Disorder-Aggressive
Family	Undersocialized Conduct Disorder-Unaggressive
Fears	Socialized Conduct Disorder
Worries	Separation Anxiety Disorder
Self-Image	Overanxious Disorder
Mood	Oppositional Defiant Disorder
Somatic Concerns	Depression
Expression of Anger	
Thought Disorder	

Note. Adapted from "The Development of a Child Assessment Interview for Research and Clinical Use" by K. Hodges, J. Kline, L. Stern, L. Cytryn, and D. McKnew, 1982, *Journal of Abnormal Child Psychology, 10,* p. 181. Copyright 1982 by Plenum Publishing Corporation. Adapted by Permission.

the boy referred for concentration problems who had been sexually molested. In addition, the interview provides information that will help in treatment planning, such as the need to include the parents in treatment, potential reinforcers available to the child for use in a reinforcement contingency program, and the child's willingness and motivation to cooperate in subsequent treatment.

The interview's flexibility permits the interviewer to alter how questions are asked. If an initial attempt to obtain information is unsuccessful, the interviewer can rephrase the question (e.g., by making it more concrete or by giving response alternatives from which the child selects an answer), shift to another topic and return to the first topic at a more opportune time, or alter the way the child responds (e.g., by pointing or drawing a picture rather than by answering verbally). Bierman (1983) gives an example of reducing the child's perception of a question's threat by having the child answer for a pretend character rather than for himself or herself. For example, if a young girl is hesitant to answer a direct question about why she stays outside at recess but doesn't play, the interviewer can present a situation with dolls in which two girls are playing and a third girl is watching. The interviewer asks the girl, "Why do you think this girl is watching instead of playing?" Bierman (1983) also cautions the interviewer that a child's unwillingness to respond to a question may reflect the child's attempt to defend against the threat of harm or loss (anxiety) that the question elicits. If the interviewer forces the issue by encouraging or pressuring the child to answer the question, the child may assume a more defensive and less adaptive posture. During the interview, the interviewer must be sensitive to the child's emotional reactions and gauge the child's willingness to express feelings and thoughts about topics raised in the interview.

Techniques for reducing threat in interviewing require flexibility. For example, if a child is unable or unwilling to express feelings with words, the interviewer can describe some situations and ask the child to point to the picture that shows how he or she would feel in that situation. The interviewer can reduce the complexity and the threat of the question by providing the child with alternatives and suggesting that other children may feel the same way the child feels. For example, "All children sometimes get mad at their moms. Do you tell your mom you are mad at her, or do you do something that lets her know you are mad?"

Some children find it easier to express thoughts and feelings in the context of a game, such as the Talking, Feeling, and Doing Game (Gardner, l983). The game provides a familiar social context to school-age children. Children are more capable of communicating their thoughts and feelings when they are provided with a familiar context (Melton & Thompson, 1987).

Facilitation of the Therapeutic Relationship

When the interview is likely to be followed by a counseling relationship, the interview facilitates the reciprocal communication necessary to effective counseling (Bierman & Schwartz, l986a). Similarly, if a child feels involved in the assessment process, the child is more likely to cooperate with the treatment that follows the assessment (Witt, Cavell, Heffer, Carey, & Martens, l988). For example, when a girl reports in the interview that she feels lonely and wants more friends, and this information is used to select the treatment goal of improving the child's friendship-making skills, she is likely to cooperate with the treatment. Research on treatment acceptability suggests that children's perceptions of the acceptability of an intervention affect intervention effectiveness (Turco, Elliott, & Witt, 1985). Thus, obtaining children's perceptions of the need for treatment as well as their preferences for different intervention activities is likely to result in greater cooperation, which in turn is likely to result in greater treatment effectiveness.

On the other hand, if a child's initial contact with the psychologist involves a relationship in which the psychologist has a high level of interpersonal control, as is necessary in standardized testing, the child is likely to find it difficult to assume control in the counseling relationship. Yet counseling depends on the child's active participation by sharing experiences, thoughts, and feelings. When children experience little control in a conversation with adults, they reveal little of their thoughts, feelings, or intentions (Wood & Wood, 1983).

If testing is indicated, it is better to begin with an unstructured or semistructured interview. Once the child assumes the more passive role of providing answers to the examiner's questions, it is difficult for the child to shift to a more collaborative role.

RELIABILITY AND VALIDITY OF CHILD INTERVIEW DATA

Questions concerning the reliability and validity of child interview data can best be answered by addressing several more specific questions: Do children report accurately on their experiences? Are their reports reliable? Does information obtained from child interviewing demonstrate concurrent validity (i.e., does it correlate with information obtained from other assessment strategies)? Do interview data have treatment utility (i.e., do they contribute positively to treatment planning, implementation, or evaluation)? Although these questions are interrelated, each is discussed separately here for purposes of emphasis.

Accuracy of Child Report

It is important to begin a discussion on the accuracy of child report with the statement that many of the potential benefits of the child interview do not depend on the veracity of children's reports. As discussed earlier, the interview permits opportunities to observe important child characteristics, such as social reasoning, logical thinking processes, thematic development, emotional responsiveness, and social skills. These observational benefits do not depend on the accuracy of a child's report. More critical to this discussion, however, is the fact that a child's self-perceptions and perceptions of his or her environment are clinically important even if factually inaccurate. For example, the child who believes that there is no relationship between effort and achievement outcomes is unlikely to expend much effort on academic tasks. Although the child's belief may be inaccurate, it is an important determinant of his or her achievement behaviors. An intervention that does not change the child's attributions is likely to be of limited effectiveness. Similarly, a high school boy who is a star on the track team and an honor roll student may feel like a failure and experience a sense of hopelessness. An objective analysis of his situation is likely to be quite at odds with his self- appraisal. Nevertheless, his self-appraisals may lead him to become depressed.

Witt et al. (1988) report an actual case involving a hospitalized schizophrenic adolescent boy who thought he was God. The behavioral treatment program in the hospital involved removing all attention to him when he talked about himself as being God and attending to his more appropriate verbalizations.

> As expected, the rate of inappropriate behavior reduced in frequency and, after about 2 weeks, disappeared altogether. As the patient was about to be dismissed from the hospital, one of the psychologists said to him, "You have really improved here. When you came into the hospital you actually thought you were God and now you don't think that way anymore do you?" The patient replied, "Oh yes I do think I'm God but no one wants to talk with me about it!" (p. 388)

The authors noted that the patient's improvement was not likely to continue after release from the hospital unless his self-perception were to change also.

Even though we recognize that children's reports are clinically meaningful, even if inaccurate, it is still important to know at what age children can be expected to report on events and experiences accurately. A definitive answer to this question is difficult for two reasons. First, what criteria do we use to establish "the truth"? Determining the accuracy of child report data on the basis of its agreement with adults assumes that adults' perceptions are correct. As discussed below, this assumption is often erroneous. Second, the accuracy of children's reports depends, in large part, on the way information is obtained from children. In the past, researchers were quick to blame the children for inaccurate data rather than to question the appropriateness of their interviewing procedures to the children's developmental characteristics. For example, Edelbrock, Costello et al. (1985) employed a highly structured interview format with children, in which children answered "yes" or "no" to questions about the presence or absence of symptoms. They concluded that children under the age of 10 are not reliable in reporting on their own symptoms, except for fears, and that their reports must be interpreted with considerable caution: "Our findings suggest that symptoms reported by young children should not be taken at face value for purposes of diagnosis, treatment selection, or treatment evaluation" (p. 273). Our conclusion, however, would be that children's answers to highly structured questions do not permit children to communicate as effectively as when developmentally sensitive interviewing approaches are used.

Reliability

Not surprisingly, most information on the reliability of child interviews is available for the more structured diagnostic interviews, in which the interviewer asks a specified series of questions and responses are scored objectively. Unless a child's responses are assigned some number, it is difficult to compute a reliability coefficient. The available evidence supports the conclusion that these interviews possess adequate interrater and test–retest reliabilities (see Paget, 1984; Witt et al., 1988). More specific information concerning reliability for the diagnostic interview schedules is reported in Chapter 3.

Because of the flexibility of the unstructured interview, it does not yield quantitative data necessary for computing reliability coefficients. In the unstructured interview, the way topics are covered and the way questions are phrased differ both between interviewers and between interviews conducted by the same interviewer. The only evidence of the reliability of unstructured interviews comes from studies that compare diagnostic impressions, judgments of overall functioning, or lists of problems detected in the interview. In one of the few studies of the reliability of the unstructured interview, Hay, Hay, Angle, and Nelson (1979) found good agreement between interviews in the total number of problems detected; however, they demonstrated poor agreement concerning the specific nature of the problem.

In investigating the test–retest and interrater reliability of a semi-structured diagnostic interview, Rutter and Graham (1968) found that global ratings of maladjustment, based on two different raters' interviews with children on two different occasions (1 to 30 days apart, mean of 12 days) were highly reliable ($r = .84$). Again, there was fair or poor agreement on specific symptoms, especially those pertaining to anxiety and depression.

Concurrent Validity

Most of the validity research on child interviews has examined the relationship between child and parent report of symptoms (Edelbrock, Costello, et al., 1985; Herjanic, Herjanic, Brown, & Wheatt, 1975). These investigators concluded that children are accurate in reporting factual information (e.g., whether they wet the bed or have repeated a grade), but inaccurate in reporting judgments (e.g., whether they fight often).

Evaluating the accuracy of child interview data in terms of parent–child agreement is problematic. Garber (1984) and Kazdin (1987) concluded that parents are less accurate than children in reporting on children's internalizing symptoms (fears, depression, anxiety, self-evaluations), but that parents and teachers are better informants concerning children's overt behaviors (see also Edelbrock, Costello, Dulcan, Conover, & Kalas, 1986). The prevailing view concerning the lack of correspondence between child and parent report is that each source of information provides distinct, important information. Garber (1984) advocates the use of multiple informants because they provide diverse information. The lack of agreement among informants, she states, suggests "that the assessment and classification of childhood disorders should be based on multiple sources that can be combined in such a way as to produce a more complete and accurate picture of the child" (p. 44). Kazdin (1987) recommends the use of both child and parent report for assessing depression, because the diagnosis of depression requires information about subjective states (e.g., self-esteem, feelings of worthlessness), about which the child can more accurately report, and overt behavioral signs (sleeping and eating disturbances, lack of participation in activities previously found pleasurable), about which the parents may be more accurate reporters.

Worchel et al. (1990) compared teacher-rated, peer-rated, and self-rated measures of depression in adolescents. They found that teacher and peer ratings showed moderate agreement, but that both had nonsignificant or low correlations with self-reported depression. Thus, their results support Kazdin's conclusion that self-reports and reports of others measure different aspects of depressive symptomatology. Obtaining high agreement between child and parent reports may be less important than determining which informants provide the most clinically useful information regarding which aspects of the child's functioning.

Inconsistency between parent and child reports may be clinically significant in itself. There has been no research to date on the meaning of high and low consistency between parent and child report. The degree of agreement within parent–child dyads may provide useful information predictive of other adjustment indices or indices of family functioning. Recently, Victor, Halverson, and Wampler (1988) found that a measure of agreement between parent–teacher triads correlated with important child characteristics. Thus, they advocate viewing disagreement as an important individual-difference variable in relations, rather than as error variance in measuring child characteristics.

Another reason why parental report data may be inaccurate, and therefore inappropriate criteria against which to judge child self-report data, is the well-established finding that parental reports of child adjustment, temperament, and functioning are moderately related to maternal psychopathology and marital discord (Compas, Howell, Phares, Williams, & Giunta, 1989; Kazdin, 1987; Martin, 1988). Thus, parental perceptions of child functioning indicate as much about the parent's functioning (including anxiety, depression, stresses, level of social support, and marital relationship) as they do about child behavior.

The most critical issue in evaluating the validity of child report data is not its correspondence with parental report, but its ability to predict other important criteria. In this regard, child and parent reports of child depression predict different criteria. Thus, they are both valid, but different. Child reports of depressive symptoms correlate with suicide attempts and suicide ideation, attributional style, hopelessness, self-concept, and child-rearing practices of the parent (see Kazdin, 1987). Parent reports correlate with social withdrawal, overt signs of expressed affect, and family dysfunction (Compas et al., 1989; Kazdin, Esveldt-Dawson, Sherick, & Colbus, 1985).

Because different interview measures are used to accomplish different purposes, there is no one criterion appropriate to establishing the interview's validity. Diagnostic interviews would be expected to correspond with diagnoses obtained from more complete diagnostic procedures. Rutter and Graham (1968) found that ratings of psychiatric impairment based on a 30-minute semistructured interview with the child corresponded well with ratings of impairment based on a full child study, including a detailed history from parents and a report from the child's school. Although the interview was sensitive to impairment, the child interviews did not discriminate between different types of impairment.

More recently developed diagnostic interview schedules are sensitive to different types of pathology. Scores on the CAS (Hodges et al., 1982) discriminate between groups of children differing in level of pathology (i.e., deviant or control) and correspond with maternal reports of child behavior problems. Furthermore, the relevant scales of the CAS correspond to scores on self-report measures of anxiety and depression (Hodges et al., 1982).

Interviews with a more specific focus have demonstrated the ability to discriminate between different groups of psychiatrically impaired children. For example, the Children's Depression Rating Scale (Poznanski et al., 1984), an interview measure of depression, discriminates between depressed and nondepressed psychiatric inpatients and corresponds with therapists' global ratings of depression.

Interviews used to assess aspects of children's social reasoning or problem solving have also accumulated evidence of their validity. Children's scores on the Interpersonal Understanding Interview (Selman et al., 1979) discriminate between emotionally disturbed and nondisturbed children and are related to children's naturalistic social behaviors (Gurucharri, Phelps, & Selman, 1984). The Asarnow and Callan (1985) problem-solving interview, designed for use with preadolescent children, assesses five social-cognitive skills: (1) the ability to generate alternative solutions, (2) the ability to generate nonaggressive solutions, (3) the ability to evaluate solution effectiveness, (4) planning skills, and (5) attributional processes. The interview demonstrates very high inter-rater reliability, and scores on the five social problem- solving variables discriminate between sociometrically rejected and accepted boys.

Child interviewing is used extensively in child development research. For the most part, interview schedules used to assess social reasoning, moral reasoning, concepts of friendships, and the like have not found their way into clinical practice. The child development research does, however, document the potential clinical utility of child interview data. For example, this literature reports that children's interview responses predict such important child characteristics and outcomes as peer acceptance (Gottman, Gonso, & Rasmussen, 1975; Ladd & Oden, 1979), aggression (Asarnow & Callan, 1985; Richard & Dodge, 1982), emotional disturbance (Selman, 1976; Shure & Spivack, 1972), and academic motivation (Pearl, Bryan, & Donahue, 1980). Because these interviews were designed for research rather than clinical purposes, administration procedures are standardized and relatively inflexible. Obtaining evidence of their treatment utility represents an important research priority in child clinical assessment.

Hayes, Nelson, and Jarrett (1987) define treatment utility as "the degree to which assessment is shown to contribute to beneficial treatment outcomes" (p. 963). This definition is similar to that of Korchin and Schuldberg (1981), who define treatment utility as the degree to which assessment information leads to more effective planning, execution, and evaluation of treatment.

Hayes et al. (1987) state that most measures used by psychologists have not demonstrated treatment utility. Whereas evidence of the treatment utility of interviews is lacking, certainly the constructs for which interviews are best suited, such as self-efficacy, motivation, intervention acceptability, outcome expectations, attributions, and reward preferences, have demonstrated their relevance to treatment effectiveness. For example, Elliott (1986) found that children's ratings of the acceptability of classroom interventions predicted their efficacy. Bugental, Whalen, and Henker (1977) found that impulsive and hyperactive children's tendency to attribute positive and negative outcomes to internal or external causes predicted the differential effectiveness of two interventions. Evers-Pasquale and Sherman (1975; see also Evers-Pasquale, 1978) found that socially withdrawn children's self-reported preferences for-peer interaction predicted which children benefited from a modeling intervention designed to increase peer interaction. Kirigin, Braukmann, Atwater, and Wolf (1982) found that children's satisfaction with the Achievement Place intervention predicted subsequent criminality better than evaluations of the program by staff or parents.

Hughes (1989) has extrapolated the suggestions made by Hayes et al. (1987) for estimating the treatment utility of assessment procedures to the task of establishing the treatment utility of the child interview. For example, evidence that the interview helps in the selection of treatment targets would be provided if socially rejected children were divided into two groups-one receiving a social skills intervention in which the skills taught were those targeted in an interview assessment, and the other receiving an intervention in which skills were not selected in this man- ner-and the group receiving the interview-based intervention improved more in peer acceptance. Hayes et al. (1987) and Hughes (1989) suggest several additional methods of establishing the treatment utility of the interview.

Children's Suggestibility

An issue related to the validity of children's reports is the degree to which children's reports are susceptible to suggestion. Children's re- ports of past events are often devalued because people believe that children have poor memory for events and that their memories are influenced by the power of suggestion. Children's ability to remember events accurately shows developmental progressions during early and middle childhood. These developmental changes, however, interact with the type of event remembered, the children's interest level, and the questioning strategy used by the interviewer (Melton & Thompson, 1987). For events of high personal saliencey under conditions of sponta- neous (i.e., free) recall, even children as young as 5 years of age provide highly accurate information. Under direct questioning, their recall of central information is as complete as that of adults, but more likely to be inaccurate (see Schwartz & Schwanenflugel, 1989). The implications of developmental changes in memory for interviewing are discussed in greater detail in Chapter 2. In this section, one threat to children's memory, suggestibility, is discussed. The question that requires answer- ing is this: "When can we trust children's memory of events, especially traumatic events such as sexual abuse?"

Young children are more vulnerable to misleading suggestions, espe- cially from an adult, than are older children and adults (Cole & Loftus, 1987). Several factors probably account for their greater suggestibility. First, they do not have as many detailed "scripts" for events as adults, and their scripts are less detailed (Kail, 1984). Such scripts provide a meaningful context for what is to be remembered and facilitate memory via their effects on both the storage and retrieval of information. For example, if a child has a script for going to the movies, it is easier for him or her to remember the facts that someone took tickets at the door or that the concession stand sold popcorn. The importance of scripts was demonstrated by Hess and Baker-Ward (1987), who found that pre-school children's recall of events in a game varied with their under-standing of the game: better understanding resulted in better recall of central events in the game. On the other hand, familiar scripts can distort memory in the direction of typical experience (Kail, 1984). Be-cause children are less able to know what they know and what they do not know (Kail, 1984), they are more likely to distort memory in the direction of typical experience. Nevertheless, scripts usually facilitate memory, and children's lack of embellished scripts makes it more difficult for them to remember details of an event. Thus, they are more likely to agree with erroneous information concerning events periph-eral to the central event. Children as young as 6 to 8 years old, however, are no more suggestible than adults are with respect to their memory for central events (i.e., events with high personal relevance; Goodman & Reed, 1986; King & Yuille, 1987).

Among other factors contributing to children's suggestibility are their deficits in metamemory (i.e., knowledge of what they do know and knowledge of strategies for remembering). Young children, lacking the ability to know what they know and do not know, may accept a sugges-tion as fact, especially for peripheral information (King & Yuille, 1987). Their lack of metamemory may also help explain why, in general, young children provide less complete (but more accurate) information on memory tasks that require them to recall rather than to recognize information (Schwartz & Schwanenflugel, 1989). Recall memory re-quires knowledge of strategies for retrieving information. Whereas young children's recall memory is less complete than that of older children and adults (List, 1986; Saywitz, 1987), their recognition memo-ry is nearly as good as that of older children (Perlmutter & Lange, 1978). Preschoolers perform similarly to grade school children on tasks requiring them to identify drawings presented to them 3 days earlier, whereas their recall memory is poor and continues to show improve-ments through the middle childhood years (Ceci, Toglia, & Ross, 1987).

Young children's greater facility with recognition memory poses a dilemma for the interviewer. To capitalize on the young child's better-developed recognition memory, the interviewer needs to present re-sponse alternatives from which the child selects the correct response. However, this questioning format increases the risk that the child's memory will be influenced by the questioning process. Children prov-ide more complete information with specific questions that provide structure or guidance (e.g., "Did you play in the house center or in the block corner this morning?") than with general questions (e.g., "What did you do today at school?"). The more guidance provided, however, the greater the threat of distortion and intrusion errors.

> Present evidence suggests that young children's free recall is more *accurate* than recall obtained under direct questioning, particularly for information concerning people. There is general agreement, however, that younger children will provide less *complete* accounts under free recall procedures than older children. Thus, the questioning method used by the school psychologist should vary depending on whether the aim is to obtain the most accurate or the most complete information. (Schwartz & Schwanen-flugel, 1989, p. 240)

Also contributing to young children's suggestibility are their lack of sophisticated communication skills, dependence on contextual cues, and eagerness to do and say what is expected, especially with adults (King & Yuille, 1987). Consider children's performance in the "blank lineup" memory task. In this situation, children are shown an array of photographs that does not include the person the child witnessed engage in some act. Children are asked to select the photograph of the person they saw. Typically, children younger than 12 years of age erroneously select a photograph (King & Yuille, 1987).

It will be recalled that children are highly accurate in their performance on this recognition task when the array includes the target photograph. In the "blank lineup" task, children's poor performance is probably a result of their (1) lack of knowledge of when they know and do not know something; (2) poor communication skills to describe their confusion about the task; and (3) tendency to treat a question as a requirement for an answer, based both on their eagerness to please adults and to say what is expected and on their greater dependence on nonverbal than on verbal cues in a situation. That is, children reason that if an adult asks them to select the photograph of the target person, then the correct photograph must be present. This tendency is evident even when children are told that the array may not include the target person's photograph.

These differences in children's metamemory, communication skills, reliance on contextual cues, and desire to please adults should not be viewed as obstacles to interviewing children as much as evidence of the need to alter our interviewing techniques with children. Specific strategies for interviewing young children presented in Chapter 2 include beginning the interview with general probes and little directiveness, and increasing the directiveness of questioning as needed; using a conversational interview style rather than a formal, structured one; providing a retrieval context that resembles the encoding context; reducing task demands; providing concrete retrieval cues; reducing the complexity of questions; reducing the complexity of the responses needed from children; and reducing the threat of questions.

DIMENSIONS ON WHICH INTERVIEWS DIFFER

Structure

Although interviews are often classified as structured, semistructured, or unstructured, interview structure is best thought of as a continuum rather than as a category system. At one end of the continuum are highly structured interviews, in which the interviewer has no discretion over the phrasing or sequencing of questions, and responses are limited to "yes" and "no" and are scored dichotomously. Such highly structured interviews are probably not appropriate for clinical assessment of children, but may be appropriate for epidemiological studies. The Diagnostic Interview for Children and Adolescents (DICA; Herjanic & Reich, 1982) was developed for such purposes; the DICA and its revision, the DICA-R, are reviewed briefly in Chapter 3. At the other extreme of the continuum are unstructured interviews, in which the interviewer exercises little control over the content, much less the form, of the interview. The child selects the topics, the pace, and the methods (talking, dramatic play, object play).The unstructured approach is exemplified by the play therapy interview (Axline, !969; Greenspan, 1981; Irwin, 1983) and is based on the assumption that the less one intrudes, the more the child will tell. In reality, the interviewer does provide some structure in these interviews by selecting what toys or materials to make available, commenting on selected aspects of what the child says or does, and empathizing with the feelings expressed by the child ("That looks like a scary picture").

Most interviews offer a moderate degree of structure. The interviewer selects topics to cover in the interview but is flexible in responding to topics introduced by the child, and exercises considerable judgment in phrasing and sequencing questions and in probing the child's responses. The interviewer may use hypothetical situations to assess a child's perceptions and reasoning about certain events, or concrete props (toys, reconstructive techniques, drawings) to enhance the child's ability to share his or her thoughts and feelings. The more conversational tone of low-structure interviews provides a more familiar context for children, increasing their self-confidence and communicative competence; it also establishes a communication system of shared control that promotes the children's active involvement in subsequent therapeutic interactions.

Content

Interviews differ in their breadth of coverage. Some interviews assess a wide range of child behaviors and affective reactions, whereas other interviews focus on a more in-depth assessment of particular types of problems, such as aggression or depression. Also, interviews differ in their emphasis on learning about the child's thinking processes versus learning about particular events or behaviors. For example, an interviewer who is interested in assessing a child's social reasoning ability might use an interview format similar to that described by Hughes (1989). In this interview, the event reported is less important than the child's thinking about that event (i.e., types of cues attended to, types of attributions for peers' provocations, expectancy of the success of aggressive and nonaggressive solutions, ability to generate nonaggressive solutions). In other interviews, the interviewer wants to know what types of events or behaviors have occurred and their frequency and intensity.

Reliance on Talking versus Doing

Some definitions of interviewing state that it is a verbal interaction conducted for the purpose of obtaining specific information (Martin, 1988). The child interview, however, may rely more on nonverbal behavior than on verbal behavior to obtain information. Because play is a natural medium of communication for young children, they reveal thoughts, fears, and perceptions of recurring or significant events as well as reasoning ability in their play. Because children give a great deal of weight to contextual cues in comprehending language, they communicate more competently when provided with concrete props such as toys or with opportunities to reconstruct their experience. Although older children are usually more comfortable with question–answer interview approaches, when discussing emotionally intense experiences they may become inarticulate and need the opportunity to respond in a less mature manner.

Theoretical Orientation

Not surprisingly, clinicians who adopt different theoretical orientations in their work with children tend to adopt different interviewing strategies. Interview approaches can be identified as most consistent with one of three different theoretical orientations: psychometric, psychodynamic, and behavioral. Chapters 3–6 describe each of these types of interviews in detail and present examples of each.

SUMMARY

The child interview is uniquely suited to learning about children's subjective experiences and reasoning about their world. The benefits of the child interview, however, are not automatic, but depend on the ability of the interviewer to adapt the process to a child's level of ability. This adaptation requires knowledge of developmental changes in children's linguistic, cognitive, and psychosocial functioning. The next chapter discusses these developmental changes and offers practice guidelines for interviewing children at different developmental levels.

2

Developmentally Sensitive Interviewing

Children perceive, conceptualize, and reason about other people, themselves, and events in ways that are qualitatively different from those of adults. Their abilities to understand what people say to them and to express themselves develop as they grow. These developmental progressions, as well as changes in children's motivations, goals, and coping strategies, affect their performance in the interview, including their ability and willingness to share their thoughts and feelings. Knowledge of developmental changes in children's communicative competence, cognition, and psychosocial functioning is essential to developmentally sensitive interviewing. The purpose of this chapter is to suggest implications of these developmental changes for interviewing children. Following Garbarino, Stott, and the Faculty of Erikson Institute (1989), we offer these implications as practice guidelines rather than as rules. Because the cardinal prerequisite of sensitive child interviewing is flexibility, any list of strategies for interviewing would be unhelpful. The specific strategy an interviewer employs should depend not only on the child's developmental level, but also on the purpose of the interview, the child's relationship with the interviewer, the interview setting, and the interpersonal styles of the child and the interviewer.

Instead of offering a list of procedures for interviewing children, we offer numerous suggestions for developmentally sensitive interviewing and one caution: Interviewers should not take it for granted that children give the same meaning to words that adults do. Because children reason about people and the world in qualitatively different ways and use language differently, adults cannot assume that they know what a child is thinking or feeling, based on what the child says and does.

Adults need to try to put themselves in the child's place (e.g., "What might the child think about why I am asking this question?") and to obtain clarification and elaboration from the child through gently probing the child's responses and offering comments that encourage the child to elaborate on short, ambiguous responses.

THE INTERACTIVE NATURE OF COMPETENCE

Certainly children's communicative competence increases with age. However, competence in interview situations is best viewed as a function of developmental age plus the child's motivations, the familiarity of the interview situation and materials used, the question-asking strategies of the interviewer, and the relationship with the interviewer. We believe that the interviewer has a considerable responsibility for the completeness and accuracy of a child's communication. Adults who are fluent with a variety of interview approaches and aware of children's linguistic capabilities, cognitive characteristics, and motivations are likely to be successful in helping children share their complex and rich subjective experiences.

The interactive nature of the child's competence and of the interview situation is supported by research conducted within the last 15 years on preschoolers' cognitive competencies. Earlier research conducted by Piaget had found preschool children incapable of taking the perspective of another person or of considering two dimensions of a problem situation at the same time. More recently, researchers have demonstrated that preschool children's apparent cognitive limitations are artifacts of the way they are questioned. For example, Piaget's finding that preschool children's perspective-taking ability is quite limited was based on the "three-mountain task" (Piaget & Inhelder, 1969), in which a child is shown a model containing three mountains, complete with such details as trees, lakes, houses, and snow. After carefully viewing the model from each side, the child is seated in a chair and a doll is seated in turn at chairs positioned differently around the table with the model. When children under 6 or 7 are asked to describe what the doll sees, they describe the display from their own perspective. Piaget and Inhelder concluded that young children are unable to take the perspective of another person, reflecting their "egocentrism" and inability to "decenter" from their own point of view.

Other researchers (Borke, 1975; Donaldson, 1978) have found that young children's difficulty with the three-mountain task is at least partially a result of their unfamiliarity with the situation and materials used. For example, Martin Hughes (1975, cited in Donaldson, 1978) presented children with a model of four "rooms," created with two interlocking "walls." The experimenter placed a boy doll in one room and a policeman at different positions in the model. When the experimenter asked children whether or not the policeman could see the boy and where the boy could hide so that the policeman could not see him, most children between the ages of 3 1/2 and 5 years answer correctly, demonstrating the ability to take the visual perspective of another. Hughes postulated that his results differed from those of Piaget and Inhelder because children are more familiar with the situation he presented than they are with the three-mountain task. Although children probably have not hid from a policeman, they have played hide and seek. Thus, the policeman task made human sense.

> The *motives* and *intentions* of the characters are entirely comprehensible, even to a child of three. The task requires the child to act in ways that are in line with certain very basic human purposes and interactions (escape and pursuit)—it makes *human sense*. (Donaldson, 1978, p. 17)

A second example of increasing children's apparent competence by modifying a task was provided by McGarrigle (cited in Donaldson, 1978), whose results challenged Piaget's claim that preoperational (roughly ages 2 to 6) children's failure to solve so-called "class inclusion" problems was a result of their inability to "decenter" (i.e., to consider more than one dimension of a problem at a time). In a typical class inclusion task, the child is shown a number of objects that are familiar to the child, such as candies or beads. The objects can be divided into two readily apparent subclasses, such as red and white candies or wooden and plastic beads. For example, the child is presented with six candies, four of them red and two of them white, and is asked, "Are there more red candies or more candies?" Most children under 6 or 7 will answer, "More red candies." The question requires the child to think of the class (candies) and the subclasses (red and white candies) at the same time—a feat Piaget believed to be beyond the cognitive grasp of the preoperational child. McGarrigle suspected that children's difficulty was a result of their not understanding the question. McGarrigle used four toy cows, three of them black and one of them white. He laid all the cows on their sides and said they were sleeping. He then asked both the standard class inclusion question ("Are there more black cows or more cows?") and a modified class inclusion question ("Are there more black cows or more sleeping cows?"). By adding the adjective "sleeping" to the second question, the experimenter emphasized the total class of cows in a way not done in the standard question. Whereas only 25% of 6-year-olds correctly answered the first question, 48% correctly answered the second question. Many children who did not demonstrate the ability to decenter in the standard question format were able to do so when the question was changed. Importantly, the change in the question did not change the essential feature of the task, which requires the ability to reason simultaneously about a class and its subclasses.

In his review of research on preschool children's cognitive competencies, Flavell (1985) concluded that research using developmentally sensitive ways of inquiring about children's reasoning has demonstrated that "the young child's mind is more coherent, better organized, and generally less confused than we used to think it was" (p. 53).

Recognizing the interactive nature of children's competence, when a child's answer appears irrational or silly, the adult interviewer should ask, "What changes in the interview procedure might enable the child to respond in a more capable, meaningful way?" It may be helpful for the interviewer to try to figure out what the question means to the child, remembering that the intended and received tasks may not be the same (King & Yuille, 1987).

Development occurs in different domains. Next, development in communication, cognition, and psychosocial functioning are reviewed, with an emphasis on implications of these changes for sensitive interviewing.

DEVELOPMENT OF COMMUNICATIVE COMPETENCE

It is obvious that children's vocabulary, syntax, and knowledge of language pragmatics change with age. Even children as young as 4 years of age know this fact, as demonstrated in the finding that 4-year-olds alter their speech (words, syntax, length, and pragmatics) when speaking to babies, peers, and adults (Shatz & Gelman, 1973). The purpose of this section is not to provide an overview of language development in the preschool and grade school years; several excellent sources on language development are available (e.g., Lindfors, 1987). Rather, the purpose is to selectively review aspects of children's progress in social communicative competence that are most important to having conversations with young children. "Social communicative competence" refers to a child's ability to use language to affect social outcomes. It both depends on and reflects a child's increase in general cognitive and language skills. Growth in social communicative skills is most rapid in the preschool years, but it continues through middle childhood.

Flavell (1985) described the growth of social communicative competence as learning

> how to converse as well as to talk—that is, how to maintain focus on a single topic during an extended verbal interchange with another person. They

[children] gradually become able to go beyond the here, the now, and the real in what they converse about. They gain command of new and cognitively more advanced types of speech acts....For instance, they eventually find out that language can be used not only to assert, request, and question, but also to express psychological states ("I'm sorry"), to commit oneself to future actions ("I promise I'll come"), and even to bring about new states of affairs by verbal declarations ("I quit"). (p. 259)

Children also learn to fill in the gaps or to draw inferences, and to adapt their speech to different purposes, settings, and speakers (Flavell, 1985).

Children's Understanding of Questions

Whereas adolescents and adults are able and willing to respond to open-ended questions of the nature "Tell me about your family," such a directive yields a blank stare or, at best, a string of unrelated associations from young children. Preschool children have a hard time sustaining conversation and need frequent specific probes and empathic comments in order to communicate effectively. Questioning young children is a subtle art, requiring a combination of open-ended questions ("What will the mother doll do now?"), specific questions that avoid leading ("What do you like about school?"), and a generous sprinkling of "extenders" ("Oh" and "umm" and "I understand"). Questions that are asked in a familiar setting and that are related to ongoing activities (e.g., "There must be a good story to go with that picture") are more likely to encourage responses. This chapter includes several specific recommendations for phrasing and sequencing questions.

Following are two dialogues with preschool children that illustrate the difference between developmentally sensitive and insensitive interviewing. In the first interview, the adult makes the common error of asking too many questions and asking "forced-choice" questions that elicit one-word answers. The child is drawing a picture of a house.

ADULT: What grade are you in?

CHILD: I'm in kindergarten.

ADULT: Did you have a fun time at school today?

CHILD: Yes.

ADULT: Did you play outside?

CHILD: Uh-huh.

ADULT: What did you play?

CHILD: In the sandbox.

ADULT: Did you ride the bus to school?

CHILD: No.

ADULT: Do you like school?

CHILD: (*Keeps drawing, no answer*)

In the second dialogue the adult limits the use of questioning, relates the question to the child's activity, and comments on the child's activity and verbalizations, encouraging the child to share thoughts and feelings. The child is drawing a picture of a house.

ADULT: I wonder who lives in that house.

CHILD: A mommy, daddy, boy, and baby.

ADULT: Mmmmm.

CHILD: The daddy got hurt.

ADULT: What happened to the daddy?

CHILD: A robber came in the back door and shot him.

ADULT: Oh!

CHILD: My daddy left. He could have beat up a robber.

ADULT: Your daddy was strong.

CHILD: He was real strong. Sometimes he was stronger than he wanted to be. (*Pause*) He hurt Mommy. But he didn't mean to and he was sorry.

Adults, perhaps as a method of compensating for children's conversational limitations, often err by assuming too much control in conversations with children. Wood and Wood (1983) point out that questions are an exercise in control (p. 161), especially questions that limit the range of the child's response (i.e., forced-choice questions). Wood and his colleagues (Wood, MacMahon, & Cranstoun, 1980) studied 24 teachers' conversations with preschoolers and found that 50% of all conversational initiatives on the part of teachers were in the form of questions. Furthermore, most of these questions could be answered in single words. They also found that children of teachers who used the most questions were least likely to ask questions of the teacher, answer the teacher's questions, elaborate on their responses, or offer spontaneous comments. "In general, we found that the linguistic initiative shown by young children went down as a function of how often they were questioned" (Wood & Wood, 1983, p. 151).

In a follow-up study, Wood and Wood (1983) investigated the relationship between question asking and the quality and quantity of children's responses. Using a case study methodology, they studied the conversations between an experienced, capable preschool teacher and six pupils. The teacher purposefully altered her questioning style during different conversational sessions with children, which were audiotaped, transcribed, and coded for purposes of testing several research hypotheses. Of particular importance to this discussion are the following findings. Children showed most initiative (i.e., spontaneous comments, elaboration, and other contributions) in low-control sessions (sessions in which the teacher used fewer direct questions of the nature, "What color are your shoes?" or "Did you have a good time?"), and more comments and reflective statements. Children's responses were also lengthier in low-control sessions. When the teacher used a high proportion of closed-ended and forced- choice questions, children responded with short, unelaborated answers and did not show initiative by bringing up topics, elaborating, commenting, or asking questions. The researchers also investigated the relationship between the demand of questions and the quality of children's responses. High-demand questions ask for explanation, interpretation, and generalizations, such as "Why do you think he was sad?" or "What do you think will happen next?" Although high-level questions tended to elicit high-level responses from children, sessions with lots of "wh-"questions produced the fewest high-level responses from children.

> We thus have the situation where demanding questions will produce "the goods" they require, but the attempt to simply pack more of them into a session does not bring about any perceptible increase in the amount of reasoning, hypothesizing [sic], remembering, or describing what goes on. (Wood & Wood, 1983, p.159)

Wood and Wood explained their findings in terms of children's willingness to provide explanations and descriptions on their own initiative. "If a teacher seeks to get children talking and thinking through question after question, then she is unlikely to hear children spontaneously elaborate on the theme of conversation or go beyond her questions to add more information" (p. 160). "Too many questions therefore not only make children passive and terse, they also tend to depress their performance" (pp. 159-160).

These findings are especially noteworthy, given research demonstrating that children's spontaneous recall is more accurate (although less complete) than is their cued recall (King & Yuille, 1987). Thus, the frequent use of direct questions results in passive children and unreliable information.

In interviewing children, especially preschool children, a combination of open-ended and direct questions may be helpful. The interviewer should ask a few relatively open-ended questions and comment on the child's responses or encourage the child to elaborate. If the interviewer needs specific information from a child that is not yielded by open-ended questions and the ensuing conversation, direct questions may elicit the necessary details.

The following dialogue occurred during an interview one of us (Jan Hughes) had with a 9-year-old boy referred for nausea on school mornings.

JH: All boys have things they like and don't like so much about school. What about school do you like?

MIKE: Math.

JH: Umm. In 4th grade math gets pretty hard.

MIKE: Yeah. I'm in the top group and I've made 100s on every test this 6 weeks, so far.

JH: You're really doing great, and you seem pleased with yourself about math.

MIKE: The teacher lets me help other kids in class when I finish my math, because I'm so good. Math is easy! Dad says I might be an engineer, like him, if I want to.

JH: I can understand why math is your favorite subject. And what about school do you not like so much?

MIKE: (*pause*). Reading.

JH: Lots of kids find that reading can be tough.

MIKE: It's okay. But I hate it when Miss Phillips makes us read out loud.

JH: Oh. Sounds bad.

MIKE: If I know we're going to read out loud, I say I have to go to the bathroom.

JH: You try to avoid having to read out loud. You really don't like doing that.

MIKE: Yeah.

JH: When you think you're going to have to read out loud in classes, have you noticed how your body feels?

MIKE: What do you mean?

J_H: Well, when you have to do something you really don't like, you might feel a little scared, and your body might feel scared, too.

M_IKE: Like my tummy getting all hard. It feels like a grapefruit landed in my gut.

J_H: Yeah, like that.

Gaining Familiarity with the Child's Experience

In order to frame questions that elicit responses from a child, it is helpful if the adult has some familiarity with the situation described by the child. However, when adults ask questions to which they know the answers, children are unlikely to respond. Wood et al. (1980, pp. 121–122) investigated the relationship between preschool children's communicative competence with their mothers and the children's perceptions of their mothers' knowledge of the conversation topic. One group of mothers played with their 4-year-olds in a playroom stocked with attractive toys. A second group of mothers watched their children play over a video recorder, and a third group of mothers did not watch their children at all while their children played in the playroom with an adult. At the end of the play session, each mother had refreshments with her child and attempted to coax her child into talking about what he or she had been playing with, how the child had played, what the child had enjoyed, and so forth. Children who had played with their mothers were the most resistant to describing their play sessions. Because they knew their mothers knew the answers to the questions, the questions seemed test-like and manipulative. The children whose mothers were genuinely naive about the play session were also at a distinct disadvantage. Compared to the mothers who had watched their children play, these mothers did not possess the familiarity with the play setting to ask intelligent questions. Children this age are limited in their ability to recall specific events without considerable support and structure from another person, and these mothers were unable to provide much structure.

An interviewer should avoid asking questions to which it is apparent to the child that the interviewer knows the answer. The test-like nature of the questioning process stifles the child's motivation to communicate. Such questioning practices are at odds with communicating respect for the child and with establishing a climate of mutual exploration. However, interviewers should attempt to know something about the events to which children are referring, in order to provide the structure children require to share their experiences completely and accurately.

Often questions need to be modified in order to make them easier to understand or to make it easier for the child to answer. Several authors suggest that the interviewer can reduce the complexity of questions by reducing the complexity of the stimulus (the question itself) or the response (Yarrow, 1960; Witt et al., 1988; Bierman, 1983).

Reducing Stimulus Complexity

In addition to selecting words within the vocabulary of the child and reducing the length of questions, the interviewer can reduce the complexity of questions by using concrete referents, using incomplete sentences and stories, and providing response options.

Concrete Referents. Pictures and manipulatives serve as concrete referents for events referred to in questions. For example, if the interviewer is interested in the child's ideas about sex-role typing, he or she can present pictures of toys and a boy and a girl doll, and ask the child which toys the girl doll (and then the boy doll) would choose to play with. The multiple-choice nature of the task reduces the cognitive demands placed on the child of remembering different toys and mutually evaluating them with respect to gender preferences. Feelings are especially difficult for children to report. Questions of the sort, "How do you feel about your parents' divorce?" are typically unproductive. Instead, the interviewer can obtain the desired information by presenting a picture of a mother and a father on one side of a door and a girl on the other side. The interviewer says, "Here are a mother and a father. They are talking about getting a divorce. What do you think they are saying?" Additional questions include "What do you think will happen?" "What do you think the girl might be thinking?" "What do you think the girl might be feeling?" "Have you felt that way?" The interviewer will want to avoid asking questions one after the other, and to comment on the child's responses with understanding statements such as "I can understand how a girl might feel that way."

In interviewing a boy about his reaction to a new baby at home, the interviewer can present a doll play scenario involving mother, father, boy, and baby dolls. "Here are mother, father, boy, and a new baby. What will be different at their home, now that the baby has come?" "How does the boy feel about having a new baby?" "Have you ever felt that way?" "What did you do when you felt that way?"

Another example of using drawings to refer to feelings involves the interviewer drawing pictures of three different faces: happy, sad, and mad. After the child has labeled each picture with the feeling it represents, the interviewer asks the child to describe one time when he or she felt that way.

Drawings can be used to help the child report on his or her thoughts in a situation. For example, after having a child with high test anxiety draw a picture of taking a test at school, the interviewer draws a cartoon-like bubble coming out of the child's mouth and says, "Let's fill this bubble in with things you might be thinking when you are about to take a test."

Incomplete Sentences and Stories. Bierman (1983; Bierman & Schwartz, 1986) recommends using incomplete sentences and incomplete stories to reduce a question's complexity. When using incomplete sentences, the interviewer asks the child to complete a series of sentences, such as "Sometimes at night I worry that..." and "I'm happiest when..." The child can read the sentence stems and can write his or her responses, or the stems can be read aloud by the interviewer and answered aloud by the child. This approach is particularly effective with middle school children who are comfortable with task- oriented approaches. When the interviewer reads the stems and records the child's responses, the interviewer has the opportunity to comment on responses, encouraging elaboration on selected topics. Sentence completion techniques are discussed further in Chapter 8.

The incomplete-story approach is similar. The interviewer selects topics relevant to the child's concerns and introduces the task by saying something like the following: "Okay, now I have this story we're supposed to fill out together. I'll read the story and then you think of an answer to fill in the blanks, okay?" (Bierman & Schwartz, l986a, p. 274). For example, the interviewer tells the beginning of a story about a boy reading a book after his mother told him to go to sleep. The mother comes into the boy's bedroom and discovers the him reading the book. After this part of the story is presented, the interviewer asks the child, "What does the mother say or do?" "What does the child say or do?" "What happens next?" "Is that what would happen in your family?"

Providing Response Options. A third strategy for reducing task complexity is to present alternatives from which the child selects a response. Instead of determining the child's reinforcement preferences by asking, "What sorts of things do you like to do?", the interviewer can present the child with a list of potential reinforcers and have the child indicate on a scale of 1–10 how much he or she likes each one. Alternatively, depending on the child's reading level and verbal fluency, the interviewer can present a written list of reinforcers for the child to rate (Witt et al., l988).

Reducing Response Complexity

Some of the examples above of reducing the complexity of the question entail modifying the response requirements by permitting a pointing response or permitting a shorter response. Another technique for reducing the complexity of a child's response is permitting the child to enact a situation with props instead of describing it. "Show me" directives to children are particularly effective in eliciting script knowledge (i.e., knowledge of recurring events).

Having children enact a situation places fewer demands on their verbal skills. Children use words in different ways than adults do. This difference may cause children to think they have told adults something that the adults did not understand the children to have said. For example, a 5-year-old girl who tells the interviewer that her grandfather kisses her goodnight may think she has told the interviewer about the sexual molestation she has experienced.

In response to the child's statement that her grandfather kisses her good night, the interviewer can present the child with family dolls and bedroom furniture and say, "Show me how this granddaddy puts this little girl to bed." After the child has responded with the dolls, the interviewer can seek clarification with questions such as "Is that how it is at your house?" "How is it the same?" "How is it different?"

Children's Metacommunication

Another characteristic of children's communicative competence with implications for the clinical child interview is their developing "metacommunication," defined broadly as their thinking about language. An aspect of metacommunication with particular relevance to the interview is children's developing ability to monitor their own language comprehension. Deficiencies in monitoring comprehension are apparent in young children's performance on referential communication tasks. Typical of this research is a study by Glucksberg and Krauss (cited in Glucksberg, Krauss, & Higgins, 1975). A speaker and a listener are seated so that they cannot see each other and are told that the objects in front of them are identical to the items in front of the other person. The speaker's job is to describe the objects well enough for the listener to identify its duplicate in his or her own set. If there are two red blocks, one square and one round, and children under 5 are told to pick the red block, they will show no hesitancy about which one to pick. They do not detect ambiguity in the instruction. For them to detect the ambiguity in the task, they would have to mentally compare what they think with what they know and detect the ambiguity (Flavell, 1985). If the children are asked whether they are sure they selected the right one, they will answer yes. Furthermore, their memory for the speaker's instructions is distorted by what they thought they heard, such that they will state that the speaker told them to pick the red square block, if that is the one they selected.

Markman (1977) illustrated young children's poor ability to monitor their comprehension. Children between 6 and 8 years of age were presented orally with instructions for playing a game and performing a magic trick. They were instructed to let the experimenter know of any omissions, unclarities, or suggested improvements. Even though the instructions were blatantly inadequate and full of ambiguities, 6-year-old children did not detect the inadequacies prior to carrying out the instructions.

The implications of this research are straightforward. Asking young children to report on their level of understanding ("Do you understand?") is unproductive and developmentally inappropriate. Not only are children unable to monitor their understanding sufficiently to answer this question accurately, their desire to please the interviewer may increase the likelihood of an invalid affirmative response. When the interviewer wishes to know whether or not children understand what they have been told, it is best to ask them to explain what has been told them or to give them a task that will reveal misunderstandings. After explaining to a 7-year-old girl referred for oppositional and defiant behavior that the purpose of the initial interview was to learn more about her worries and her feelings so that she could help herself and her family to have more good times and not so many tough times, the interviewer asked her, "So, can you tell me what we're going to do today?" She responded, "You're going to find out how bad I am so you can tell my parents if I have to go to the dumb class."

Children between 6 and 11 years of age enjoy their growing ability to think about language, which accounts for their fascination with puns, riddles, secret codes, and secret languages, such as Pig Latin. A 6-year-old takes great pleasure in quipping, "Why don't you marry it?" when his mother says, "I love chocolate." The interviewer can improve rapport with this age group by the sparse use of puns and riddles.

Children's Reliance on Context

Reliance on Contextual Cues

In addition to (and partly as a result of) developmental changes in syntax, vocabulary, and metacommunication, children show changes in the relative weight they give to language in relation to contextual cues (Donaldson, 1978). This difference is exemplified in research on children's ability to solve Piagetian conservation tasks. In a typical Piagetian conservation experiment to assess conservation of length, a child is presented with two pencils of equal length, one directly beneath the other, and asked whether the pencils are the same length or whether one is longer. The child responds that they are the same. Next, the experimenter moves one pencil so that it extends farther to the right, saying, "Watch what I do" as he or she moves the pencil. Then the experimenter repeats the initial question. The typical preschooler (ages 3 to 6) is likely to respond that the pencil extending farther to the right is longer, demonstrating a failure to conserve length. Important to this discussion is research demonstrating that the child's purported failure to conserve may be a result of the relative weight the child gives to nonlanguage cues in the situation (McGarrigle & Donaldson, 1974). Consider that the child knows the experimenter did something. Perhaps the child reasons that what the experimenter did is relevant to the experimenter's next question. In fact, the child may reason that if the experimenter asked the question a second time and something has changed, the child's answer should acknowledge that something has changed. This interpretation of young children's performance on the two- pencil problem is suggested by the finding that if the experimenter displaces the pencil in such a manner that it appears to be an accident, children as young as 4 years of age solve the conservation problem.

The findings of McGarrigle and Donaldson (1974) and others (e.g., Rose & Blank, 1974) suggest that the child is responding to the whole situation, not just to the words. In attempting to make sense out of the communicative act, the child relies relatively more on contextual cues, such as the speaker's inferred intent and perceptual cues, than on language per se.

> Children's development and use of language are context-dependent—words are tied to actions and are embedded in on- going situations and relationships with those who know the children well. It is not until roughly age six or seven that children can begin to pay attention to language itself and to give verbal reports that are not necessarily dependent on external supports (people or objects) in the immediate environment. (McNamee, 1989, p. 68)

Clinicians should reduce their reliance on words out of context when interviewing children below age 8. When children are asked questions in a natural context rather than in a structured verbal format, and when questions are accompanied by concrete referents (i.e., pictures or manipulatives), the children are able to give more competent and meaningful answers.

Children's sensitivity to contextual cues makes them more vulnerable to suggestion. King and Yuille (1987) reinterpret Varendonck's classic 1911 study on children's suggestibility as an example of such context sensitivity. Varendonck asked boys in middle childhood what color their teacher's beard was. Although their teacher was clean-shaven, most of the children responded to the question with a color. Once again, in this situation, children may be responding to the whole situation and to all available cues, including linguistic, social, and pragmatic aspects of the situation. Specifically, they reason that if an adult has asked them a question, the question must make sense and they need to respond with a sensible answer.

Reliance on Familiar Settings and Activities

A familiar setting elicits more capable communication from children, as demonstrated by Labov's (1972) classic study on interviewing black children living in Harlem. Many of these children were linguistically "backward" in interviews with white school psychologists during standardized testing situations. When the same children were interviewed in their own homes by black examiners speaking in a familiar dialect, they performed more competently on standard tests and in the interviews.

It is not always possible or optimal to interview children in their homes, to speak their dialect, or to select interviewers from the same culture. However, it is usually possible to provide children time to become familiar with the interviewer and the setting, make sure they understand the purpose of the interview, and use less formal and more conversational interview approaches.

Just as play is a familiar activity for children and puts them at ease in the interview situation, paper-and-pencil tasks and board games are familiar to grade school children. The interviewer introduces the incomplete-sentence task by saying something like the following: "Here are some sentences I'd like you to finish for me. It will help me know more about how you think and feel about things. Just say whatever you think, and I will write it right here. There aren't any right or wrong answers. Here's the first one."

Children are not used to maintaining extensive eye contact with adults and seem to appreciate the opportunity to focus on manipulatives, such as a lump of clay or some Legos. Drawings are also familiar to latency-age children (roughly ages 6-12) and permit the children to avoid extensive eye contact and to rely less on their language skills. Having children draw a picture of their family members, or of anything they want, and then asking them to tell a story about the drawing is often effective. For example, Bob, age 11, was referred for underachievement in school and a generally depressed mood. When the interviewer (Jan Hughes) asked Bob to draw a picture of his family, he drew a beach scene with two people on the beach and one child in the water. He identified the persons on the beach as his parents and the boy in the water as his younger brother. Hughes asked him to help her tell a story about the picture.

Jн: A family decided to go on an outing. They decided to go to the beach. The reason they decided on the beach was....

Boв: The mother wanted to read a book without the kids bothering her. And it didn't cost anything.

Jн: Neat idea. When they got to the beach....What next?

Boв: The big brother unloaded the car.

Jн: He unloaded the car—the ice chest and umbrellas, and lots of stuff. Then....

Boв: He dropped the Diet Pepsi, and his mother was real mad 'cause that's all she likes to drink.

Jн: He dropped the Diet Pepsi and then got the rest of the stuff out and started to play. What did he start to play?

Boв: He started to play in the sand. He saw a pretty seashell but it went out with the waves. He tried to get it but it was lost. He started diving for shells. He stayed down a long time.

Jн: While he was diving for seashells, his family....

Boв: His dad is watching the little brother play, and his mom is reading. Nobody notices that he is under water a long time.

Jн: Nobody notices him at first, and then....

Boв: It is time to eat and they can't find him. He drowned.

Jн: Oh. He drowned because no one noticed. (*long pause*) The story gives me a sad feeling. I wonder if you sometimes feel nobody is noticing.

DEVELOPMENT OF COGNITION

Children's linguistic development mirrors their general cognitive development. Among the numerous cognitive skills attained during the preschool and grade school years discussed in this section are the following: the development of the symbolic function and emergence of play; the ability to distinguish between appearance and reality; the ability to "decenter" from one's own perspective; memorial abilities; and social cognitive abilities.

Development of the Symbolic Function

Between the ages of 18 and 24 months, children learn that one thing can stand for another. This knowledge is essential to the development of language, play, and deferred imitation. When the child uses words to stand for an object or pretends a block of wood is a train engine, the child is exercising the essential human capacity of symbolic thought. The ages between 2 and 6 are a time of rapid development of play, through which the child both manifests symbolic thought and further develops and refines it.

Fein (1979) charted four developmental trends apparent in children's play between 2 and 6 years. First, in general, play becomes less dependent on concrete and realistic props. For example, a 2-year-old pretends to eat with an actual spoon, a 3-year-old requires a spoon-like prop, and a 4-year-old can pretend to eat without the assistance of concrete props (using his or her finger for a spoon). Second, at first, the child is both agent and recipient of pretend actions (e.g., pretending to feed himself or herself); next, others and objects are included as recipients and then as agents in play (e.g., the child feeds the doll and then the doll feeds another doll). Third, social play replaces solitary play by 3 years of age. Fourth, sociodramatic play increases through age 6 and increasingly involves elaborate and reciprocal roles and complex themes and plots. After age 6, play declines and is replaced with mastery activity, such as sports and school learning.

The interviewer should capitalize on play as the child's natural medium of expression between the ages of 2 and 6. When working with very young children, the interviewer should provide realistic props, whereas older children can "make do" with objects that bear little resemblance to their real identities. Children between the ages of 4 and 6 enjoy dramatic play, and providing a dollhouse and family dolls, telephone, and kitchen objects encourages sociodramatic play that may reveal important aspects of a child's family environment. Children this age can respond to suggestions to pretend a certain type of play, such as playing school, and will often include the interviewer in the play ("I'll be the teacher, and you be the student").

Bateson (1976) suggests that play is as powerful as it is in eliciting children's thoughts and feelings because it permits children to distance themselves from anxiety-producing events and thoughts by pretending that they are someone else's problems or thoughts. For example, when a little girl makes a bad mommy send the new baby away, she is communicating her wish that the new child would disappear in a way that does not threaten her self-esteem.

In initial sessions with Brandon, age 6, Brandon repeated destructive themes in his play with the dollhouse. Repeatedly, the father doll tried to get into the house and was shot by burglars or policemen, fell off the roof, or stepped on a bomb. Brandon's father had died of natural causes after his mother obtained a restraining order because of his abusive treatment of her. Brandon expressed in his play his angry feelings toward his father while consciously denying his anger. He could not admit his anger because he felt his anger might be responsible for his dad's death. These play interviews helped the therapist understand Brandon's aggressive behavior and predominant coping mechanisms. (Chapter 4 provides a fuller discussion of the use of play in interviews.)

The Appearance–Reality Distinction

Children's pretending in play is both a result of their emerging ability to distinguish between appearance and reality and a causative factor in their further development of this important conceptual achievement. Flavell (1986) has extensively studied children's development of the achievement–reality distinction. In a typical appearance–reality task, the child is presented with an object with certain actual properties and an actual identity that is made to look like a different object or to have different properties. For example, a child is presented with a stone that is the shape of an egg and colored white, so that it looks exactly like an egg. The experimenter establishes with the child the object's real identity (a stone that somebody painted), its real size (small), and its real color (white).

> The experimenter then said: "Okay. Now I'm going to ask you two different questions. I'm going to ask you what it *looks* like to your eyes right now, and I'm going to ask you what it *really, really* is." She then held up the fake egg and asked whether it looked like an egg or a stone, and whether it really really was an egg or a stone. (Flavell, 1985, p. 55)

The experimenter also has the child view the stone under a magnifying glass and through a blue filter, and asks similar questions about its real and perceived size and color.

Children between 3 and 4 years of age are likely to make one of two types of errors. They say that the stone *is* an egg ("phenomenism") and that the stone *looks like* a rock ("intellectual realism"). Errors of phenomenism occur when the child focuses only on the object's appearance. The child's performance on this task thus resembles the child's "failure to conserve" on typical conservation tasks, in which the child is presented with two objects identical in appearance, and then the appearance of one object is changed. The child in the conservation task is asked to compare the objects on the relevant dimension (e.g., weight, number). In both the conservation task and the stone task, the child seems to confuse an object's characteristics with its appearance. Phenomenism errors are especially likely to occur when children are asked questions concerning objects' physical properties, such as color or size. When looking at the stone through a magnifying glass, children say both that the stone looks big (correct) and really is big (incorrect).

The child who makes the second type of error, intellectual realism, seems to be ignoring the object's appearance and responding on the basis of the object's actual properties. Although the stone looks exactly like an egg, the child responds both that it is a stone (correct) and that it looks like a stone (incorrect). When the stone is viewed under the magnifying glass, the child responds that it really is small and that it looks small. Similarly, when the stone is viewed through a blue filter, the child responds that it is really white and that it looks white.

Flavell concluded that children's failures on the appearance–reality tasks illustrate their difficulty in thinking about and comparing what they *know* and what they *perceive*. When these two sources of information are inconsistent, children select one source to attend to.

The appearance–reality distinction requires going beneath the surface appearances to ferret out what something or someone is "really like." Difficulty in mastering this cognitive landmark probably accounts for the finding that a child's perceptions of people tend to be based on external characteristics (appearances), polarized (e.g., the person is either good or bad), and dependent on the child's immediate experience with the person rather than on enduring experiences. It is reflected in the child's belief that an excellent baseball player who does a bad thing can no longer be good at playing baseball (Saltz & Medow, 1971). Similarly, when viewing a videotape in which a character performs good deeds and then bad ones (or bad first and then good ones), young children recall only the good or the bad actions (Gollin, 1958).

The interviewer should remember that the child's perception of a person may reflect only part of the the child's experiences with that person. A young child may express only positive feelings toward a parent, relative, or teacher because the child has difficulty coordinating his or her different experiences with that person. It is hard for the young child to grasp that a teacher (positive-valanced role) who looks nice and does many good things also does bad things (such as ridicule or punish excessively). Of course, it is even harder for the child to accept the reality that a trusted and beloved relative such as an uncle could do such bad things as sexual molestation.

Children's self-perceptions are similar to their perceptions of others, in that they are global, evaluative, and polarized. It is difficult for the young child to admit to negative, "bad" feelings or behaviors without concluding that he or she is also "bad." The interviewer, outside a strong therapeutic relationship with the child, should avoid confronting the child with inaccuracies that are in defense of the child's self-esteem. The interviewer can reduce the threat posed by questions that elicit negative feelings by following five strategies recommended by Yarrow (1960, p. 580):

1. The interviewer can suggest in the question that other children might feel the same way. For example, "All girls sometimes get mad at their parents. What sorts of things make you feel mad?"

2. The interviewer can present two or three alternatives, each of which appears equally acceptable: "Do you think your parents expect too much of you, or do you think they expect about the right amount, or too little?"

3. The interviewer can choose words that soften an undesirable response or that makes it appear more acceptable. For instance, instead of asking a boy if he hits, the interviewer can ask, "If a boy in your class teases you, do you punish him so he stops or do you let the teacher know about it?" This example combines providing two alternatives that sound about equal in acceptability and relabeling actions to minimize their negative connotations (punishing instead of hitting and letting the teacher know instead of tattling).

4. Rather than requiring the child to admit engaging in negative behaviors or having negative feelings, the interviewer can assume that the child engages in these negative behaviors (e.g., "What sorts of things do you and your brother fight about the most?"). Clearly, this technique must be used sensitively, both to avoid damaging rapport by creating the impression in children that the interviewer thinks the worse of them and to avoid arousing anxiety in children by forcing them to admit to negative behavior. This technique is best used when preceded with a statement that shows the acceptability of the behavior, such as "All brothers fight sometimes." The interviewer can give the child an opportunity to express a positive feeling before asking a question that elicits a negative one. For example, children can be asked what they like best about school before they are asked to report on what they don't like.

Ability to Decenter

Piaget (1957) described the preschool child's thinking as "egocentric" because children apparently have difficulty assuming a perspective (visual, spatial, emotional, or cognitive) different from their own. As discussed earlier, linguistic demands of a task account in part for children's difficulty with standardized perspective-taking tasks, such as the three-mountain task, described above. Nevertheless, considerable evidence exists to support the view that children's thinking is more egocentric than that of older children or adults. "Egocentricity" is defined as a failure to distinguish clearly between one's own point of view and another's (Flavell, 1985, p. 124).

A study by Mossler, Marvin, and Greenberg (1976) illustrates the young child's egocentrism. Children between ages 2 and 6 were shown a videotape in which a good part of the information was provided by the audio portion of the videotape. Mothers were absent during this initial presentation of the videotape. Then children and mothers viewed the tape together, but the audio portion was turned off, and the children's attention was pointedly directed to this fact by the experimenter. Afterwards, the children were asked questions about their mothers' knowledge of the events in the film. Children under 5 showed no awareness that their mothers' knowledge was different from their own and attributed to her the same knowledge they had. Children 5 and 6 years of age, in contrast, were able to infer what the mothers knew and did not know on the basis of the mothers' limited perceptual experience.

Often the interviewer's task is to obtain the necessary clarification without making the child feel like an inadequate communicator. Frequent queries of the sort "Who did that?" or "Who is Jack?" may be less effective in facilitating the child's communication than waiting for the child to clarify ambiguities. The following dialogue occurred between Jan Hughes and 6-year-old Tim, as he handled a lump of clay:

T~IM~: I'm not going to be friends with Gary any more. [This was the first time Gary had been introduced into the conversation.]

J~H~: You don't feel like being friends with Gary.

T~IM~: He wouldn't let me see his forts.

J~H~: Umm.

T~IM~: And I asked him to be on my team.

J~H~: Where do you play with Gary?

T~IM~: At home. He lives next door. He's 7. We have these forts next door in a field. And we have a map. Only he made a new map with Roger and now I don't know where his forts are.

J~H~: Are you still on the same team?

T~IM~: Not now. He and Roger are on a team. They know where their forts are. So I'm going to steal their map and knock down their forts. That'll teach them!

J~H~: You are mad!

The child's tendency to attribute his or her own thoughts and feelings to others makes use of incomplete stories and play scenarios especially helpful. The stories can be presented with picture aids or acted out with dolls. The child is asked to respond for the story character; however, children's responses are likely to reflect their own experiences. This interview approach sounds similar to the use of projectives with children. For example, the Madeleine Thomas stories and Despart fables (Wursten, 1960) resemble the incomplete-story approach recommended here. However, the child's responses to the stories or other stimuli in the interview are not interpreted as signs of unconscious processes, such as drives and defense mechanisms. Rather, they are interpreted as expressions of the child's conscious thinking processes.

Memory

In Chapter 1, several aspects of children's memory development have been discussed in relation to the accuracy of children's memory and children's vulnerability to the effects of suggestibility. We have concluded that children's recall memory is more accurate but less complete than their recognition memory, and that children's knowledge structures (event schemas and scripts) become more detailed and accessible with age. These developments in memory have several implications for the interviewer.

First, when the purpose of the interview is to obtain accurate information, the interviewer should rely more on open-ended questions and reconstructive approaches to recall than on direct and specific questioning (King & Yuille, 1987).

Second, one reason why young children's unaided recall is poor is that they are deficient in strategies for retrieving memories. Strategies for remembering are referred to as "metamemorial" strategies. Thus, young children require extensive props to enhance their recall. Concrete props, such as dollhouses, that are similar to the setting in which the events to be remembered were experienced lead to more complete event recall (Goodman, 1984; McNamee, 1989).

Third, children's recall for recurring events (script memory), as opposed to their memory for events that occurred only once or a few times (episodic memory), is relatively good.

> Young children find it easier to describe a script for a familiar sequence than a memory for a specific instance of that script. In other words, young children can more easily provide the script for going to McDonalds than they can remember the specifics of their last meal there. (King & Yuille, 1987, p. 32)

Thus, asking children to recall a familiar script (such as dinnertime, bedtime, or getting ready for school) and using manipulatives or the incomplete-story technique result in more complete recall than does asking children to report on a specific experience.

Social Cognition

Social cognition is concerned with the observations and inferences we make about people's intentions, attitudes, emotions, dispositions, and other "under-the-skin" characteristics, as well as observations and inferences about such social relationships as those with friends, peer groups, and family members (Flavell, 1985). Children's ways of thinking about intrapersonal and interpersonal events change over time. Their conceptualizations of people (including themselves) and relationships are qualitatively different at different developmental levels. In Chapter 1, developmental changes in children's perceptions of people and their understanding of conflicting emotions have been discussed. In addition, the discussion earlier in this chapter on the appearance–reality distinction has reviewed children's increasing ability to distinguish a person's appearances and "true self." In general, children under 8 years of age describe people in global, polarized, evaluative, and highly self-referenced terms. Between 8 and 11 years of age, children's descriptions of people rely less on appearances, include more traits and dispositions, are less global and stereotyped, and include more abstract terms ("honest," "selfish") and more precision (e.g., "considerate" replaces "nice"). Nevertheless, their perceptions of others are not integrated into dynamic wholes, and their descriptions seem to be a string of adjectives rather than a coordinated perception. Adolescents' person descriptions reflect their attempt to integrate conflicting traits and to explain apparent inconsistencies (e.g., "She is loud and domineering, but that is an act to cover up her insecurities.") (Flavell, 1985).

> If one were to view the "child as a psychologist" who subscribes to certain positions or theories, the developmental changes, broadly put, suggest the following: prior to 7 or 8, the child conceives of persons largely as one who is both a demographer and a behaviorist would, defining the person in terms of her environmental circumstances and observable behavior; during middle childhood, persons are conceived more as a trait-personality theorist would, ascribing unqualified constancies to persons; and by the onset of adolescence, a more interactionalist position emerges in which people and their behavior are often seen as a joint function of personal characteristics and situational factors. (Shantz, 1983, p. 506)

We have already discussed the importance of respecting a child's struggle with coordinating mixed feelings by not forcing the child to admit to negative behaviors or thoughts. There are several additional implications of the child's developing person perception. First, the interviewer should not take at face value a young child's expression of positive or negative feelings toward others. Because feelings are reactive to recent situations and polarized (all or none), statements of strong negative feelings such as "I hate school" or "I hate my sister" may represent a child's momentary feeling state rather than a generalizable, stable feeling. Similarly, the child may believe that one parent is all good and the other parent, who sets limits on the child's behavior, is "mean." If the "good" parent disciplines the child, these perceptions may be reversed (Bierman, 1983).

Second, if the interviewer desires more specific information about a child's relations with others, general questions such as "Tell me about your daddy" are likely to yield an "I don't know" or a flat refusal to communicate. If such information is desired, the child might be asked to describe familiar routines, such as dinner or homework, and the interviewer can introject questions such as "And who do you ask to help you with homework?" "What happens when Dad helps you?" "What happens when Mom helps you?".

Children in middle childhood provide accurate and complete information with self-report questionnaires, which can be used in an interview or modified for interview presentation. Bierman and Schwartz (1986a) review four such questionnaires that assess children's perceptions of their relations with family and peers. The Network of Relationships Inventory (Furman & Buhrmester, 1985), developed for fifth- and sixth-grade children, is a promising example of this type of measure. Children rate different relationships (parents, teacher, friends, siblings) on six social dimensions (enhancement of worth, companionship, affection, instrumental help, intimacy, and reliable alliance) and four other qualities (relative power, conflict, satisfaction, and importance of the relationship).

Recursive Thinking

When a child is able to think about what another person thinks about him or her ("I think he thinks I like him"), the child has mastered an important social-cognitive skill. This type of thinking about one's own or another's thinking, referred to as "recursive thinking," usually emerges at about 7 or 8 years of age and continues to develop into adolescence (Flavell, 1985; Barenboim, 1978). This ability enables the child to answer questions about what other people might be thinking about him or her. "Why do you think he thought you did that?" is a question the 9- or 10-year-old child is probably capable of answering, but younger children may not be. Similarly, statements such as "I thought you knew I meant X" and "I thought you knew I was joking" can be understood by the child who has developed recursive thinking.

Recursive thinking improves the child's ability to purposefully deceive others into misattributing the child's actual beliefs, attitudes, intentions, feelings ("If I laugh about being called fatso, she will think I don't care"). In the interview, the child may present himself or herself in a "false"manner for any of several reasons, including pleasing the interviewer, protecting self-esteem, or being loyal to family or friends. Establishing a trusting and accepting relationship with the preadolescent and adolescent child is essential to obtaining authentic responses. Conveying the purpose of the interview, dispelling the child's apprehensions about the interview, and spending time establishing the relationship are especially important to interviewing this age group.

PSYCHOSOCIAL DEVELOPMENT

Children's Self-Esteem and Coping

A child's self-esteem is the child's subjective evaluation of his or her personal worth. It consists of a combination of general and specific thoughts and feelings concerning the self (i.e., one's self-concept and one's overall experience of cohesiveness and well-being; Demos, 1983). Although different theorists have identified different aspects of self-esteem (see Harter, 1983), one's self-judgments of competence versus incompetence and self-judgments of acceptance (or relatedness) versus rejection (or isolation) emerge as the two major dimensions (Stott, 1989). "I am capable and lovable," the credo of school-based self-esteem enhancement programs such as Magic Circle (Bessell & Palomares, 1967), incorporates these two basic self-concepts.

Self-esteem develops as a result of a child's interactions with his or her environment. Children who have experienced nurturing, accepting caretakers and who have had opportunities to succeed in their mastery attempts generally have a positive self-concept. Children who have experienced humiliation, rejection, and failure generally have feelings of low self-worth and vulnerability. "Out of the interaction of a child's experiences and characteristics comes a perspective on himself, or self-esteem, and a set of strategies and tactics for dealing with the world, or coping mechanism" (Stott, 1989, p. 18).

Self-esteem affects achievement striving, use of coping strategies (including defense mechanisms), interpersonal competence, and willingness and ability to communicate. Of particular interest to this discussion is the influence of a child's self-esteem on the child's communication and behavior in the interview.

When persons experience a threat to their self-esteem, they respond in ways intended to preserve their feelings of self- worth. Ways of coping with threats to one's self-esteem include positive coping strategies, such as exploration, asking for assistance, and taking credit for and pride in one's accomplishments, as well as defensive strategies (Stott, 1989). Defense mechanisms are coping strategies that are usually unconscious and include denial, regression, repression, projection, and displacement (A. Freud, 1937). Children, perhaps because of their more limited repertoire of coping strategies or more frequent experience of threat, rely more on defense mechanisms than adults do. Defense mechanisms are not necessarily maladaptive. In fact, they serve useful purposes in enabling children to maintain positive feelings about themselves and their ability to cope with a situation. For example, a 5-year-old girl may project her feelings of resentment toward a new baby to another sibling, enabling her to protect herself against the anxiety associated with acknowledging these "bad" feelings. Denial in seriously ill children helps them cope with the enormity of their situation by making it seem more manageable (Worchel, Copeland, & Barker, 1987).

Clara, age 5, illustrates the potential positive aspects of defense mechanisms. Between the ages of 2 and 4, Clara experienced recurring sexual molestation by multiple adults, in which her mother participated. Clara had been removed from her home because of neglect and placed in a foster home, pending a court hearing to determine permanent custody. Only after a year of being separated from her mother and being involved in psychotherapy did Clara relate the sexual abuse. When Clara entered therapy, she relied on denial and an exaggerated need for control as her ways of coping with her experiences. These coping strategies permitted Clara to maintain her feeling of cohesiveness and safety. Clara was very controlling in the initial sessions, putting each colored marker back in its box after using it, telling the interviewer where to sit and what to do, putting each toy up before she selected a different toy, and refusing to do many of the things asked of her (e.g., when asked to draw a picture of a girl, she refused, stating that she was going to draw a picture of a balloon; when offered a raccoon puppet to play with, she told the examiner to put it in the drawer and never to get it out again). By establishing control over her environment, Clara was protecting herself from her past experiences of helplessness when she was hurt. At first, Clara refused to talk about her mother. Then she talked about a "bad" mother in her play, and a real "good" mother, clearly stating that the bad mother was "only pretend." Finally, after a year of therapy, she said that her real mother had been bad to her and dramatically depicted the abuse in her drawings. After she admitted the abuse, she began to show less rigidity and more spontaneity in her play.

Despite Clara's extreme sexual abuse, her behavior in her kindergarten class was appropriate, and she extended herself emotionally to her foster mother. Her defenses appeared to be helping her cope with her past experiences. After she felt safe in her new home and safe with the therapist, she replaced the denial and control with less defensive and more adaptive coping strategies.

Respecting Children's Defenses

The interviewer should respect children's use of defense mechanisms and should not confront children with their use of denial, projection, or other defenses outside an ongoing therapeutic relationship; even within such a relationship, defenses should be confronted only if they are interfering with positive coping. The following example illustrates the risks inherent in tearing down a child's denial. Six-year-old Katy had been wetting her pants at school and avoiding interacting with her classmates. The school counselor was aware of the fact that Katy's mother, a single parent, had abandoned Katy and her 4-year-old sister 3 weeks earlier. The mother had dropped them off at her parents' house for a "few hours" and had not returned. Her whereabouts were unknown. Initially Katy was cooperative in the interview, choosing to color as she talked with the counselor. When asked to draw a picture of her family, Katy drew her sister, her mother, and herself. The counselor asked, "Does your picture show the way things used to be at home or the way things are now?" Katy seemed puzzled, and the counselor asked whether Katy's mother lived with her right now. Katy responded, "Yes. My mom went on a trip but she will be back tomorrow." When the counselor pushed by asking Katy if her mother had called her or told her good-bye, Katy crawled under the table, refusing to talk during the rest of the session. Katy was using denial to protect her from the anxiety associated with admitting that her mother had left her. When her defenses were torn down, she felt vulnerable and was no longer willing to communicate.

It is not necessary that the interviewer agree with the child's self-protective but untrue view of reality. Often an empathic statement that conveys to the child both respect for the child's struggle to cope and acceptance of the child's feelings will shore up self-esteem and lead the way to more open communication. For example, Richard, 9 years old, lived with two alcoholic parents about whom he worried a great deal. During the first session, Richard regaled the interviewer with accounts of his playground toughness. At school, he had a short temper and got into frequent fights. His tough demeanor allowed him to deny his fears and worries. The interviewer commented, "You seem to enjoy tackling problems head on instead of just worrying about them," giving Richard an opportunity to acknowledge his fears while not tearing down his defenses.

The case of Nellie offers a second example. Nellie's mother had been in and out of psychiatric hospitals several times during the child's 6 years. Nellie had never known her father. When Nellie's mother was with her, they lived in low-rent hotels and moved frequently. In the interview, Nellie described a life with her mother that was quite at odds with her reality. She told the interviewer about the birthday party her mother was planning for her, all the toys her mother had bought for her, and the times they played together. The interviewer commented, "I think most girls would want fancy birthdays and lots of time to play with their mothers," accepting Nellie's wishes without confronting the truthfulness of her report.

Establishing an Accepting Relationship

When children feel respected, accepted, and safe in the interview, they respond more freely and honestly. The child's relationship with the interviewer is the most important determinant of the child's communicative competence and openness. Referring to the child interview in developmental research, Yarrow (1960) stated, "The interview is distinguished from other data gathering research approaches commonly used with children by its dependence on an interpersonal relationship. This is a source of strength as well as difficulty" (pp. 561-562). Furthermore, the more sensitive the information sought in the interview, the more important is the relationship. "An interview that probes feelings, attitudes, and deeply personal orientations requires a deeper level of relationship in terms of warmth, sensitivity, and responsiveness than one concerned primarily with obtaining factual data" (p. 569).

Following are suggestions for building a relationship with a child that is characterized by mutual respect and warmth—one in which the child feels accepted and safe.

Listening

The successful interviewer depends more on listening skills than on questioning skills. Through listening, the interviewer shows respect for the child and a genuine desire to listen to the child's ideas. Through listening, the interviewer encourages children to express themselves fully and nondefensively. As a result of being listened to, children develop a clearer understanding of their thoughts and feelings and greater self- confidence in handling problems.

Empathic listening is an active process that includes both nonverbal and verbal behaviors. An empathic response validates and accepts the child's experience. It does not introduce new content or offer advice. Rather, it reflects, or mirrors, the content and the feeling expressed by the child. It can be a restating of what the child says, or it can offer a link between seemingly isolated statements made by the child. The important thing is that the child feels understood and is encouraged to share his or her thoughts and feelings with the interviewer. Consider the following examples of reflective listening.

CHILD: (*Tearing up a drawing he is dissatisfied with*) I'll never get this right.

INTERVIEWER: You weren't pleased with your drawing, and you're feeling discouraged.

CHILD: (*After arguing with Johnny*) I hate Johnny. I don't care if I ever play with him again.

INTERVIEWER: I can see you're really mad with Johnny right now.

CHILD: (*Near tears*) That mean old Mrs. Jones. She gave me so much homework I'll miss all of my favorite TV programs.

INTERVIEWER: You have a lot of homework. It must be hard to work all day at school and then to have homework, too.

CHILD: The teacher makes me do dumb stuff [exercises for learning problems] all the time. The other kids don't do the dumb stuff, and I hate it.

INTERVIEWER: Some of the stuff your teacher gives you to do feels like dumb stuff, and you don't like that a bit. And the fact that the other kids don't have to do it bothers you, too.

CHILD: (*After talking about parents fighting, the child stops abruptly, in mid-sentence.*)

INTERVIEWER: It's scary when people are angry with each other.

In each of the examples above, the interviewer responds reflectively to the child's statement and behavior. A reflective response does not add anything new to what the child expresses. It rephrases what the child has expressed, or it describes what the child is doing in the interviewer's own words. It may rephrase the content of what the child says ("You have a lot of homework"), or it may reflect the child's feeling, either directly or indirectly expressed by the child, or both. When reflecting a feeling that the child has not directly stated, the interviewer should be tentative in suggesting that the child may be expressing a particular feeling. Children (and adults) do not like to be told in an authoritarian manner how they are feeling, but they do feel accepted and understood when an adult picks up on their feelings and summarizes them in a questioning rather than an "expert" manner.

Nonverbal listening behaviors include smiling, appropriately timed nodding, maintaining a relaxed but interested physical posture, matching one's facial expression to the feeling the child expresses, and maintaining frequent (but not constant) eye contact. With children, interviewers should keep their eyes on the children's level (or close to it). Stooping or sitting in a child-size chair communicates to a child the interviewer's genuine interest in "getting his or her point of view."

The child is helped to feel accepted when the interviewer adapts his or her language to the child's. A therapist, trying to find out how a 10-year-old boy who defecates in his pants feels just before he defecates, uses the child's language in asking questions. If the boy uses the word "poop," the therapist uses that term.

Beginning the Interview

How to begin the interview depends on the nature and purpose of the interview and the developmental level of the child. In general, it is important to provide some time for the child to explore the interview setting. Young children might bring something from home (e.g., a craft project, pictures of pets, a favorite doll) to the first interview as a way of making the setting more familiar. Because the child is the expert on what he or she brings, the child is likely to assume some control in the interview rather than to respond passively.

The child should be told the purpose of the interview. The nature of the explanation and the amount of detail provided will differ according to the child's age and the interview's purpose. We find that children respond more cooperatively when they are treated as individuals who are capable of understanding what is expected of them. With children under 8, we often introduce ourselves as "worry doctors—people who help kids and their parents with things that they are worried about."

The following explanation was given to an 8-year-old referred for a personality evaluation:

> Your parents and your teacher told me that you don't seem as happy as other boys, and you keep pretty much to yourself. I want to help you feel better. Today we'll talk some, because no one else can tell me how you feel about things but you. I'll ask you to answer some questions in a booklet about how you think and feel about different things. Then I'll ask you to make some drawings for me, and we might make up some stories together. You will have a chance to ask questions as we go along. Do you have any questions right now?

It is important that the child be capable of answering the first questions asked in the interview. First questions should not involve problem areas and often ask for factual information, such as "What grade are you in?" and "Who is in your family?" The interviewer will want to avoid establishing a test-like format early in the interview; this can be done by alternating questions with comments on the child's responses and requests for elaboration. When children feel confident of their ability to perform adequately in the interview, they will attempt harder questions that they might otherwise have refused to answer. Providing a lump of clay, Legos, or some colored markers and paper permit the latency-age child to avoid prolonged eye contact, which is uncomfortable for children unfamiliar with adult-like conversations.

Phrasing and Sequencing Questions

Specific strategies for reducing the threat of questions have been offered earlier in this chapter. It is also important to avoid "why" questions. The interviewer who asks a boy why he avoids using the toilet when he needs to have a bowel movement or a girl why she stole $5.00 from the teacher's desk will probably not receive a helpful answer, and the child may feel threatened or incompetent. Children are often not aware of the motives underlying their behaviors. Furthermore, "why" questions are threatening and increase a child's resistance. Often "why" questions can be rephrased as "what" questions: "What about using the toilet is unpleasant?" "How do you feel when you use the toilet?" "What did you do with the money?" "What do you like most (and least) about your teacher?"

Appropriate sequencing of questions in the interview is important. In addition to gradually increasing the difficulty and threat posed by questions, the interviewer should shift from open-ended questions to more specific questions. Wood and Wood (1983) note that questions are an "exercise in power" (p. 161). Questions that highly restrict the possible responses of children place the adult in control of the interaction. Children may respond to this threat to their autonomy and self esteem by refusing to respond at all or by giving short, terse answers (Beer, 1989). Beer goes on:

> They respond better to open, indirect questions which leave a substantial (but not infinite) range for response, and to questioning sequences that let the child exert some control by initiating and terminating the discussion of new topics at least as much as the adult. Having said (with adult encouragement) what they would like to say about a given topic, children will respond to narrow and directed probes. Their position in the flow of the interview is of the utmost importance in maintaining an appropriately balanced relationship and in facilitating the adult's receipt of information. (p. 188)

Beer also recommends embedding questions into actions, topics, and drawings that the child introduces.

Accepting the Child's Feelings

Rephrasing or restating children's stated or implied feelings helps children feel that the interviewer accepts their feelings. In addition, children may need to be told that feelings do not make things happen and that lots of other children experience similar feelings. Often it is helpful to relabel a child's expression of feeling, as when telling a boy who cries or states that he is sad, "It is brave to own up to feelings rather than to pretend you don't have them" (Lewis, 1985, p. 10).

Handling Lies

Piers (1989) draws a distinction between taking children's statements seriously and taking them verbatim. Children lie for many reasons, including anxiety about their feelings or perceived failures, a felt need to gain some advantage, a desire to maintain self-esteem, or a wish to avoid disapproval. It is important to look for reasons for a child's lying (Hughes, 1987). Young children may deny wrongdoing or bad feelings because their dichotomous and polarized thinking about people makes the admission of bad behavior or feelings devastating to their self-esteem. Some children lie to protect themselves against the painful knowledge of their actual situation. As noted earlier, confronting a child with the untruthfulness of statements is likely to be damaging to the relationship and to the child's self-esteem.

Dealing with Children at Different Levels of Personality Development

Although preserving self-esteem is important at each developmental level, children at different levels of personality development respond differently to the interview situation and require different approaches.

Preschool

The typical 3- to 6-year-old is eager for adult approval. This desire to please can both help and hinder the interview. It helps because the child is more likely to cooperate with the interviewer's request. It hinders the interview if the interviewer asks leading questions: The child will agree with the interviewer out of a desire for approval. Also, the young child's ego is not well developed, and the child may agree with the interviewer more because of his or her dependency on the interviewer than because he or she truly agrees. Therefore, the interviewer must be careful not to present one alternative to a question as more desirable.

Some preschool children have difficulty separating from their parents. Rather than requiring that a child accompany the interviewer alone, the interviewer should be accepting of the child's feelings and permit the parent to be present during the first part of the interview. After the child has an opportunity to feel comfortable with the interview situation, the interviewer can suggest, "Mrs. Smith, I'd like you to fill out some papers for me now while Johnny and I play and talk some more. There is a place for you to sit in the waiting room." Looff's (1976) handling of separation fears in a 5-year-old girl demonstrates sensitivity and acceptance.

At the appointed hour, I could hear Beth crying loudly "I don't want to!" out in the hallway. Her mother led her gently but firmly into my waiting room and sat down in a chair near the door. As I greeted them, Beth crawled into her mother's lap, buried her face in her mother's shoulder, clung tightly, and sobbed loudly, "I don't want to go! Please don't make me go!" At this point I said, "Gee, it looks like you're feeling very unhappy right now, Beth. You know, lots of girls and boys feel just like you do when they meet a strange doctor for the very first time. I guess your mother told you I am a different kind of children's doctor than she is [the mother was a pediatrician]. She looks in kids' ears, and down their mouths, and listens to their chests. But I don't do that. No, I'm a worry-doctor." Finger in her mouth, Beth was half looking at me from her mother's shoulder at this point. "That doesn't mean that I try to make kids worried. I'm just interested in the worries all girls and boys have growing up. One of your worries right now, I guess, is that mother will leave you. I can understand that. Lots of girls feel that way sometimes. So why don't we have mother come on in with us to my playroom until we get to know each other better. You know, until we won't be strangers anymore." (pp. 84–85)

Grade-School

The grade school child is interested in competition and mastery. The interviewer can capitalize on these developmentally normal interests and concerns by conducting the interview around or after a game. Checkers, cards, Connect Four, and other games that involve both skill and a rather large amount of luck are preferable to purely chance or predominantly skill games.

Grade school children are establishing control of their egos and will not be as easily won over as younger children. The interviewer must respect a child's autonomy and not try to be too friendly, while remaining empathic and concerned. A quiet acceptance and easy-going questions about such age-appropriate issues as school, sports, and television programs can help to demonstrate to children in elementary school that the interviewer will respect their identity as persons in their own right. The interviewer can also ask questions about a child's activities outside of the family, recognizing the child's identity as a person apart from his or her family. At this age, the interviewer should explain the purpose of the interview in more detail, emphasizing the importance of knowing the child's point of view. For example, "No one else can tell me how you think or feel about things, so it is very important that I talk with you, and not just with your parents, or your teachers, or anyone else."

When interviewing children 7 years old and older, it is important to discuss confidentiality. Of course, the degree of confidentially provided to the child depends on the interviewer's purpose and the context of the interview. Regardless of the degree of confidentiality provided, the child at this age should be told what will be shared and with whom it will be shared. A preadolescent's resistance in the interview may be the result of his or her concern that the interviewer will tell the parents or teacher everything that is said. The preadolescent may be reluctant to express feelings or thoughts that are negative toward these people or to admit to behaviors that may be punished.

SUMMARY

This chapter has reviewed children's development in the areas of communication, cognition, and psychosocial functioning, and has discussed implications of these changes for the clinical child interview. The recommendations offered have been relatively broad ones, applicable to more than one interview approach. In Part II, strategies that are more specific to a particular theoretical orientation or interview approach are discussed.

II

APPROACHES TO CLINICAL CHILD INTERVIEWING

3

Structured Diagnostic
Interviews

The development of structured diagnostic interviews for children is a reflection of the advances made in the assessment of childhood psychopathology (Kazdin, 1989). Beginning with the efforts of Rutter and Graham (1968), the development of structured child interviews has continued to generate interest and activity among researchers and clinicians.

The interest in diagnostic interviewing parallels the advances being made in a number of areas of child assessment and diagnosis. An obvious example is the increasing data base that supports the utility of child self-report in assessment and diagnosis (Hughes, 1988; Witt et al., 1988). Another example is the shift toward more specific diagnostic criteria for the determination of childhood disorders. The second edition of the *Diagnostic and Statistical Manual of Mental Disorders* (DSM-II; American Psychiatric Association, 1968) contained limited categories of childhood disorders, which were broadly defined. Over the years more specific and detailed diagnostic criteria for classifying children have been made available, and these changes are reflected in the diagnostic categories contained in the DSM-III (American Psychiatric Association, 1980) and the DSM-III-R (American Psychiatric Association, 1987). Having an explicit set of criteria by which to make diagnostic decisions may reduce the variance associated with clinical judgments based on vaguely defined categories. However, there has also been an increase in the number of categories of childhood disorders. Increasing the number of categories may also decrease agreements among clinicians as to the most representative diagnosis a child should receive (Costello, 1989). Using the specific diagnostic criteria available in the DSM-III and DSM-III-R, numerous researchers have developed structured interview schedules for children as a tool for the systematic and objective evaluation of childhood disorders. Such efforts represent advances in the standardization of diagnostic classification.

In this chapter, four diagnostic interviews for children are reviewed. The interviews selected for review have been the subject of numerous reviews (Edelstein & Berler, 1987; Orvaschel, 1985, 1989; Witt et al., 1988), were readily available for review, and are representative of the advances being made in the development of structured diagnostic interviews. The establishment of adequate psychometric properties is a key component in the development of any assessment tool, and the interviews discussed in this chapter have been designed to yield quantitative data that can be used to evaluate reliability and validity. Given the recent development of these instruments, it is not surprising that evidence of their reliability and validity is limited. Although we recognize the numerous obstacles to evaluating the psychometric properties of structured interviews, we believe that such an evaluation is possible (see Costello, 1989; Hughes, 1988; Witt et al., 1988).

DEGREE OF STRUCTURE

Diagnostic interview schedules differ along a number of dimensions. In organizing our discussion of these interviews, we have grouped them into two categories: highly structured and semistructured.

The unstructured diagnostic interview, which is not considered further in this chapter, is not governed by a fixed set of guidelines or procedures. In such interviews the child supplies the stimuli to which the examiner responds. The role of the examiner is to follow the child's lead and explore and interpret the child's behavior and thematic production. In more structured approaches, the examiner assumes more responsibility for the organization of the interview. By controlling the stimuli to which the child can respond, the examiner can control the format for responding (forced choice or scale rating), the areas that are assessed (home, school, friends, etc.), and the way in which the responses are organized (symptoms vs. syndromes).

Highly Structured Interviews

Highly structured diagnostic interviews contain precise guidelines for administration and scoring. Like standardized tests, structured interviews require strict adherence to procedures for asking questions, rating responses, and ordering items. Such procedures contribute to the systematic and objective collection of quantitative data that can be used to document reliability and validity. It also allows for the acquisition of normative data. Although a high degree of structure can enhance standardization, it can also make the interview rigid and inflexible, which may reduce its sensitivity to the very sources of information that the interview is uniquely capable of supplying.

Semistructured Interviews

Semistructured interviews offer the flexibility to make adjustments in the administration of the interview on the basis of the characteristics of the individual child. By providing more flexible procedures for administration, the examiner can adjust the language, tempo, and content of the interview to fit the child and create a more conversational approach to the interview. Often the decision to make alterations in the interview format is a matter of clinical judgment. However, the clinician must keep in mind the introduction of modifications to standardized procedures, based on clinical judgments, represents a threat to reliability and validity.

Choosing an Interview Schedule

Each of the interviews included in this chapter provides DSM-III or DSM-III-R diagnoses, and the authors of each interview provided evidence of the its reliability and validity. However, the development of each of the interviews was guided by different purposes and procedures. As with the selection of any assessment tool, the choice of the most appropriate diagnostic interview is based on a number of variables. When choosing an interview schedule, the clinician needs to consider the purpose of the interview, the psychometric properties of the interview, the data it provides, the populations for which it is most appropriate, the level of training necessary to administer it, and the time and resources required for its use. These and other characteristics are reviewed in our discussion of each interview.

HIGHLY STRUCTURED DIAGNOSTIC INTERVIEWS

The Diagnostic Interview for Children and Adolescents—Revised

Description

The Diagnostic Interview for Children and Adolescents—Revised (DICA-R; Reich & Welner, 1989) is the most recent revision of the Diagnostic Interview for Children and Adolescents (DICA) (see Table

**TABLE 3.1. Diagnostic Interview for Children and Adolescents—
Revised (DICA-R)**

Age range: 6–17 years

Forms: Child, adolescent, and parent

Interview format: Brief joint interview with parent and child followed by
   separate interviews with different examiners

Number of items: 267

Administration time: Approximately 60 minutes

Training requirements: Trained interviewer recommended

Degree of structure: Highly structured

Scores obtained: Symptom scores
                 Total symptom scores

Diagnostic information: DSM-III-R, Axis I diagnoses

Diagnostic decisions: Keyed to DSM-III-R criteria

Reliability data^a: Interrater agreement

Validity data^a: Parent–child agreement
                  Agreement with hospital discharge diagnoses

---

^{a}Currently available only for the original DICA.

3.1). The DICA was modeled after the adult Diagnostic Interview
Schedule (DIS) developed at the National Institute of Mental Health
(Robins, Helzer, Croughan, & Radcliff, 1981). Parallel interviews with
children 6–17 years of age (DICA-C) and parents (DICA-P) determined
diagnostic classification according to the DSM-III criteria.

   The revisions contained in the DICA-R make the interview compat-
ible with DSM-III-R diagnoses. There are three versions: the DICA-R-C
for children 6 to 12 years of age, the DICA-R-A for adolescents 13 to 17
years of age, and the DICA-R-P for parents of children 6 to 17 years of
age. The versions are identical except for differences in wording between the child and adolescent versions in order to make the items age-
appropriate. Wording for the parent version is changed so that the
referent for the items is "my child" rather than "I." The DICA-R also
differs from the DICA in that the wording of the items has been
modified to produce a more conversational style of interaction between
the examiner and the respondent.

Administration and Scoring

The adolescent and child versions of the DICA-R contain 267 items.
The average time for administration of the DICA is 60 minutes, and the

time required for the administration of the DICA-R interviews is assumed to be similar. Many of the diagnostic categories contain "skips"; that is, if there are only "no" responses to the initial items in a category, the examiner can move to the next section.

The interviews begin with a 12-item joint interview with the parent (or parents) and child to obtain demographic data. After this task is completed the parent(s) and the child are separated and both are interviewed separately by different examiners.

Responses are coded for on the basis of the presence or absence of the symptoms covered in the interview. Although the responses "sometimes" and "rarely" can be coded, the authors suggest that the examiner attempt to elicit a "yes" or "no" response. The "sometimes" and "rarely" responses are used as criteria for determining severity. The DICA-R has attempted to provide some of the flexibility contained in semistructured interviews by including structured probes for use with ambiguous responses. The training manual provides a flowsheet for the procedures to be used for structured and open-ended probes.

The items are arranged according to DSM-III-R Axis I disorders and cover symptoms related to disruptive behavior disorders, anxiety disorders of childhood or adolescence (also including simple phobia, obsessive–compulsive disorders, and posttraumatic stress disorder), eating disorders (anorexia and bulimia), elimination disorders, psychoactive substance abuse disorders (alcohol, cigarette smoking, glue sniffing, marijuana, and street drugs), depressive disorders, somatization disorder, and psychoses.

The final portion of the interview includes an assessment of psychosocial stressors. After the interview is completed there is an observational checklist for the clinician to fill out, as well as space for clinical impressions. Diagnoses are determined by using the DICA-R scoring criteria presented at the end of the interview booklet.

Although the DICA-R can be administered with a minimum of training, the authors cite research that suggests that the careful training of interviews can enhance the reliability and validity of the interview (Reich & Welner, 1989). In addition to the training manual, the authors have developed a training videotape and are also available to conduct training seminars. Computerized versions of the DICA-R are currently being developed.

Psychometric Properties

Reliability and validity data on the original DICA include interrater agreement, parent–child agreement, and comparisons of interview diagnosis with hospital discharge diagnosis. Updating earlier studies by

Reich, Herjanic, Welner, and Gandhy (1982), Welner, Reich, Herjanic, Jung, and Amado (1987) examined the psychometric properties of the DICA. With 27 inpatient psychiatry patients ages 7–17, interrater reliability for the DICA-C ranged from .76 for anxiety disorders to 1.00 for attention deficit disorders and conduct disorders. Agreement between the DICA-C diagnoses and the hospital discharge diagnoses was 81.5%. Parent–child agreement was based on DICA-P and DICA-C interviews with 84 outpatient children (7–17 years of age) and their mothers. Results were reported for diagnostic categories in which there were 10 or more subjects. Kappa values ranged from a low of .49 for enuresis to a high of .80 for conduct disorder. Because of differences in parent–child reporting patterns, the use of parent agreement is a questionable method of determining validity (Witt et al., 1988). However, the items on which parent–child pairs agree and disagree are of interest. Not surprisingly, a study of parent–child agreement on the DICA by Herjanic and Reich (1982) showed that highest agreement was obtained on items relating to factual, observable events and behaviors. Mothers reported more behavioral problems, and children reported more unobservable internal states (e.g., depression, anxiety, somatic complaints). These findings lend support to the proposition that children may be better reporters of their internal affective states than their parents and that the inclusion of child self-report data is a useful tool in the assessment of childhood disorders.

Reliability studies of the DICA-R are currently being conducted. Given the similarity between the DICA and the DICA-R there is little reason to expect the results of reliability and studies of the DICA-R to differ significantly from those obtained for the DICA. Although no published data are available, the authors report that agreement on diagnosis and symptoms is good (Reich & Welner, 1989).

SEMISTRUCTURED DIAGNOSTIC INTERVIEWS

The Schedule for Affective Disorders and Schizophrenia for School-Age Children

Description

The Schedule for Affective Disorders and Schizophrenia for School-Age Children (Kiddie-SADS or K-SADS; Puig-Antich & Chambers, 1978) (see Table 3.2) is a semi-structured diagnostic interview that is a downward extension of the adult version of the Schedule for Affective Disorders and Schizophrenia (SADS) developed by Endicott and Spitzer

TABLE 3.2. Schedule for Affective Disorders and Schizophrenia for School-Age Children (K-SADS)

Age range: 6–18 years

Forms: K-SADS-P (Present Episode)
K-SADS-E (Epidemiologic—lifetime episodes)
Both available in child and parent versions

Interview format: Parent(s) interviewed first, followed by the child interview; both interviews conducted by the same examiner

Number of items: Over 100

Administration time: Approximately 60 minutes for each interview

Training requirements: Trained interviewers with clinical experience

Degree of structure: Semistructured

Scores obtained: Symptom scores
Subscale scores

Diagnostic information: DSM-III-R, Axis I diagnoses

Diagnostic decisions: Clinical judgment

Reliability data: Interrater agreement
Test–retest

Validity data: Parent–child agreement
Identification of depression in prepubertal children

(1978). The interview is now available in two versions. The Kiddie-SADS-Present Episode (K-SADS-P) is designed to obtain diagnostic information regarding current episodes of psychiatric disturbance in children and adolescents ages 6–18. The Epidemiologic version (K-SADS-E) was developed to assess lifetime episodes of psychopathology in children and adolescents ages 6–17 (Orvaschel, Puig-Antich, Chambers, Tabrizi, & Johnson, 1982). The K-SADS-P and K-SADS-E cover symptoms and syndromes that can be used to establish the following DSM-III-R diagnoses: major depression, dysthymic disorder, schizoaffective disorders, schizophrenia, schizophreniform disorder, brief reactive psychosis, paranoid disorders, schizotypal personality, attention-deficit hyperactivity disorder, conduct disorders, overanxious disorders, separation anxiety, phobic disorder, obsessive–compulsive disorder, depersonalization disorder, panic disorder, eating disorders, and substance abuse disorders. Both the K-SADS-P and K-SADS-E are designed to be administered by clinicians with experience and training in diagnostic assessment. For diagnosing disorders that require a detailed past history (attention-deficit hyperactivity disorder, psychoses, etc.) both versions of the K-SADS need to be administered.

Administration and Scoring

The procedure for administering both versions is the same. The parent or parents are interviewed first, followed by an interview with the child. It is recommended that one clinician conduct both the parent and child interviews. It takes approximately 60 minutes to conduct each interview.

The K-SADS-P is designed to be used for diagnosing disorders that have appeared within the last year. The K-SADS-P begins with a brief unstructured interview. During this time demographic information is obtained and the examiner attempts to ascertain the presenting problems, including their onset and duration.

The unstructured interview is followed by a series of questions regarding specific symptoms and their severity. Rating of severity is made according to specified criteria using a 6- or 7-point scale. "Skip" functions are provided for most of the diagnostic categories to allow the examiner to proceed with the interview when it is clear that the informant does not report symptoms consistent with a particular diagnostic category. Two ratings are made for symptoms that are reported to be present. One rating is used to indicate the severity of a symptom at its worst during the present episode (PE). The other rating is made for the severity of the symptom during the last week (LW). In a repeated-measures design, ratings of symptom severity can be compared to assess change and/or treatment effect. Sample questions are provided for each item to be rated. These questions are available as a guide, and examiners are free to ask whatever questions they deem necessary to achieve an accurate rating for an item.

After the interview, the examiner fills out a brief observational checklist and rates the child on a global assessment scale. Diagnostic decisions are based on summary ratings of the responses made by the informants and the clinical judgment of the examiner. During the interviews there may be discrepancies between the report of the parent(s) and that of the child. When these discrepancies involve parental reports of the child's observable behavior, such as suicide, fire setting, or truancy, the authors of the K-SADS suggest that the examiner confront the child and ask why the parent(s) would report such events. If the clinician cannot resolve the difference in the informants' reports in this way it is suggested that the clinician meet with the informants jointly and discuss the reasons for the differences in reports. Ultimately, it is up to the clinical judgment of the examiner to decide how best to respond to and code symptoms where disagreements exist.

The K-SADS-E is designed to provide a lifetime assessment of psychiatric disorders. Questions are organized around diagnostic categories, and the examiner attempts to ascertain information on the chronology, treatment, severity, and functional impairment of DSM-III-R disorders. Again, the parent or parents are interviewed first, followed by an identical interview with the child. As with the K-SADS-P, diagnostic decisions are based on summary ratings of the informants' reports and the clinical judgment of the examiner. Because the K-SADS-E is a lifetime assessment, its authors recommend that the clinician assess the referred child's sense of time before starting the interview. In many cases the parents may be a better source of information than the child about such temporal issues as onset, duration, and treatment of psychiatric disorders. According to Orvaschel and Puig-Antich (1987), children and adolescents are more accurate reporters of conduct disorders and substance abuse problems, and parents are more reliable sources of information about oppositional defiant disorder and attention-deficit hyperactivity disorder. The reports of both sets of informants are necessary for the accurate diagnosis of mood and thought disorders.

The K-SADS-E interview begins with gathering demographic data and completing a short general health history. This is followed by a 5- to 10-minute unstructured interview in which the examiner makes inquires about the child's school functioning, peer relations, activities, and family relations. The formal interview begins with an inquiry into treatment history and moves into sections related to specific diagnostic categories. Symptoms are rated as to whether they are present or absent. Severity ratings are made for the diagnostic category and not for the individual symptoms that comprise the category. Therefore, the K-SADS-E is not as sensitive a measure of change or treatment effect as the K-SADS-P.

Psychometric Properties

Limited reliability and validity data are available on the current versions of the K-SADS-P and K-SADS-E. Chambers et al. (1985) investigated the interrater reliability, test–retest reliability, and parent–child agreement for the symptoms, subscales, and diagnostic categories of the K-SADS-P. Subjects were 52 children ages 6 to 17 years who were referred to a pediatric outpatient clinic. Children and parents were interviewed by one of three pairs of raters, using a test–retest design. Retesting was conducted within 72 hours. Adequate interrater reliability was reported across depressive symptoms with intraclass correlation coefficients (ICCs) of .86 for parent interviews and .89 for the child interviews.

Test–retest reliability for individual symptoms yielded ICCs that ranged from .09 for hypochondria to .89 for conduct disorder (average

$r = .54$). For scale ratings, test–retest reliability ranged from .41 for anxiety disorders to .81 for depressive disorders (average $r = .68$). Finally, test–retest reliability kappa coefficients for diagnoses ranged from .24 for anxiety disorder to .70 for nonmajor depressive disorders (average $r = .53$). Parent–child agreement was moderate for depressive, anxiety, and psychotic disorders and highest for conduct disorder.

Validity studies using earlier versions of the K-SADS have been mostly restricted to the investigation of depression in prepubertal children. The K-SADS has been used to demonstrate the effectiveness of imipramine treatment for children with a major depressive disorder (Puig-Antich, Chambers, Halpern, Hanlon, & Sacher, 1979). However, the effect was seen in only 6 out of 13 subjects. In another study 2 out of 4 children identified as being depressed were found to show cortisol hypersecretion, which is believed by some to be a neuroendocrine marker of depression (Puig-Antich et al., 1979). Because of the small sample sizes in these studies, the results need to be interpreted cautiously.

A validity study of the K-SADS-E (Orvaschel et al., 1982) compared K-SADS-E diagnoses with previous diagnoses using the K-SADS. It was found that diagnoses were the same for 16 of the 17 subjects.

TABLE 3.3. Child Assessment Schedule (CAS)

Age range: 7–16 years

Forms: Child and parent

Interview format: Brief unstructured interview with parent(s), followed by CAS interview with the child; parent version of the CAS available.

Number of items: 320

Administration time: Approximately 60 minutes

Training requirements: Interviewers with clinical experiencerecommended

Degree of structure: Semistructured

Scores obtained: Content scores
                        Symptom scores
                        Total symptoms score

Diagnostic information: DSM-III-R, Axis I diagnoses

Diagnostic decisions: Keyed to DSM-III-R criteria

Reliability data: Test–retest
                    Interrater agreement

Validity data: Parent–child agreement
               Discrimination among inpatient, outpatient, and normal groups

The Child Assessment Schedule

Description

The Child Assessment Schedule (CAS) is a semistructured diagnostic interview appropriate for children ages 7–16 years (Hodges, 1987). The most recent version of the CAS incorporates DSM-III-R diagnostic criteria (see Table 3.3). A parallel parent version is also available.

The CAS is thematically organized according to the content areas of school, friends, activities and hobbies, family, fears, worries and anxieties, self-image, mood and behavior, physical complaints, acting out, and reality testing. Diagnostically related items are included throughout the content areas.

Administration and Scoring

The interview is divided into three sections. In the first part of the interview there are approximately 75 items that relate to the content areas described above. Responses are scored "yes," "no," "ambiguous," or "no response." The CAS is designed to obtain data about functioning within the last 6 months to 1 year. Administration time is approximately 60 minutes.

During the second part of the interview, those items that indicate the presence of symptoms related to DSM-III-R diagnostic categories are further queried to determine the onset and duration of the symptoms. The final section of the interview contains 53 observational items that are recorded by the examiner after the interview is completed.

DSM-III-R diagnoses that can be made on the basis of the CAS include disruptive behavior disorders, anxiety disorders of childhood or adolescence, elimination disorders, depressive disorders, phobic disorders, obsessive–compulsive disorder, and schizoid disorder. In order to make group comparisons, symptom total scores and content scores can be generated. A computer program has been developed that can produce diagnoses based on a computer algorithm, as well as an analysis file and a diagnostic report.

The manual that accompanies the CAS provides instructions for its administration and scoring. It includes consideration of developmental factors in conducting the interview, such as the attention span of the child and the child's understanding of time. Guidelines are also provided for the use of probes in clarifying responses and for dealing with such problems as irrelevant comments and off-task behavior.

The developers of the CAS recommend the use of examiners with clinical experience, even though diagnostic concordance has been reported between the CAS and the K-SADS when lay examiners have been used (Hodges, McKnew, Burbach, & Roebuck, 1987).

Psychometric Properties

Numerous studies of the psychometric properties of the CAS have been conducted. Studies of interrater and test–retest reliabilities have provided substantial support for the reliability of the CAS. In three studies correlation coefficients were .90 or above for the CAS total score, with individual content and symptom complex scores showing moderate to high reliabilities (Hodges et al., 1982; Turner, Beidel, & Costello, 1987; Verhulst, Althaus, & Berden, 1985). In a study of test–retest reliability, correlations for symptom scores, diagnostic categories, and content areas were all significant at p < .01 (Hodges, Cools, & McKnew, 1989). In the same study, adequate test–retest reliabilities were obtained for the diagnoses of conduct disorders, oppositional defiant disorder, major depressive episode, dysthymia, and separation anxiety disorder.

The validity of the CAS has been determined using a variety of procedures. In two studies CAS total scores and symptom complex scores showed significant differences among groups of psychosomatic, behaviorally disturbed, and healthy control children (Hodges, Kline, Barbero, & Flanery, 1985; Hodges, Kline, Barbero, & Woodruff, 1985).

Validity has also been demonstrated in studies examining the relationship of the CAS to self-report measures of depression and anxiety (Hodges et al., 1982). The depression symptom complex score of the CAS was found to correlate significantly ($r = .53$) with the scores on the Children's Depression Inventory, and the CAS anxiety symptom complex score was found to correlate with scores on the State–Trait Anxiety Inventory for Children ($r = .54$).

In addition, the CAS has been used to evaluate responses to treatment intervention. Bousha (1985) used the CAS to evaluate the effectiveness of psychotherapy with children with externalizing behavior problems. When compared to a waiting- list control group the treatment group showed significant decreases on the CAS total score as well as the conduct disorder scale score. These effects were also observed on other dependent measures, including the Child Behavior Checklist.

The Interview Schedule for Children

Description

The Interview Schedule for Children (ISC) is a semistructured interview schedule that is suitable for children and adolescents ages 8 to 17

TABLE 3.4. Interview Schedule for Children (ISC)

Age range: 8–17 years

Forms: Form C (intake)
 Follow-Up Form (re-evaluation)
 Diagnostic Addenda
 All forms available in parent and child versions

Interview format: Parent(s) interview, followed by child interview with the same interviewer

Number of items: Approximately 200

Administration time: For Form C, 1 1/2–2 1/2 hours for parent version; 45 minutes–1 1/2 hours for child interview; slightly less for Follow-Up Form

Training requirements: Experienced clinician with training in ISC administration

Degree of structure: Semistructured

Scores obtained: Symptom scores

Diagnostic information: DSM-III, Axis I and Axis II diagnoses

Diagnostic decisions: Clinical judgment

Reliability data: Interrater reliability

Validity data: Parent-child agreement
 Longitudinal studies on the course of childhood depression

(see Table 3.4). The initial version of the ISC appeared in 1974 and was designed to assess symptoms reflective of childhood depression (Kovacs & Beck, 1977). Revisions of the ISC were made on the basis of pilot testing and the current version of the interview appeared in 1979. There are two versions of the ISC: Form C is used for intake while the Follow-Up Form is used for re-evaluation. Form C and the Follow-Up Form are used to interview both the parent and child. The ISC yields symptom ratings as opposed to differential diagnoses.

The primary utility of the ISC is in assessing affective symptomatology, especially those pertaining to depressive disorders. Diagnostic addenda have been developed to broaden the scope of the interview so that additional DSM-III diagnoses can be obtained. The range of symptoms covered by the ISC makes it possible to diagnose nearly all DSM-III Axis I and Axis II disorders. At the present time modifications have not been made to fit the interview to DSM-III-R diagnoses. Diagnostic decisions are based on symptom ratings obtained from parent and child interviews and on the clinical judgment of the examiner in collaboration with the other members of the assessment team. Therefore, the use of the ISC requires an experienced clinician who is familiar both with the ISC and with DSM-III diagnostic criteria. According to the developer of the ISC, it takes at least 6 months to train an experienced clinician to use the interview schedule properly (M. Kovacs, personal communication, June 1989). Thus, its use is limited by the intensive training requirements.

Administration and Scoring

The interview form contains specific instructions for the administration of the interview. Parents are interviewed first, followed by the child interview. The same examiner can conduct both interviews. Form C of the ISC takes between 1½ and 2½ hours to complete with parent(s), and 45 minutes to 1½ hours with the child. The time necessary to conduct the Follow-Up Form is reported to be shorter than the time needed for Form C (Kovacs, 1985).

The semistructured nature of the ISC is evident in the flexibility it offers the clinician in the ordering and mode of presentation of items. For example, if the child should spontaneously mention areas of difficulty the examiner can proceed to the appropriate section of the interview and continue the inquiry. The examiner is also free to group the symptoms according to content areas (e.g., affective symptoms, symptoms relating to conduct, etc.). In cases where a child may be shy and withdrawn it is acceptable to use drawings to help elicit the desired information. For younger children a number of methods can be used to facilitate accurate responding. If a child appears uncomfortable responding to an item (particularly those reflecting negative affect and behavior) the use of hand gestures to indicate the magnitude of the symptoms is suggested. Double-check items are included throughout the interview. Such questions ask the child to elaborate on initial responses in order to verify their accuracy.

Most symptoms are rated on a scale from 0 ("none") to 8 ("severe"). For the ISC Diagnostic Addenda, symptoms are rated only for their presence or absence, with no provision for recording symptom severity. Spaces are provided on one interview schedule to record parent and child responses as well as the examiner's overall rating of the symptom in question. Where there are discrepancies between the parent and child reports the examiner is instructed to use his or her clinical judgment to arrive at a rating for the item. The time interval for assessing current functioning varies according to the content of the symptoms in question. The presence and intensity of symptoms in affect, cognition, activity level, and thought processes are rated for the 2 weeks preceding the interview. The 6-month period prior to the interview is used to evaluate behavior problems.

The ISC begins with a brief 10-minute unstructured interview during which time the examiner attempts to elicit information on the child's present difficulties. After obtaining these data the examiner proceeds with the formal interview schedule. After the interview the examiner completes a behavioral observation form, followed by ratings of items related to the examiners phenomenological impressions of the child. Finally, the examiner rates the child's highest level of adaptive functioning during the past year and records his or her diagnostic impressions.

Interrater reliability has been reported to be satisfactory for most of the ISC items (Kovacs, 1985). Pairs of interviewers conducted ISC interviews with 35 school-age children and their parent(s). Both of the interviewers were present during the interviews; one interviewer conducted each interview while the other observed. All of the interviewers had clinical experience and at least 7 months of training in the use of the ISC. Symptoms demonstrated adequate interrater reliability with coefficients ranging from .64 to 1.00 (average r = .89). Interrater agreement for the observational items was lower than the agreement for the symptoms, with coefficients ranging from .50 to .96 (average r = .78). Subjective impressions of the examiners showed the least agreement, with a range on the five items between .57 and .89 (average r = .77). Continued investigation of the interrater reliability of the ISC is planned and will utilize videotaped interviews to determine interrater agreement (Kovacs, 1985).

Validity data have been reported on longitudinal studies of childhood depression (Kovacs, Feinberg, Crouse-Novak, Paulauskas, & Feinstein, 1984). When the ISC was used to make DSM-III diagnoses differing rates of recovery were found among groups of children diagnosed as having a major depression, dysthymia, or an adjustment disorder with depressed mood. Parent–child agreement in a sample of 75 psychiatric inpatients ages 8–13 ranged from .02 to .95, with an average coefficient of .61 (Kovacs, 1983). Items that assessed observable behaviors showed the highest parent–child agreement, while agreement was lowest for items that assessed affective symptoms.

CONCLUSION

The development of structured diagnostic interviews represents an important development in the study of childhood psychopathology. Structured interviews improve our ability to identify symptoms and syndromes that occur in childhood disorders in that they provide the opportunity to quantify and collect data in a systematic manner. Such efforts are good empirical practices and hold the promise of assisting in the determination of empirically valid and reliable descriptors of childhood disorders.

Another attractive feature of structured diagnostic interviews is their emphasis on the importance of child self-report. By recognizing the value of information that the individual child can offer we move closer to providing comprehensive and meaningful data that will enhance our ability to diagnose and treat childhood disorders.

The variety of interview schedules reviewed in this chapter should provide some information on the range of options available to the researcher or clinician interested in childhood disorders. An instrument such as the DICA-R offers the opportunity to examine a wide range of behaviors and symptoms. The K-SADS and the ISC are especially useful in the assessment of depressive symptomatology in children, and the CAS can provide a useful survey of a child's functioning across a number of significant contexts.

Although these developments are welcome, much more is left to be done. It is important to keep in mind that structured diagnostic interviews are in a state of continual change as is the entire field of the diagnostic classification of childhood disorders. Although structured diagnostic interviews are not yet widely accepted in clinical practice, we hope that the continuing efforts being made to establish their reliability and validity will hasten the time when they become a significant part of the assessment of childhood psychopathology.

4

Psychodynamic Approaches to Child Interviewing

Psychodynamic approaches to child interviewing encompass a variety of theories and techniques related to what Tuma and Sobatka (1983) refer to as "traditional" psychotherapies. Broadly conceived, psychodynamic, relationship, and client-centered therapies are all derivatives of classical psychoanalysis. As Kovacs and Paulauskas (1986) have noted, all these approaches are similar in that they view psychopathology as the result of developmental, dynamic, intrapsychic, and relational disruptions that can best be ameliorated through a relationship with a helping professional whose focus is the individual child.

A central feature of psychodynamic approaches to child interviewing is the emphasis placed on the relationship between the child and the clinician. It is through this relationship that the child comes to gain trust in the process of revealing maladaptive thoughts and feelings and to achieve a level of functioning that is developmentally appropriate for the child's age. The establishment of a therapeutic alliance with the child is viewed as a necessity and is achieved through the clinician's efforts to be genuinely interested in, respectful of, and empathic with the child (Axline, 1947; Gardner, 1979). The therapeutic alliance provides the child with an opportunity to express wishes, fears, and conflicts, which in turn enables the clinician to identify, label, and interpret the child's unconscious thoughts, feelings, and behaviors. Adaptive functioning is enhanced as the child begins to integrate and express unconscious conflicts in a more appropriate fashion. The therapeutic relationship also promotes the emergence of the transference reaction in which the child projects aspects of past and present relationships and experiences onto the clinician and the therapeutic setting (Trad, 1989).

THE DEVELOPMENT OF PSYCHODYNAMIC
INTERVIEWING APPROACHES

The development of psychodynamic approaches to child interviewing can be traced back to the early works of Freud and his followers. In 1909 (the same year of his first and only visit to the United States), Freud published his paper "Analysis of a Phobia in a Five-Year-Old Boy." As most readers will know, the boy was "Little Hans," and his phobia consisted of a fear of horses. Freud only saw Hans on one occasion, and the analysis was conducted by Hans's father, Max Graf. Graf sent Freud detailed notes on the analysis, and Freud provided feedback on how the analysis should be conducted.

In response to repeated suggestions from Freud that Hans be told the facts about pregnancy and birth, Graf provided the following report:

'On April 24th my wife and I enlightened Hans up to a certain point: we told him that children grow inside their Mummy, and are then brought into the world by being pressed out of her like a "lumf", and that it involves a great deal of pain.

In the afternoon we went out in the front of the house. There was a visible improvement in his state. He ran after carts, and the only thing that betrayed a trace of his anxiety was the fact that he did not venture away from the neighbourhood of the street-door and could not be induced to go for any considerable walk.

On April 25th Hans butted me in the stomach with his head, as he has already done once before [p. 42]. I asked him if he was a goat.

"Yes," he said, "a ram." I inquired where he had seen a ram.

HE: "At Gmunden: Fritzl had one." (Fritzl had a real lamb to play with.)

I: "You must tell me about the lamb. What did it do?"

HANS: "You know, Fräulein Mizzi" (a school-mistress who lived in the house) "used always to put Hanna on the lamb, but then it couldn't stand up then and it couldn't butt. If you went up to it it used to butt, because it had horns. Fritzl used to lead it on a string and tie it to a tree. He always tied it to a tree."

I: "Did the lamb butt you?"

HANS: "It jumped up at me; Fritzl took me up to it once....I went up to it once and didn't know, and all at once it jumped up at me. It was such fun—I wasn't frightened." This was certainly untrue.

I: "Are you fond of Daddy?"

HANS: "Oh yes."

I: "Or perhaps not."

Hans was playing with a little toy horse. At that moment the horse fell down, and Hans shouted out: "The horse has fallen down! Look what a row it's making!"

I: "You're a little vexed with Daddy because Mummy's fond of him."
HANS: "No."
I: "Then why do you always cry whenever Mummy gives me a kiss? It's because you're jealous."
HANS: "Jealous, yes."
I: "You'd like to be Daddy yourself."
HANS: "Oh yes." (Freud, 1909/1955, pp. 87–89)

From this passage we are able to get some glimpse of how Freud believed psychoanalysis could be applied to children. Although numerous criticisms could be leveled against the management of Hans's case, it is important to keep in mind that this effort was among the first in the development of child psychotherapy.

Freud later (1922/1955) commented that when the case of Hans was published there was an outcry among his contemporaries that the analysis of such a young child was likely to have devastating psychological consequences. The belief was that the opening of the unconscious in the child would leave the child overwhelmed by intense affects and anxiety. In a postscript to the case of Hans, Freud (1922/1955) described a meeting with Hans when he was 19 years old. Freud had not seen Hans since the analysis and was pleased to report that in regard to the concerns of his critics"....none of these apprehensions had come true. Little Hans was now a strapping youth of nineteen. He declared that he was perfectly well, and suffered from no troubles or inhibitions" (p. 148).

Freud was pleased with the case of Hans. Not only had Hans's phobia been alleviated but the content of the analysis provided what Freud believed to be a confirmation of his theory of infantile sexuality. However, the cause of child analysis and therapy would not be further championed by Freud. For a variety of reasons, the analysis of children was viewed as less of a priority than the analysis of adults and was seen as an activity more suitable for women and lay analysts. This attitude is reflected as late as the 1950s, as evidenced by the following passage from Walker (1957):

> Child psychotherapy is a field in which the merits of the non-medical therapist are undisputed, even in the U.S.A. Most child psychotherapists are women, who not only derive particular satisfaction from working with children but also seem to secure a quicker response from young children than men can. Many of these women have a University degree or diploma in psychology, but work under the general supervision of a psychotherapist with a medical qualification. (pp. 172–173)

During the 1920s Hermine von Hug-Hellmuth (1921), Melanie Klein (1926/1948), and Anna Freud (1926/1974) all published works on the applications of Freudian theory to the treatment of children. Hermine von Hug-Hellmuth, an elementary school teacher and an associate of the Vienna Psychoanalytic Association, was one of the first to apply psychoanalytic methods to the treatment of children. Echoing the concerns of those who felt that analysis may prove too threatening to the young child, Hug-Hellmuth (1921) noted:

> A proper analysis according to psycho-analytical principles can only be carried out after the seventh or eighth year. But even with children at this early age the analyst must, as I will show later, turn aside from the usual routine, and satisfy himself with partial results, where he thinks that the child might be intimidated by too powerful a stirring-up of his feelings and ideas, or that too high demands upon his powers of assimilation are being made, or that his soul is disturbed instead of freed. (p. 289)

Some of the ways in which Hug-Hellmuth turned aside the usual analytic routine included seeing children in their homes, not requiring children to lie on a couch and avoid eye contact with the therapist, and not expecting children to gain full insight into their unconscious impulses and affects. This last point represented the beginning of the use of an important technique in child psychotherapy—namely, that of play. To Hug-Hellmuth the expression of conflicts through symbolic acts served the same function as insight in adults. When working with young children, Hug-Hellmuth (1921) believed that "the analyst can often pave the way by sharing in play activities, and thus he can recognize several symptoms, peculiar habits, and character traits; and in the case of these very young patients, very often play will enact an important part throughout the whole treatment" (pp. 294–295).

Though differing in their approaches to child analysis, Anna Freud and Melanie Klein recognized the importance of play as a vehicle that allowed children to express what they could not or would not say in words. In the treatment of adults, fantasies, wishes, and conflicts could be revealed through free association and dreams. For children such processes could be revealed through the medium of play. Thus the concept of the primacy of play in both elucidating and reducing conflicts was established.

THE POWER OF PLAY

A common assumption underlying psychodynamic approaches to child interviewing is that play allows children to project aspects of their personality and conflicts onto materials that are given symbolic meaning.

Used in this way, play represents a language or form of communication that reveals the inner world of the child (Irwin, 1983). For the clinician the "work" of play is to observe and decipher the symbolic meaning of the child's play.

Another commonly held belief among psychodynamically oriented clinicians is that play reflects a child's attempt at mastery (Ericson, 1950). In "Beyond the Pleasure Principle" Freud wrote,"...in their play children repeat everything that has made a great impression on them in real life, and that in doing so they abreact the strength of the impression and...make themselves master of the situation" (1920/1955, p. 17).

There are numerous ways in which play can serve to reduce anxiety and provide the child with a sense of mastery over conflicts. To begin with, the projective power of play creates a situation where children can exert control and authority over issues that may seem insurmountable in reality. Consider the following example from a 10-year-old boy, Tom. Tom's mother had recently been killed in an automobile accident as a result of another driver's failure to yield at a stop sign. Tom frequently complained of stomach aches but no medical basis for his symptoms could be established and a psychological consultation was requested. During the initial interview Tom refused to discuss anything pertaining to his mother or the accident. When given the opportunity to choose toys from the cabinet Tom selected toy cars and Legos and proceeded to build a town. Each house had a garage and a car. After the town was built, Tom took two cars and used them to destroy the town.

Tom: This is a bad town. The drivers are destroying everything. This is an evil town.

Interviewer: It seems like a lot of bad things happen here.

Tom: Yeah, and I'm going to build a good town.

Tom proceeded to rebuild the town and took the cars out again.

Tom: Now this town, this is a good town. People drive good and don't have accidents.

Interviewer: It would be nice to live in a town where bad things didn't happen to people.

Play can also allow for the expression of hostile feelings that the child may feel are unacceptable. For example, a child who is angered over the birth of a sibling can express hostility through aggressive play with a doll without having to verbally acknowledge the hurt and anger felt over perceived rejection.

The child seen for consultation may feel anxious and uncomfortable talking to an adult stranger who asks personal questions. The opportunity to play with toys and games or draw pictures can provide a means of relieving tension and build rapport, as the case of John demonstrates. Twelve-year-old John was referred for a consultation because of school failure and oppositional behavior. He was virtually mute during the interview and stared out the window rather than talk to the interviewer. Finally, the interviewer said, "Well, I can understand not wanting to talk. How about a game of checkers?" John agreed and became very involved in the game. However, when it appeared that he was about to lose the game, John became more sullen:

JOHN: This is a stupid game, you win.

INTERVIEWER: The game's not over yet.

JOHN: There's no point, you're going to win. I'm not any good at this.

INTERVIEWER: It's frustrating to think you are going to lose, but you have made some really good moves.

JOHN: Let's play again. Maybe I'll beat you. I play checkers with a friend of mine at school and sometimes I beat him.

Yet another benefit of play is the opportunity it affords the child to project thoughts and feelings onto objects as if the thoughts and feelings resided in the objects rather than in the child (Garbarino et al., 1989). Such a projection can keep the child at a distance from feelings and experiences that are perceived to be emotionally overwhelming, as in the case of Ann.

Ann was a 7-year-old girl who had been sexually abused by both her natural father and a foster father, and living in her second foster home. Ann's new foster mother was concerned about Ann's frequent nightmares and fearful behavior. During the interview Ann moved about in her seat and appeared nervous. When shown the toy cabinet she quickly reached for the stuffed animals.

ANN: I like these animals. I have a lot of stuffed animals in my room. I sleep with them and there are so many that they almost take up the whole bed.

INTERVIEWER: Wow! That sure is a lot.

ANN: Some of them I've had a long time.

INTERVIEWER: So some of them have lived in a couple of different houses with you?

ANN: Yeah, I even take them with me if I go on a trip.

INTERVIEWER: You take all of them?

ANN: Well, I should, but mostly I just take the Pound Puppies.

INTERVIEWER: Are they your favorites?

ANN: Kinda. You see, Pound Puppies, they don't have a home and they need someone to take care of them.

INTERVIEWER: What happened to their mom and dad?

ANN: Well, uh, I don't know. I guess they didn't take care of them right. I don't know, they're just Pound Puppies.

THE DEVELOPMENT OF PLAY

If play behavior is seen as a symbolic activity it would follow that the child has developed the capacity for symbolic thought. Numerous researchers have attempted to delineate the stages of play development, and these efforts are providing a meaningful framework for understanding how and what children can tell us about themselves and their development.

During the first 2 years of life, an important milestone is the development of what Piaget (1962) termed the "symbolic function". The development of the symbolic function makes it possible for the child to engage in representational thought which allows for the development of language and pretend play. Research on the development of children's play (for a review see McCune-Nicolich, 1981) indicates that play moves through a series of sequences: Simple meaningful acts (picking up a glass to drink) lead to pretend activities (pretending to drink from a toy cup) that eventually form complex sequences (having a tea party).

As children mature, their play becomes more sophisticated. Clearer distinctions are made between reality and fantasy: the capacity for perspective taking emerges (Flavell, Green, & Flavell, 1986); and interactive play increases (Corsaro, 1979; Iwanaga, 1973). As perspective taking increases play behavior becomes less egocentric, and person fantasy comes to replace object and animal fantasy (Field, De Stefano, & Koewler, 1982; Sarnoff, 1976). For the school-age child, advances in cognitive ability also allow for participation in more structured game-type play activities. Structured games not only match the school-age child's increased intellectual abilities, but also provide a means of assimilating cultural expectations for rule-governed behavior (Garbarino et al., 1989).

Based on psychoanalytic principles and her observations of children's play behavior, Anna Freud (1937) outlined a sequence of play development beginning in infancy. Infant play is dominated by autoerotic activities involving stimulation through the mouth and skin. An Infant makes no distinction between his or her body and the body of the mother and both can be a source of gratification. As a first step toward the recognition of the self as a separate person, the attachments to the body of the mother are transferred to an object (such as a blanket, teddy bear, etc.), which serves as what Winnicott (1951/1965) termed a "transitional object."

Transitional objects begin to be replaced by toys, which serve to gratify instincts and sublimate drives. Toys are used for activities such as filling and emptying, opening and closing, and piecing together as representations of the functions of body parts. Moving toys and construction-type toys serve as an expression of the growing child's sense of mastery and competence.

Mastery over play activities leads to pleasure in task completion, which serves as a foundation for the transition from play to work. The ability to plan, construct and use toys in a meaningful way represents a shift from the pleasure principle (where toys are used for immediate gratification) to the reality principle (where impulses are controlled and gratification is delayed). While the younger child uses toys to put wishes into action, the maturation of the school-age child enables him/her to achieve this through daydreams. Games also provide a means for gratification at this stage, but likewise represent adherence to the reality principle as they require cooperative group behavior and the control of aggression necessary to achieve a desired outcome.

Still further along the line of play development, hobbies appear as a midway point between work and play. Whereas hobbies provide the satisfaction and pleasure derived from play, they also require the ability to plan and delay gratification. Hobbies such as collecting coins, stamps, and dolls require the child to continually seek information and acquire objects over time. Ultimately, the achievement of these developmental tasks provides the child with the abilities necessary for learning and adapting to the demands of society.

THE PLAY ROOM

A variety of opinions exist on the appropriate setting for the play interview, but one aspect is clear: The play space should be safe. "Childproofing" or making the play area safe requires the interviewer to arrange an area and provide materials that will not physically harm the child or allow the child to destroy objects of value. Failure to establish such an environment is bound to lead to power struggles between the interviewer and the child and to increase limit setting by the interviewer.

There are no hard and fast rules as to the type of room used to conduct the play interview. Many would consider a separate play room essential, but it is not a necessity, nor is it always feasible. Extra office space, whether in a public facility (school system, mental health clinic, etc.) or a private practice, is often at a premium, and the interviewer is often forced to make the best of what is available.

While the interviewer does not always have a choice as to where to conduct a play interview, he or she does have a choice as to what types of materials will be available for the child to use during the interview. Psychodynamically-oriented clinicians emphasize toys and materials that will enhance thematic development and elicit themes related to drives and defenses (Krall, 1986; Spiegel, 1989). The following discussion describes items that are frequently utilized in play interviews:

Dolls and Puppets

Figures such as dolls and puppets can allow the child to enact stories that reflect concerns regarding the self and/or relationships to others. Hand puppets can facilitate role playing because they can be easily manipulated. Children will often identify with attributes of a puppet' or doll's character, and a mix of animal and human figures is useful. For example, a child may use a lion puppet to express feelings of power and strength, while a police puppet may be used to express concerns centering around appropriate behavior and punishment. Baby dolls are often used by children to convey themes related to feeding and nurturing. Toy soldiers are also popular toys for eliciting themes about good and bad behavior and attributes. Nearly all children play with puppets and dolls, and their use in a clinical setting is not likely to seem foreign or threatening to the child.

Dollhouse

Dollhouses can be helpful in enabling the child to communicate about family issues. The child may use a dollhouse to represent current issues in the home or to fantasize about how he or she would like things to be. This can often be seen in the play of children whose parents are divorced. For instance, Sam was a 9-year-old boy whose parents had been divorced for a year.

SAM: This is goin' to be a two story house.

INTERVIEWER: Is your house a two-story house?

SAM: No, but I wish it was. I'd like a two story house.

INTERVIEWER: Who lives in this house?

SAM: Well, this is the mom, a son, and a baby. They're going to be in the kitchen eating.

INTERVIEWER: Is there a dad?

Sam took a toy car and drove it up to the house.

SAM: "Here comes the dad. He doesn't live here but he's coming to eat."

Sam then took army men and positioned them around the house.

INTERVIEWER: "What are they doing?"

SAM: "They're trying to get in the house and fight."

A battle ensued and the dad fought the soldiers off.

INTERVIEWER: That was a big fight.

SAM: Yeah, and the dad got hurt, but he'll be all right. He's done eating and he goes back to work (*driving him away in the car*).

Sam's dollhouse play suggested that he was experiencing a variety of concerns related to his parents' divorce. There were themes regarding the satisfaction of basic needs (eating), the need for safety (being attacked and protected), and concern for his father (fighting, being hurt). As with the interpretation of any play activity, the possible meanings of play themes should be considered hypotheses regarding adjustment rather than absolute representations of reality.

Transportation Toys

Cars, boats, and airplanes are toys that most children enjoy and that encourage the expression of mobility. Transportation toys can be used by children to represent fleeing a threatening scene or pursuing a desired object or person. Because of their speed and power, transportation vehicles may also elicit themes related to the expression of control issues and regulation of impulses.

Toy Telephones

The presence of a play telephone may allow the child who is reluctant to discuss or play out conflicts to communicate with the interviewer in an indirect fashion. Using a play phone, the child is able to control who is spoken to, what is discussed, and how long the conversation lasts. It is a good idea to have two toy phones in the event that the child wishes to "call" the interviewer.

Construction Toys

Toys such as building blocks, Legos, and Erector Sets provide children the opportunity to use their imaginations to construct objects of their own choosing. Such activities have projective value because the building production is guided by the children themselves. Construction activities also serve to enhance mastery as children can experience a sense of pride and accomplishment in their ability to make something. A traditional psychoanalytic interpretation of building activity is that it reflects genital modes of expression. In his well-known book, *Childhood and Society*, Erikson (1950) noted that boys tended to construct and adorn towers and then knock them down, while girls tended to build simple enclosures and gates. Based on his clinical observations Erikson believed that this was symbolic of the genital organs and typical of cultural norms that expect males to be aggressive and striving while females are expected to be domestic.

Play-Dough and Sand

Soft materials like Play Dough and sand can be considered a type of sensory toy because they encourage tactile manipulation. The soft and malleable quality of Play Dough makes it easy for the child to quickly change the appearance of or destroy objects and figures. This play provides children the opportunity to project and express feelings and wishes toward objects and figures without having to acknowledge their intent openly.

The use of sand in play interviewing was popularized by the British analyst Margaret Lowenfeld (1970). She developed a method for allowing children to express their conflicts by having them construct a make believe world using a sand tray and toy figures. Lowenfeld and others (Aoki, 1981; Sjolund, 1981) have devised methods for assessing personality variables based on children's sand world productions much in the same way that the Thematic Apperception Test (TAT; Morgan & Murray, 1935) is used to assess adult personality. The assessment value of sand play is related to a clinician's theoretical beliefs. As with most projective techniques, the information provided by the child is best utilized as a source of possible hypotheses that can be confirmed by comparisons with other sources of data.

For some children, particularly those who experience prohibitions (either internally or externally) about being messy, playing with clay may help free the child to reveal feelings and attitudes that may not otherwise be expressed.

Aggression Toys

By design toys such as guns, swords, and bobo dolls easily elicit aggressive play. Aggressive play with these types of play is expected and the interviewer is cautioned about overemphasizing the presence of hostility when these toys are used. When the interviewer is attempting to determine whether aggressive play is diagnostically significant, it is important to consider the frequency and duration of the aggressive play. Does the child persist in aggressive play for the majority of the session? Will the child continue to choose aggressive toys and activities even when other activities of interest are offered? Can the child control his or her aggressive play? Does aggressive play lead to increasing levels of aggression and violence? Have others (parents, teachers) reported that the child displays excessive aggressive behavior? Affirmative answers to these types of questions would indicate that a child's aggressive behavior is diagnostically significant. Just as it is important to evaluate the presence of excessive levels of aggression, it is equally important to note the absence of aggression. A child may ignore aggressive toys or use them only in benign ways. A noticeable lack of aggressive play with aggressive toys may be indicative of prohibitions against the expression of anger and a reflection of passive and depressive tendencies.

Crayons, Paints, and Markers

Although some children may feel more comfortable communicating through toys, others may prefer drawing or painting. The projective value of drawing is seen in the popularity of such techniques as the Draw-A-Person Technique (Levy, 1980) and the House–Tree–Person Test (HTP; Buck, 1948). The use of projective drawings is based on the belief that the child projects unconscious wishes, needs, and conflicts onto the figures drawn (for a more complete description of projective drawings, see Hammer, 1980). Formal projective techniques such as the HTP require the child to draw figures that are then analyzed according to a number of dimensions (such as size, shading, location, action, etc.)

and interpreted to reveal aspects of the child's personality and emotional functioning. In the child interview formal projective drawing techniques may be administered in order to gain an understanding of the dynamic forces acting upon the child, or the interviewer can allow the child to choose drawing as an activity and to produce drawings of his or her own choice.

From a psychodynamic perspective the toys and activities described above serve to provide children the opportunity to express themselves and reveal their inner life through a medium they enjoy (play), using materials (toys) with which they are familiar. It is important to recognize that while toys and play are enjoyable and familiar to children, they may not be so for adults. The interviewer needs to be aware of the toys and activities with which he or she would not be comfortable. In other words, if an interviewer is concerned with getting Play Dough into the carpet, it is best not to have it available. Individual differences exist in interviewers' preferences for and comfort with various toys and activities, and there is no universal equipment list. However, interviewers who have too many restrictions on what is acceptable in the play interview will not be effective in facilitating communication with children.

THE INITIAL INTERVIEW

A variety of principles and practices exists for conducting the initial interview. Beginning with the first contact with the parents, the clinician will have to make a series of decisions on how best to proceed. Since psychodynamic theory places a significant emphasis on the relationship between the child and the clinician, it is incumbent upon the clinician to ensure that a facilitating relationship with the child is established. As a first step it is important to consider the means by which the child arrives at the clinician's office. Children are not likely to request the services of a helping professional. Usually the concerns of significant adults in a child's life are what prompt a referral for services. The child's understanding of the interview process and its purpose is most likely to be vague at best. One of the first tasks for the interviewer is to be sure that the child is provided with some basic understanding of why he or she is being seen. This task can be accomplished during the first contact with the parent(s).

Once the presenting problem has been clarified, the interviewer should discuss with the parent(s) what the child will be told about the interview. If the parents have already discussed the visit with the child, it is important to find out what they have told the child. If the information they have given the child is misleading ("You're going to play with a new friend"), untrue ("We're going to the park"), or punitive ("You have to go because you've been bad"), the interviewer needs to assist the parent(s) in providing the child with a nonjudgmental, honest, and clear explanation for the visit. The type of information the child should receive does not need to be any more elaborate than something to this effect: "We are worried about how unhappy you feel when you go to school, and we are all going to visit with someone who talks to lots of kids who are unhappy going to school." The parent(s) should then be willing to answer any questions the child may have about the visit. If the clinician is a psychologist or psychiatrist who is addressed as "Dr.," the child may believe that he or she is going to get a shot or some form of a medical procedure. In such a case it is important to inform the child that this type of doctor does not give shots, look in their ears, etc. The child can be told that this type of doctor is a "worry doctor" or a "talk doctor" who wants to help kids and families with their worries or problems.

An issue to consider is whether the person conducting the interview is going to be the same person who continues to see the child if psychotherapy is recommended. In cases where the child is referred by a therapist for a diagnostic evaluation, it will need to be made clear that the interview process is a time-limited one and that further contact with the interviewer is not likely to occur. In such cases it is not prudent for the interviewer to draw the child into an emotionally dependent relationship, as the child is likely to feel rejected and angry when the contact with the interviewer is ended. At the end of brief diagnostic interviews Goldman, Stein, and Guerry (1983) recommend that, "The focus should be on helping the child feel better about his ability to communicate effectively rather than on how good contact with the interviewer feels" (p. 93).

Given the emphasis that psychodynamically oriented clinicians place on the relationship between the interviewer and the child, it would follow that if psychotherapy is recommended, the clinician who conducted the interview should also be the person to conduct the therapy. This practice makes sense for a number of reasons. First the initial interview process may last more than one session; it is not uncommon in many settings for a child to be seen two or three times before recommendations and a treatment plan are developed. Often during the process the child develops some sense of rapport and trust with the interviewer. The interviewer is also likely to develop an attachment to the child and an understanding of the child's style of relating, as well as of the issues that brought the child in for services. These are essential ingredients in the therapeutic process and, in a sense, the therapeutic process has already begun.

Among psychodynamically oriented clinicians, there are disagreements about who should be seen first by the interviewer. Gardner (1979) notes that traditional theory recommends that the child be seen first, in order to convey to the child that he or she has a special relationship with the clinician that is separate from the parents. However, Gardner believes that it is best to see the family together first since it lowers the child's apprehension about being alone with a stranger and provides an opportunity to observe family interaction.

Spiegel (1989) believes that when one is seeing a young child it is advisable to see the parents first, because they can provide the more accurate information on background history. With an older child who can talk about problems, Spiegel indicates that seeing the child first may be warranted, as it will convey the message that the child's communication is confidential.

Considerations in planning the first interview are discussed in Chapter 5. Typically, in our own work we prefer to see the family first for a brief intake interview, followed by an interview with the child. During the family or parent–child interview, developmental and background information is reviewed (much of which can be gathered from parent questionnaires obtained before the interview), and the presenting problem is discussed. This practice serves a number of purposes. First, the child is part of an interpersonal network that includes the parents. Seeing everyone together the conveys message is that the problem is shared by and affects everyone in the family. We believe that this practice also lets the parents know that their thoughts and feelings are important and that their participation is desired. By inviting the parents to participate in the process, we feel that we are building rapport that will facilitate the parents' willingness to comply with our recommendations following the intake process. Seeing the family together can also demonstrate to the child that the interviewer is sensitive and responsive to the concerns of the child. Consider the following excerpt from an initial interview with 10-year-old John and his family:

INTERVIEWER: Tell me more about the concerns that brought you here today.

MOTHER: Well, as I said over the phone, we're worried about John's attitude. He seems to want to make us mad. He doesn't do what we ask, and getting him to do homework has become such a battle that we have practically given up making him try. He may fail and he doesn't seem to care. I've told him how foolish he'll feel if he has to repeat a grade and how his friends will make fun of him...

FATHER: I can't understand how any kid would want to fail, but John seems determined to undermine our efforts to help him out. He seems to think that we're against him but we're only doing what we think will help. I've talked to him, yelled, spanked him, and taken away his privileges and nothing seems to help. If he would just show some effort or interest this would all be a lot better.

INTERVIEWER: I can sense how frustrated you feel with all this. You want John to care about his responsibilities and you want to help, but you don't know how to reach him.

MOTHER: It's like Chuck said. He thinks we're against him and we're not, but he has to show some effort.

INTERVIEWER: You know, John, it sounds like your parents are stuck. They are saying that they want to help you, but the way they say it makes me think that you must really feel picked on. It sounds like they come down pretty hard on you... (*John is looking at the interviewer and the mother laughs.*)

MOTHER: Yeah, we're real ogres aren't we John.

INTERVIEWER: I bet.

JOHN: They keep saying, "Oh, you're going to fail" and stuff but I'm not doing that bad.

FATHER: Two F's and a D is not doing that well.

INTERVIEWER: I bet we could get into an argument just like you do at home, but I'll tell you what: Let's skip the argument for now, and how about you and I (*to John*) spend some time together and see if we can figure out some ways to help your mom and dad stop bugging you and help you with your grades, Okay?

JOHN: Yeah, that's O.K.

INTERVIEWER: Okay with you? (*to parents*).

FATHER: That's why we're here.

In this segment, the interviewer has reacted to the concerns of both the parents and the child. The alliance with John was established by making statements that were addressed to his feelings of being picked on by his parents. Children may expect the interviewer to side with the parents and reflect the concerns and attitudes of the parents. By not doing so, the interviewer can send a message to the child that the child's feelings are important and deserve consideration. This attitude does not imply that the interviewer believes that the child is right and the parents are wrong. Rather it communicates that everyone has feelings and opinions, that these deserve to be heard, and that a mutually satisfying solution is possible.

Once the interviewer is alone with the child, the formal interview begins. The play interview begins by allowing the child to examine and explore the toys and activities available in the play room. If the interviewer does not have a separate play room a small table and chairs along with a cabinet of toys is sufficient. Such a setup has an advantage with older children, who may feel immature playing with toys. If at some point in the interview children desire to play or draw, the materials are immediately available, and the transition from talking to play can be made quickly and easily.

The degree of structure involved in the psychodynamic interview varies as a function of the circumstances. Although it is generally agreed that the interviewer should allow the child to "set the stage" for the play interview (Axline, 1947; Greenspan, 1981; Spiegel, 1989), there are times when the interviewer will want to assume control of the structure of the interview. For the aggressive and difficult-to-manage child, the interviewer may need to set clear limits and help the child to maintain control over his or her behavior. Timid, shy, or anxious children may need to be gradually induced to participate in the process through such means as drawing pictures or talking about benign topics such as their favorite activities and interests. If the purpose of the interview is to gather information regarding a specific question (such as whether the child has been sexually abused), the interviewer will have to provide and direct activities that are aimed at answering the question.

The purpose of the play interview is to elicit information from the child that will aid in determining the nature of the problem, in order to provide the parents and/or the referral source with a plan of action. It is also important to provide the child with a sense of being understood and respected. The next section describes a framework for conducting the psychodynamically oriented interview.

THE OBSERVATION OF PLAY

Whereas psychodynamic approaches to child interviewing emphasize the expression of internal experience and conflict through play, numerous other dimensions of development that can also be observed in the play of children referred for psychological evaluation. When one is considering the multiple lines of development that contribute to play behavior, it is easy to see how the play interview can be a useful tool in the assessment process.

The determination of the specific lines of development to be observed during the child interview vary as a function of the clinician conducting the interview. Numerous guidelines exist for conducting the psychodynamic child interview (Behar & Rapoport, 1983; Garbarino et al., 1989; Greenspan, 1981; Trad, 1989) and the following outline presents a general observational framework. However, such guidelines are only useful when the examiner has a working knowledge of age-appropriate expectations for children.

Physical and Neurological Status

Beginning with the first contact with the child, it is important to note the child's general appearance. Do the child's height and weight appear appropriate to the child's chronological age? What does the child's grooming suggest about the child's attention to his or her body and the parents' concern for the child's public appearance? Observation of the child's gait, posture, and activity level can provide information on the integrity of the skeletal muscular and central nervous system. During the interview, fine motor skills can be assessed through observations of the child's ability to manipulate objects such as pencils and crayons, while gross motor ability can be assesed from activities such as tossing a ball or beanbag. Information regarding visual–motor integration can be gathered by observing the child's facility with construction activities such as putting a puzzle together.

Cognitive Development

Indications of the child's general level of cognitive development can be observed through a variety of activities. Verbal ability can provide clues as to the child's general level of language development. Are the child's speech and grammar age-appropriate? Does the child understand questions and directions? Problem-solving ability can be observed in such activities as building a structure or solving a puzzle. For the younger child, observations of the child's ability to recognize colors, shapes, and objects provide data on cognitive functioning. For the older child, estimates of cognitive ability may be based on the child's fund of information and the child's activities and interests. For example, James, a precocious 4-year-old boy, told the examiner in detail about his interest in and knowledge of dinosaurs, including the various species and their eating habits. In addition, James was able to explain alternative hypotheses regarding the extinction of dinosaurs. However, the informal estimation of a child's cognitive ability should never be used as a substitute for standardized intellectual assessment.

Psychosocial Development

Psychodynamic approaches to child interviewing emphasize aspects of the child's affect and behavior that are believed to reflect the structure of the child's personality. A number of dimensions are included in such an evaluation.

Affect

An important consideration in the child interview is the child's emotional state as revealed by his or her mood and affect. Children often have difficulty verbalizing affect, and feeling states are often communicated nonverbally. For example, a sad child may sit slumped in a chair, avoiding eye contact with the interviewer and remaining unresponsive to invitations to play. Anxious children may move about restlessly, pick at their skin, or fiddle with objects. The arousal of affect during play activities can serve as a source of information as to what topics or events may be upsetting to the child.

For example, Pam was a 6-year-old girl who became fearful of attending school after witnessing her father being assaulted by a group of gang members. During the play interview she used colored markers to draw a den of rabbits. When she completed the rabbits she began to draw a giant who was going to step on the rabbits. As Pam started to explain how the giant was going to flatten the rabbits, she became increasingly anxious and began to scribble all over the page. Pam then put the markers down and said she needed to use the bathroom.

Interpersonal Relations

A child's relationships to others and his or her feelings about these relationships plays a crucial role in the psychodynamic approach to child interviewing. Theory and research on child development continues to highlight the importance of the infant's attachment to the primary caretaker as a key determinant of psychological adjustment (Ainsworth, Blehar, Waters, & Wall, 1978; Mahler, Pine, & Bergman, 1975; Main & Goldwyn, 1984).

Within a psychoanalytic framework, Mahler et al. (1975) have described the process by which the infant develops from a state of total dependence on the mother to a recognition of the self as separate from the mother. This process, referred to as "separation–individuation," includes age-specific stages of development in the infant's ability to tolerate increasing separation from the mother, leading to the development of autonomy. Disruptions to the process of separation and individuation are hypothesized to contribute to various forms of psychopathology (Mahler et al., 1975).

The Strange Situation procedure developed by Ainsworth et al. (1978) assesses patterns of attachment by observing infants' reactions to a brief separation and reunion with their mothers. Research studies using the Strange Situation procedure have found that attachment patterns can be classified as "secure," "anxious-avoidant," or "anxious–resistant."

Children with secure attachments demonstrate proximity-seeking responses to reunion and their mothers are reported to be responsive caregivers. Behavioral manifestations of anxious–avoidant patterns of attachment include a child's avoiding the mother following reunion while not avoiding strangers, and engaging in limited affective exchange with the mother. Anxious–resistant children show marked distress over separation from their mothers and may continue to be distressed upon reunion, including seeking contact with their mothers through aggressive means such as hitting and kicking. These patterns of attachments in the first few months of life have been shown to be related to patterns of attachment at 1 year of age (Ainsworth et al., 1978). Researchers have also found that early attachment styles have implications for future adjustment. For example, it has been demonstrated that secure attachments are related to good interpersonal relationships and flexible problem-solving skills (Arend, Gove, & Sroufe, 1979; Matas, Arend, & Sroufe, 1978; Waters, Wippman, & Sroufe, 1979).

In the context of the child interview, patterns of attachments can be observed in the way the child and mother negotiate the process of separation. It is not necessary to conduct a formal Strange Situation procedure to observe attachment behavior. Reactions to separation can be observed in a number of ways. The mother may separate from the child to meet with the interviewer; the interviewer may invite the child into the interview without the parent; or the parent may be asked to leave the interview room without the child after a joint interview has been conducted. In any of these situations, information on attachment patterns can be gained by observing how the parent handles the separation ("I'll be right outside if you need me," "Stay here and don't fuss," "Will you be all right?," etc.), how the child reacts to it (does the child accept it, resist, cry, act indifferent, etc.?), and how parent and child respond to being reunited (do they show interest in each other or are they aloof?).

The child's style of relating to the interviewer is also an important source of information regarding interpersonal development. The child's attitude and behavior toward the interviewer can typify styles of relating to other adults in the child's interpersonal world. A child who enters the interview session and begins ordering the interviewer around and dominating the activity of the session may be displaying a strong need for control; another child may acquiesce to the wishes of the interviewer and be reluctant to initiate any activity. A more traditional psychoanalytic view is that the child's style of relating to the interviewer is a manifestation of a transference reaction, in which the child projects conflicts with other important adults onto the interviewer (Trad, 1989). From this perspective, the child who attempts to control the interviewer may be expressing conflicts with a caretaker who, the child believes, is unable to provide structure and nurturance. Similarly, passive children may be projecting onto the interviewer the experience of being controlled by adults to the extent that they are fearful of independent action.

It is important to keep in mind that the interview is an interpersonal process. Thus, the interviewer brings his or her own conflicts and concepts of relationships into the session (i.e., countertransference). The interviewer who possesses a strong need for control may overpower the child who is eager to play and relate and may thus lose sight of the purpose of the interview, just as the indulgent interviewer may find it difficult to set limits and may thus inadvertently encourage limit-testing behavior in the child.

Thematic Development

Thematic development and its relationship to personality derives from Freudian concepts of projection. Although "projection" has become best known as a defense mechanism, Freud also used the term to refer to perceptual distortions (also referred to as "apperceptive distortions") that revealed personality dynamics (Bellak, 1954). Dreams and free associations are examples of projective perceptual distortions that contain thematic material, which, when analyzed, reveals conflicts within the individual.

The acceptance of the importance of thematic development in revealing personality dynamics contributed to the development of numerous projective techniques designed expressly to elicit thematic material. Perhaps the best-known of these techniques are the TAT (Morgan & Murray, 1935) and the Children's Apperception Test (CAT; Bellak & Bellak, 1949). The TAT, designed for personality assessment of adults and adolescents, contains pictures of people in various situations; the respondent is asked to tell a story about each picture. The pictures are designed to represent areas of conflict for the individual and the stories that are produced are analyzed for themes which give clues to the individual's personality structure. The CAT is similar in nature to the TAT, with the exception of the stimulus pictures. The 10 stimulus pictures that comprise the CAT depict animal figures in a variety of situations. Eight of the 10 pictures are anthropomorphic, such as Picture 10, which depicts a puppy across the knee of a full-grown dog in a bathroom. The pictures that are set in a naturalistic setting include Picture 6 (a den of sleeping bears) and Picture 7 (a tiger attacking a monkey in the jungle).

Haworth (1966) reports that the use of animal pictures was based on the psychoanalytic belief that children more readily identify themselves with animals than with people. Thus, the animals in the CAT pictures are shown in situations designed to elicit themes representative of children's significant relationships and drives. However, numerous studies have shown that children frequently produce as much if not more clinically significant material with human than, animal pictures (Murstein, 1963).

Numerous studies of the CAT's reliability and validity have been conducted (for a review see Haworth, 1966). In general, studies of construct and concurrent validity, and of interrater and test–retest reliability, have been limited by the use of small sample sizes and a lack of standardized scoring criteria.

Thematic development in child interviewing involves the observation of the structure, sequence, and content of the child's communications with the interviewer. From a psychodynamic perspective, the materials the child uses and the stories or themes that are developed with them constitute the cornerstone for understanding a child's inner world. As Greenspan (1981) has noted, "Attention to thematic development will tell you a great deal about the child's characterological structure as well as the specific conflicts that the child may be experiencing at the time you are assessing him or her" (p. 29).

Adults are better able than children to express their experiences and conflicts through words, and, in the absence of a thought disorder, can generally present a logical sequence of events and their reactions to them. The cognitive and emotional immaturity of children makes such clarity and cohesion more difficult to achieve. Rather, children are able to express troubling aspects of their lives through symbolic actions and activities that can vary greatly in their complexity and meaning.

For instance, Jane was a 6-year-old girl referred for psychological services because of separation anxiety. In the month preceding her contact with the interviewer, she had frequently feigned illness to avoid school and aggressively resisted her mother's attempts to get her to school. When Jane entered the interviewer's office, she voiced concern and anxiety about her mother's well-being in the waiting area. Jane worried that her mother might leave the office to run to the store and have an automobile accident. After checking twice with her mother, Jane was assured that her mother would not leave the waiting area. Jane then sat quietly in a chair and offered the interviewer the opportunity to look at a few of the toys she had brought to the office.

When given the opportunity to explore the interviewer's toy box, Jane brought out two animal hand puppets and began a dialogue with them. When the interviewer inquired as to what they might be talking about, Jane said they were going to play a game and invited the interviewer to play along. The game involved Jane's hiding one of the puppets in the office and having the examiner hunt for it with the other puppet. Jane said that the hidden puppet was the baby and the other puppet was the mommy. At first the hidden puppet was placed in locations that made it easy for the interviewer to spot. Gradually the hiding places became more difficult to detect. Jane appeared to enjoy the game greatly and took delight in the interviewer's concern for finding the hidden puppet. However, whenever the interviewer commented that it was difficult to find the puppet, Jane would quickly provide "warm" and "cold" clues to indicate the interviewer's proximity to the hidden puppet. Jane ended the game when the interviewer reminded her that the session was almost over. After asking how much time was left in the session, Jane took a small basketball from the toy box and asked the interviewer to play basketball with her using the trash can as a basket. Jane laughed as she played and this continued until the end of the session.

The thematic development of Jane's play is fairly clear. Initially, Jane verbalized her concerns about her mother's well-being and continued to develop this theme in her play. Jane's game of hide and seek appeared to be a means of communicating and trying to master the fear associated with increased distance and separation from her mother. The urgency of the issue, and Jane's ability to tolerate the anxiety associated with her separation fears, allowed her to play out this theme without interruption. When told that the session was almost over, Jane was able to shift to another, less threatening game and leave the interview in a positive mood.

Not all children can present a theme as organized and coherent as Jane's. For example 8-year-old Ron was abandoned by his mother (a heroin addict who later committed suicide) when he was 14 months old. An uncle with whom he lived for 5 years routinely physically and sexually abused him. During the first grade Ron was placed in a residential treatment facility because of his uncontrollable and aggressive behavior. Ron was seen for an evaluation for placement after having spent 18 months in the treatment facility. Despite the chaos in his life, Ron obtained a Verbal Scale IQ of 122 and a Performance Scale IQ of 136 on the Wechsler Intelligence Scale for Children—Revised (WISC-R; Wechsler, 1974). The diagnostician reported that during the testing Ron frequently tested limits and needed a great deal of structure and encouragement to complete the testing.

During the play interview Ron was unable to sit still and explored the interviewer's office without regard to the interviewer's comments. Upon finding a toy helmet and gun, Ron began to shoot everything in sight including the interviewer. The interviewer decided to set limits on Ron's behavior after he knocked over the telephone and began shooting and banging on the wall. It was explained to Ron that he could choose what to play with, but he was not allowed to injure himself or the interviewer and he could not destroy the furniture. Next, Ron took a baby doll out of the cabinet, made believe it was crying, and threw it on the floor. He proceeded to remove all the toys from the cabinet and asked for more toys. Ron seemed unable to choose any one activity. He took a deck of cards out of the cabinet and asked the interviewer to play. He began playing a game that was unfamiliar to the interviewer; when asked to explain the game, he threw the cards around the room and instructed the interviewer to pick them up. It appeared that Ron was unable to structure himself, so the interviewer structured the session by removing the toys and providing Ron with paper and markers to draw with. Ron drew a soldier-type figure who carried guns, arrows, and knives but also had an arrow shot through his head and heart. When asked to describe his drawing, Ron said it was a warrior and began to stab it with a marker.

The case of Ron is a disturbing one. Although the overall theme of his play strongly projected violence, it was also highly chaotic and lacking in continuity. Ron's age and intelligence suggested that he was capable of more elaborate thematic production, but his intense rage limited his ability to do anything but act out his rage through aggressive play. Nevertheless, Ron's play was diagnostically significant. Ron's behavior strongly suggested that he had difficulty modulating and controlling his aggressive feelings and needed structure and limits to help him stay in control.

CONCLUDING REMARKS

Psychodynamic approaches to child interviewing represent a broad spectrum of theories and practices that are rooted in traditional psychoanalytic concepts and practices. Out of this tradition, the play interview has emerged as a key component in the assessment of the psychosocial adjustment of children. For the psychodynamically oriented clinician, the play interview allows for the observation of the lines of development that correspond to the child's emotional growth and development. Play is believed to be a reflection of unconscious forces and interpersonal experiences that contribute to the development of the child's personality and view of the world.

The advantages of the psychodynamic play interview are similar to those of any type of unstructured interview. The play interview generally follows from the child's lead. The child is free to choose the activities that constitute the interview, and the interviewer is available as a participant/observer (Spiegel, 1989). By observing what the child chooses to play with and how the child plays, the interviewer begins to get a picture of key themes that may be contributing to disturbances in adaptive functioning.

A disadvantage of the psychodynamic interview is the reliance it places on subjective judgment. In a sense, the psychodynamic play interview can be thought of as analogous to a projective test. In the play interview the child is presented with an ambiguous situation (free play) and the interviewer bases hypotheses about the child's social and emotional functioning based on interpretations of the symbolic meaning of the child's play. The same criticisms regarding the lack of psychometric adequacy of projective techniques (Prout & Ferber, 1988) can also be applied to the play interview.

Research on the reliability and validity of the play interview is limited, but the studies that have been done indicate that play behavior is reflective of actual behavior in everyday life (Behar & Rapoport, 1983). Perhaps the best way to conceptualize the play interview is to consider it as a sample of behavior that serves as a means of developing hypotheses regarding psychological adjustment. The validity and utility of the hypotheses can then be evaluated through formal and informal procedures (e.g., cognitive assessment, parent reports, behavioral observations). Overall, the process should be one that contributes to the delineation of problem areas and aids in the planning of effective treatment.

5

Principles of Behavioral Interviewing

CONCEPTUAL AND METHODOLOGICAL ADVANCES IN BEHAVIORAL ASSESSMENT

The increased importance of interview data in the behavioral assessment of childhood disorders in recent years reflects conceptual and methodological advances in the field of behavioral assessment. "Behavioral assessment" is no longer synonymous with the direct observation of behavior; rather, it refers to the use of multiple methods to assess a greatly expanded range of person and situation variables that empirical investigations have found to be important to the development, maintenance, and treatment of childhood disorders. Child behavioral assessment is "a problem-solving strategy that seeks to assess multiple child and family characteristics utilizing a variety of methods" (Mash & Terdal, 1988, p. 18). These assessment procedures reflect a multivariate view of children's behavior disorders—a view that recognizes that children's and parents' perceptions of events mediate behavior and behavior change, and that children's behaviors occur within interlocking systems of interactions. Thus, behavior assessors attempt to assess children's and parents' perceptions, beliefs, and thinking processes and family interactions (especially parent–child interactions), as well as the children's problematic behaviors and the immediate contexts in which these behaviors occur. In such a broad-based assessment scheme, parent, child, and family interviews are essential components of the behavioral assessment of childhood disorders.

Not only have parent and child interviews become more frequent in behavior assessment, but the purposes and nature of these interviews have also changed. In early work in child behavior assessment, interviewing primarily involved asking parents to report on the antecedents and consequences of specific target behaviors. The purpose of the interview was to develop a functional analysis of target behaviors (Gross, 1984; Nelson & Hayes, 1981). After the parents generated a list of problem behaviors and the interviewer helped the parents define each problem in terms of specific and observable behaviors, the interviewer asked the parents to report on situational variables temporally associated with the occurrence of these behaviors and on environmental events that followed the behavior (and, presumably, maintained the behavior). This functional analysis of behavior targeted specific child behaviors and their functional relationship to antecedent and consequent events.

The narrow approach to behavioral interviewing characteristic of early behavioral assessment can best be understood in the context of behavioral intervention approaches that were prevalent at the time.

> Early behavioral approaches to the treatment of child and family disorders involved the specification of target behaviors and their alteration through the arrangement or rearrangement of antecedent and consequent stimulus events in a manner loosely conforming to the learning principles encompassed under the operant, classical, and observational learning paradigms. [These included] a focus on easily defined and observable events, current behaviors and situational determinants, and the child as the primary target for assessment and treatment. (Mash & Terdal, 1988, p. 7)

The complexity of contemporary models of childhood disorders has broadened the types of interventions encompassed under the term "behavior therapy" to include interventions that focus on children's and parents' perceptions, expectancies, beliefs, and problem-solving processes, as well as children's interactions in multiple social networks.

Until recently, interviewing in behavior assessment did not routinely include a child interview, as children were considered unreliable reporters of their own behavior and the environmental events that elicited and maintained their behaviors (Atkeson & Forehand, 1981; Edelbrock, Costello, et al., 1985; Gross, 1984). The veracity of parental reports was suspect, too, and were relied on as necessary but impure substitutes for direct observation, the "hallmark" of behavior assessment (Bellack, 1979). Referring to behavior assessment's emphasis on direct observation, Gross (1984) notes that direct observation "is not always possible, and, at times, the patient's verbal report or the verbal report of significant others is the only base on which to perform a behavioral analysis" (p. 62).

Behavior assessment and therapy underwent major conceptual and methodological changes in the 1980s, and these changes are reflected in the purposes and methods of behavior interviewing. In this section of the chapter, conceptual and methodological advances in behavior assessment are summarized, and implications of these advances for behavior interviewing are discussed.

Broadened Definition of Context

A vast amount of research conducted within the past two decades has proven the importance of a wide range of contextual variables in the development, maintenance, and treatment of children's behavior disorders. Conceptual models of behavior disorders are based on an expanding research base that implicates the interplay of multiple variables in the development and treatment of childhood behavior disorders. Consequently, the behavioral assessment of children's disorders involves a greatly expanded range of assessment variables. The child is now viewed not only as an individual influenced by specific antecedent conditions and reinforcement contingencies, but also as part of a larger network of interacting social systems. The assessment of childhood problems necessarily involves the assessment of these systems and subsystems, including family interactions and child interactions with parents, siblings, teachers, and peers.

Whereas some system factors are implicated in only one or a few disorders, other system factors are relevant to a wide range of childhood problems and should be routinely assessed when a child presents with disturbed behavior, affect, or learning. For example, marital discord is related to both externalizing and internalizing child behavior disorders (Barkley, 1988; Kazdin, 1988) and should be routinely assessed. Lack of social support available to mothers is implicated in child abuse (Wolfe, 1988); family cohesion is strongly implicated in the behavioral adjustment of children diagnosed as having attention-deficit hyperactivity disorder (Barkley, 1988); a reliance on punitive disciplinary approaches and poor monitoring of child behavior are associated with childhood aggression, conduct disorder, and delinquency (Patterson, 1982; Patterson & Stouthamer-Loeber, 1984); and family food dynamics are related to childhood obesity (Foreyt & Goodrick, 1988).

Whereas early behavior assessors defined context in terms of contemporaneous behaviors and their controlling variables, today behavior assessors view behavior as being influenced by a wider range of contextual variables, including variables that are temporally and spatially distant from the setting in which the problem behavior occurs. Parental personality and adjustment, family climate, peer group relationships, marital discord, and social support are examples of controlling variables that do not comprise part of the immediate context for problem behaviors but that enter importantly into empirically driven theoretical models of behavior disorders. For example, maternal depression is associated with child noncompliance to maternal directives and with high rates of maternal criticism (Brody & Forehand, 1986; Dumas, Gibson, & Albin, 1989). Attributional biases characterize both abusive parents (Larrance & Twentyman, 1983; Watlington, 1990) and parents of children with attention-deficit hyperactivity disorder (Watlington, 1990): These parents are more likely to infer that their children acted with the intent to annoy them in situations in which the children's negative behavior is ambiguous as to intentionality, and to explain their children's negative behaviors as a result of trait-like dispositions rather than as a result of situational factors. These attributional biases are thought to mediate parents' punitive behavior toward their children.

The expanded social and temporal context includes a focus on individuals' cognitive, behavioral, and affective responses within the context of ongoing interactions. In a family interview, behavior assessors have the opportunity to observe family communication, problem solving, and patterns of interaction that define family structure. The parameters of structure to be assessed in family interviews include family boundaries, alignments, and power (Aponte & VanDeusen, 1981). For example, diffuse boundaries and excessive closeness between a parent and child (a boundary problem referred to as "enmeshment"), are associated with psychosomatic disorders (Minuchin, Rosman, & Baker, 1978). A lack of closeness (disengagement), especially father under-involvement with children, is associated with externalizing disorders (Patterson, 1982). A child's quality of interactions with peers is also implicated in a wide range of disorders, including delinquency (Roff, Sells, & Golden, 1972), depression (Strauss, Forehand, Frame, & Smith, 1984), and school underachievement (Green, Forehand, Beck, & Vosk, 1980).

Thus, contemporary models of childhood behavior disorders are complex, multidimensional, and empirically driven. Because these models define parameters to be assessed, behavior assessment practices have become multivariate. The target behavior paradigm and the emphasis on the functional analysis of behavior have been replaced with multivariate models of disorders that emphasize a range of contextual variables, including both contemporaneous variables and variables that are temporally and spatially distant.

Reconceptualization of Target Behavior

The target behavior paradigm in behavior assessment has been replaced with a "general set of problem-solving strategies encompassing a wide range of system variables and a greater variety of methods than were characteristic of earlier work" (Mash & Terdal, 1988, p. 8). The earlier emphasis on assessing target behaviors produced many valuable outcomes, including the development of assessment procedures with high interrater reliability, the determination of functional relationships between behaviors and environmental events, stronger assessment— treatment links, and the continuous measurement of intervention effectiveness. However, the target behavior paradigm also limited the development of treatment-valid behavior assessment methods. Because target behaviors were selected without regard for conceptual models of various disorders, all undesirable behaviors were considered equally appropriate targets for intervention, with little regard for determining which behaviors (or cognitions) would produce the greatest amount of desired change. In addition, the target behavior paradigm did not lend itself to a focus on cognitive and affective mediators of behavior.

As behavior therapists incorporated a focus on cognitive and affective variables into the treatment of behavior disorders, the inadequacies of the target behavior paradigm became more obvious. In 1979, Goldfried addressed limitations of the target behavior paradigm:

> One of the big problems with behavior assessment—and with behavior therapy in general—is that we have no "theory" to guide our work. Although we have developed a detailed technology for assessing and modifying the "behavior of interest," we need to have clearer direction as to what behaviors to be interested in, as well as their parameters and determinants. (p. 21)

Today, behavior assessors select variables to be assessed on the basis of conceptual models of the clients' problems. These models are hypotheses about the relationships among the clients' symptoms and multiple person and environmental variables, and are based in part on empirical evidence. For example, a clinician encounters a 7-year-old boy who wets his bed and opposes his parents' authority. Rather than viewing the nighttime enuresis and the noncompliance as two target behaviors of more or less equal importance, the clinician develops a hypothesis concerning the relationship between the two behaviors. In this case, the clinician hypothesizes that the child's nighttime enuresis is a result of poor parenting practices and that a focus on improving child compliance will be more effective than a focus on the enuresis. This hypothesis is based, in part, on research documenting that bedwetting decreases when child compliance increases during parent training (Nordquist, 1971).

Perhaps another case will illustrate the clinical decision-making process that characterizes contemporary behavior assessment. Consider a situation in which an 8-year-old boy, Chris, is referred by school personnel for psychotherapy because of aggressiveness. An interview with the teacher reveals that Chris, an academically capable student, is disliked by his peers, frequently starts fights, and purposefully disturbs others. An interview with Chris's mother reveals that the mother relies excessively on punitive control strategies with Chris and demonstrates a lack of positivity toward him. Furthermore, the clinician determines that the mother lacks a meaningful support system and experiences a high level of stress. Two primary stressors are finances and conflict with her own mother, with whom she finds it necessary to live, and who is highly critical of her and undermines her authority with her son. The clinician hypothesizes that the lack of support and stress are causally related to the mother's parenting practices, which are causally related to Chris's aggressiveness. Based on research conducted by Bierman and Schwartz (1986b) the clinician also hypothesizes that at school, Chris's classmates respond more negatively and less positively to Chris than to other boys, even when Chris's behavior is appropriate. Thus, Chris's aggressive behaviors are viewed as multiply determined within the context of interlocking systems (peer group, mother–child, family).

Deciding where to begin an intervention depends on assumptions about the pattern of interactive influences among these variables. The task in this case is not to find the "root" cause of the aggressiveness, but to identify the point in this interactive system of variables that has the greatest potential for producing positive behavior change. These hypotheses constitute a model of Chris's problems that suggests the most advantageous point(s) in the system in which to intervene. In this case, the clinician decides to focus on establishing a support system for the mother prior to implementing parent training. This decision is based in part on research documenting that parent management is least effective with mothers lacking a social support system (Dumas & Wahler, 1983). Concurrently, the clinician consults with the teacher regarding a contingency management system for fighting and increasing opportunities for cooperative peer interaction.

Another change in target behavior selection involves a greater emphasis on response classes (e.g., aggressiveness or oppositional behaviors) than on single behaviors (e.g., hitting or lying). Because response classes have greater temporal and situational stability than single behaviors do, a change in the frequency of the class of behaviors is likely to reflect a more basic and clinically significant change than a change in a circumscribed behavior. Early critics of behavior therapy stated that even if the target behavior changed in the desired direction following a behavior intervention, another problem or symptom would replace it. Although evidence for symptom substitution is generally lacking, an emphasis on narrowly defined target behaviors may result in less stable and meaningful change than an emphasis on the class of behavior to which the target behavior belongs. For example, fear of dogs may exist within a response class that includes a number of avoidant behaviors. As we learn more about constellations of behaviors, response covariation, and developmental psychopathology, we are better able to select assessment foci that will result in stable and meaningful change.

Today, behavior assessment targets include unobservable events (i.e., cognitions and affective responses) as well as observable behavior. Interviews and other self-report measures are most frequently used to assess these covert processes. The specific cognitive processes assessed should depend on an empirically driven theory or model of the disorder. For example, when assessing a depressed child, the clinician may want to assess the child's tendency to make cognitive errors (such as those detailed by Beck, 1967, 1976), attributional style, prevalent mood, optimism, self-concept, changes in the degree of pleasure experienced while engaging in activities that were once found pleasurable, and changes in attention and worrying.

Broadened Range of Assessment Methods

The reconceptualization of target behaviors and the incorporation of cognitive and affective variables in models of behavior disorders have led to less reliance on direct observation. Interviews and self-report questionnaires are no longer viewed as poor substitutes for direct observation but as essential components of behavior assessment. Recognition of the limitations of direct observation (e.g., reactivity of direct observation, issues of practicality) have contributed to the shift to alternative assessment methods. Mash and Terdal (1988, p. 6) emphasize that "to omit direct observation from assessment is not to abandon a behavior assessment approach."

Behavior assessment is defined in terms of certain assessment principles rather than in terms of a specific assessment procedure. These principles include the importance of contextual information; a systems orientation to assessment; a reliance on empirically driven theories of behavior disorders; a relatively greater emphasis on contemporaneous variables than on historical events: a high priority on linking assessment data to treatment decisions; a relatively greater focus on specific situations than on traits with broad situational and temporal stability; priority given to specific behaviors, cognitions, and affective responses; and the view that behaviors are important in their own right and not as indices of a more "real," underlying cause.

Incorporation of Diagnostic Practices

In the early years of behavior assessment, clinicians eschewed diagnostic practices. This disenchantment with diagnostic practices was a result of several factors, including the association of psychiatric diagnosis with traditional assessment procedures; the priority given to target behaviors over constellations of symptoms; the low priority given to psychometric properties of behavior assessment procedures (reliability, norms, and validity were considered largely irrelevant to direct observation methods); and an idiographic rather than nomothetic orientation to assessment. As behavior assessment evolved and the classification systems relevant to childhood behavior disorders improved, diagnostic procedures were incorporated into assessment practices. The third edition of the *Diagnostic and Statistical Manual of Mental Disorders* (DSM-III; American Psychiatric Association, 1980) contained approximately four times as many categories appropriate for use with children as the second edition did. Both DSM-III and its revision (DSM-III-R; American Psychological Association, 1987) provide more objective and behaviorally oriented diagnostic criteria. In addition, DSM-III differs from earlier versions in its multiaxial approach to classification. In addition to providing a psychiatric diagnosis (Axis I), it is possible to classify an individual along several dimensions. Children are assessed in terms of developmental disorders they may exhibit (Axis II), any physical condition that may be relevant to their disorder (Axis III), the severity of psychosocial stressors experienced during the previous year (Axis IV), and the highest level of adaptive functioning displayed during the past year (Axis V). Because diagnostic criteria are more objective and multidimensional diagnoses are recommended in DSM-III-R, behavioral assessors rely more heavily on it. The diagnostic interviews reviewed in Chapter 3 are based on DSM-III-R criteria and are recommended by behavior assessors (e.g., Kazdin, 1988).

PLANNING THE BEHAVIORAL INTERVIEW

Published Interview Guides

There is no single guideline for conducting a behavioral interview. Several behavior assessors have suggested interview formats (Goldfried & Davison, 1976; Gresham & Davis, 1988; Kanfer & Grimm, 1977; Kanfer & Saslow, 1969; Lazarus, 1976; Stuart, 1970; Turkat, 1986; Wolfe, 1988). Although these interview formats differ in several ways, they all recognize the importance of specifying the problem(s) and

TABLE 5.1. Components of Problem Identification

  I. Explanation of problem definition purpose
   A. Sets tone for interview
   B. Gives overview of what is to be accomplished
   C. Focuses upon client behaviors
   D. Establishes that consultee owns the problems

 II. Identification and selection of target behaviors
   A. Defines behaviors in specific operational terms
   B. Establishes discrepancy between observed performance
   C. Prioritizes behaviors in terms of importance to consultee

III. Identification of problem frequency, duration, and intensity
   A. Focuses upon objective features of behavior
   B. Compares behavior rates with other clients in classroom
   C. Provides feedback to consultee regarding normal expectations for behavior of concern

 IV. Identification of conditions under which behavior occurs
   A. Specifies antecedent conditions
   B. Specifies consequent conditions
   C. Specifies sequential conditions

  V. Identification of required level of performance
   A. Determines consultee expectations for behavior
   B. Sets goals or objectives for terminal behavior rates
   C. Specifies time lines for meeting behavioral goals

 VI. Identification of client's strengths
   A. Establishes if consultee recognizes any positive value in child
   B. Detects irrational ideas of consultee
   C. Identifies potential client reinforcers

VII. Identification of behavioral assessment procedures
   A. Explains rationale for data collection
   B. Determines what will be recorded C. Determines who will record behavior
   D. Determines how behavior will be recordedE. Determines when and where behavior will be recorded

VIII. Identification of consultee effectiveness
   A. Models problem-solving skills for consultee
   B. Evaluates consultee's previous problem-solving problems
   C. Assesses consultee's motivation for solving problems
   D. Identifies logistical problems that may interfere with intervention plan

 IX. Summarizes and identifies methods and times of future contacts
   A. Summarizes important points discussed in interview
   B. Sets time for next interview
   C. Provides means of contacting consultant and consultee regarding problem behavior, recording methods, and functional analysis of behavior

Note. From "Behavioral Interviews with Teachers and Parents" by G. Gresham and C. Davis, 1988, in E. S. Shapiro & T. R. Kratochwill (Eds.), *Behavioral Assessment in Schools: Conceptual Foundations and Practical Applications* (p. 468). New York: Guilford Press. Copyright 1988 by The Guilford Press. Reprinted by permission. Adapted by Gresham and Davis from "Assessment in Behavioral Consultation: The Initial Interview" by J.C. Witt and S. N. Elliott, 1983, *School Psychology Review, 12,* 42–49. Copyright 1983 by National Association of School Psychologists. Adapted by permission.

conducting an analysis of antecedent and consequent stimulus events. The major differences concern the comprehensiveness of the interview and the degree to which the interviewer adheres to an operant approach. Stuart's (1970) and Gresham and Davis's (1988) behavior interviews represent the target-behavior-focused, operant approach. Stuart's interview involves the precise specification of problem behaviors, followed by an assessment of four classes of antecedents (instructional, discriminative, potentiating, and facilitating) and four classes of consequences (positive, aversive, extinguishing, and negatively reinforcing). Gresham and Davis's interview, designed for interviewing teachers, is also recommended for interviewing parents. Table 5.1 provides the content of the first interview, in which the problem is identified and a functional analysis is begun. Table 5.2 provides a guideline for conducting this interview, which is highly directive and focuses on the functional analysis of specific target behaviors.

Lazarus (1976) and Goldfried and Davison (1976) recommend more comprehensive interviews. Lazarus's interview includes an assessment of the client's behavior, affective, sensory, interpersonal, cognitive, imagery, and drug experiences. The acronym BASIC-ID refers to these modalities, which are then targeted in his multimodal treatment approach. Goldfried and Davison recommend covering the points listed in Table 5.3 in their interview, which can be completed with an adult client or with a child's parents.

Goldfried and Davison recommend incorporating Rogerian interview techniques, such as reflection of feelings and interacting in a warm and empathic manner with the client, in order to establish a therapeutic relationship with the client. Turkat (1986), on the other hand, believes that empathy and warmth are not necessary to the behavior interview and advocates a more directive, problem-focused approach: "One can not be empathic if one does not understand the specifics of a problem" (p. 126). Recent research on the relationship of therapist characteristics to outcomes in psychotherapy (Lafferty, Beutler, & Crago, 1989) suggests the importance of empathy to client change in therapy, supporting Goldfried and Davison's more nondirective approach. Turkat seems to view establishing a therapeutic relationship and getting specific information as incompatible goals. Instead, we view them as complementary goals: Getting the specifics of a problem, especially specifics regarding the client's thoughts, expectancies, and affective responses, depends in part on the interviewer's ability to establish an accepting and warm relationship with the client.

All of the general guidelines for conducting the behavioral interview are helpful, in that they sensitize the interviewer to areas that may be

TABLE 5.2. The Problem Identification Interview (PII)

I. Purpose of PII

   A. Define problem(s) in behavioral terms

   B. Tentative identification of conditions surrounding the behavior: antecedent, situational, consequent

   C. Tentative strength specification—How often or severe at present vs. acceptable level

   D. Establish procedure for collection of baseline data sampling plan, what, who, how behavior is recorded, etc.

   E. Detection of irrational ideas

II. Essential interviewing behaviors

   A. Directional question to introduce discussion of problem; e.g., "Describe Diane's hyperactive behavior." "Let's see, you referred Johnny because of his poor self-concept, lack of progress, and rebellious behavior—which of these do you want to start with...?" "Describe Johnny's rebellion (self-concept or lack of progress) in the classroom."

   B. Examples of behavior question(s); e.g., "What does Charles do when he is hyperactive? What does Mary do when she is disrespectful?"

   C. Preceding conditions questions; e.g., "What happens before Mary makes an obscene gesture to the rest of the class?" "What happens before Egbert begins to hit other children?"

   D. Situational condition questions; e.g., "When does Mary...? Who is Mary with...? What is Mary supposed to be doing when...?"

   E. Consequent conditions questions; e.g., "What happens after Mary...?" "What do the other students do when Charles climbs on the radiator?" "What do you do when Egbert hits other children?"

   F. Frequency/severity questions; e.g., "About how often does Patrick refuse to do his homework?" "How many times each day or week does Charles race about the room?"

   G. Tentative definition of goal question; e.g., "How often would Patrick have to turn in his work in order to get along O.K.?"

   H. Assets question; e.g., "Is there something that Mary does well?"

   I. Question about approach to teaching or existing procedures; e.g., "How long are Charles and the other students doing seat work problems?" "What kind of...?"

   J. Summarization statement and agreement question; e.g., "Let's see, the main problem is that Charles gets out of his seat and runs around the room during independent work assignments. He does this about four times each day, and...Is that right?"

   K. Directional statement to introduce discussion of data recording; e.g., "We need some record of Sarah's completion of homework assignments—how often assignments are completed, what assignments are completed, etc. This record will help us to determine how frequently the behavior is occuring and it may give us some clues about the nature of the problem. Also the record will help us decide whether any plan we initiate is effective or not."

   L. Question about data recording and conditions; e.g., "How would it be most convenient for you to keep a record of Charles' out of seat behavior?" "What would you record?" "When would you record?" "How often?"

   M. Summary statement; e.g., "Let's see now, you'll record the number of times Danny hits other students in the hall—you'll record this in the morning before school and at noon, and you'll keep a record for one week."

Note. From "Behavioral Interviews with Teachers and Parents" by F. Gresham and C. Davis, 1988, in E. S. Shapiro and T. R. Kratochwill (Eds.), *Behavioral Assessment in Schools: Conceptual foundation and Practical Applications* (p. 469). New York: Guilford Press. Copyright 1988 by The Guilford Press. Reprinted by permission.

important to assess. The common emphasis on specifying problems and then assessing antecedents and consequences follows an antecendent–behavior–consequence (A-B-C) analysis of behavior, an essential component of developing a behavioral formulation of the problem. Nevertheless, the utility of these interview guidelines is greatly limited by their "generic" approach. Those interviews that attempt to be broad enough to apply to different problems (e.g., Lazarus, 1976) lack the specificity to guide the interview, whereas those interviews that attempt to provide specific guidance (Gresham & Davis, 1988) lack flexibility, which is the primary advantage of interview assessment. The interview format in child behavior assessment should differ according to the nature of the problem, the purpose of the interview (i.e., diagnosis, treatment planning, or evaluation of treatment), and the child's age. Thus, generic interview formats are less helpful and appropriate than are disorder-specific interview formats. The selection of the content and interview methods (e.g., family, child, or parent interview) should be based on theoretically important parameters of the problem. An interview concerning a depressed child will differ greatly from an interview concerning a conduct-disordered child, which will differ from an interview concerning an adolescent with an eating disorder.

TABLE 5.3. Goldfried and Davison's Interview Format

Physical description of the patient
Patient behavior during the interview
Presenting problem
  Nature of the problem
  Historical events
  Current situational determinants
  Organismic variables (perceptions, beliefs, affect)
  Problem dimensions
  Consequences of the problem
Other problems
Personal assets
Targets for modification
Recommended treatment
Motivation for treatment
Prognosis
Priority for treatment
Expectancies
Other comments

Note. Adapted from *Clinical Behavior Therapy* by M. Goldfried and G.C. Davison, 1976. New York: Holt, Rinehart & Winston. Copyright 1976 by Holt, Rinehart & Winston. Adapted by permission.

Most interview formats are intended for use both with adults as clients and with adults as informants on their children. Interviewing parents as informants requires a different interview format, which covers the parents' as well as the child's behaviors, the parents' expectations for and perceptions of their child, and the parent's experience of stress, available resources, and motivation for seeking treatment. Nevertheless, available general interview guidelines designed for parents focus almost exclusively on child behavior (e.g., Kanfer & Grimm, 1977; Gresham & Davis, 1988).

Developing an Initial Problem Formulation

Because the parent interview, child interview, and family interview yield different types of information and are best suited for different interview purposes, one of the first decisions the behavior assessor must make is that of whom to interview. If more than one type of interview is deemed probable, the assessor must decide how to sequence the different interviews. These decisions depend on the clinician's initial formulation of the problem. An initial problem formulation is based on information obtained in an initial intake interview, usually conducted over the telephone and taking approximately 15 minutes. Information obtained includes the nature of the problem experienced by the child; the ways in which significant others in the child's life are affected by the problem and have responded to it in the past; limited information concerning child and family characteristics (child's age, gender, and school placement, and names, ages, and living arrangements of family members); and factors leading to the request for services at this time. Following this initial contact with the parent, the clinician develops an initial problem formulation and decides whether the initial interview will be conducted with the family, the parents (with or without the child), or the child alone.

Typically, the parents and child are asked to come to the first interview. After the parents and child are interviewed together, the interviewer spends the last few minutes of the first session with the parents alone. This gives the parents an opportunity to disclose information they were reluctant to disclose in the presence of their child, and it gives the interviewer a chance to ask questions that he or she did not want to ask in the child's presence (e.g., questions about the marital relationship or about the parents' adjustment). Next, a second appointment is scheduled for the child interview.

Having the child present for at least part of the first interview is based on at least three considerations. First, the opportunity to observe parent–child interactions provides essential information about the parent–

child relationship. Second, the child's cooperation in treatment is expected to be greater if the child is involved from the beginning. The interviewer can frame problems in ways that reduce blame and minimize the child's feeling that he or she is the cause of all of the problems. If the interviewer meets with the parents alone for the first interview, the child may believe that "my parents told the interviewer all the bad stuff about me, and now the interviewer is going to 'fix' me." Third, interviewing the parent and child together facilitates open communication in the family about the problem. The interviewer communicates to the family that they can talk about these problems without experiencing terrible consequences. An open, nonblaming discussion of the problem can minimize feelings of anger and guilt and promote positive expectancies for treatment.

The following three cases illustrate how the information obtained in a brief telephone intake is used to develop an initial problem formulation and to plan for the initial interview.

Dee

Dee F., age 15, was a sophomore in a rural high school. Her mother called the therapist, upon the advice of her pediatrician. When asked to describe her concerns about Dee, Mrs. F. stated that Dee had been complaining of feeling unhappy and feeling that she was "no good." Dee had always been an above-average student, but within the past few months, her grades had declined. She was also not taking her usual care concerning her appearance, letting her hair become dirty and wearing "worn-out jeans with holes in the knees." Mrs. F. added that what had really disturbed her was that last week Dee had "cut some on her arms" and told her mother she wished she was dead. In order to assess the degree to which Dee posed a suicide threat, the therapist asked questions about past suicide attempts (none), the extensiveness of the cutting (skin barely broken), attempts to give her belongings away or to resolve old conflicts with people (none), changes in social activities (Dee continued to be involved in the drama club and basketball), and any significant losses Dee had experienced recently (none).

Questions about the family composition revealed that Dee had no siblings and lived with her mother (age 31) and father (age 38). Dee's date of birth was 5 months after the parents' date of marriage. Mrs. F. held a clerical job in a retail business, and Mr. F. was a skilled laborer employed by a rural electrical cooperative. When asked what prompted her to seek treatment at this time, Mrs. F. stated that she and Dee had always been very close. About 6 months earlier, Dee had started dating, and Mrs. F. and Dee began arguing about dating rules (e.g., curfew, types of activities, which boys she could date). Mrs. F. stated that she knew what boys that age were after, and she wanted to protect Dee from being hurt. Mrs. F. complained that Dee no longer talked with her about her friends. When asked how she and her husband had tried to handle these problems, she stated that Mr. F. was not very involved in parenting and that he had told her to do whatever she thought best. She had tried to talk with Dee, but Dee had become secretive. "She takes the phone into her room to talk now, and I have to pick up the phone and ask who it is to find out."

Subsequent to this brief telephone interview, the following initial problem formulation was developed: Dee's relationship with her mother had been overly close (enmeshed), and Dee's attempts to become more independent from her mother had aroused her mother's fears that Dee would become sexually active and perhaps pregnant. These fears caused Mrs. F. to become overly restrictive and mistrustful of Dee. Dee responded to these restrictions and lack of trust with a combination of feelings of guilt and anger.

The decision to begin the assessment with an individual interview with Dee was based on the following rationale: First, interviewing Dee individually would acknowledge her separateness from her mother. Second, Dee could report more accurately on her own feelings and experiences associated with depressive disorders than could anyone else. Third, unless Dee felt responsible for her therapy and felt that her independence would be respected by her therapist, therapy would be unlikely to be effective. Fourth, the mother's presence during an interview with Dee would inhibit Dee's openness, and meeting with Mrs. F. alone would probably give Dee the feeling that the therapist had formed an alliance with her mother and, like her mother, viewed Dee as a child.

The initial problem formulation was elaborated during the interview with Dee, in which Dee reported several symptoms of a depressive disorder. Two months earlier, Dee had had sexual intercourse while on a date. She experienced excessive self- condemnation, and her thinking evidenced many cognitive errors implicated in depressive disorders. Following individual therapy for her depressive disorder, which followed Beck's (1976) cognitive therapy for depression, Dee accepted the therapist's recommendation to include her mother in therapy to address issues in their relationship.

Cindy B

When the therapist returned Mrs. B.'s initial call, Mr. B. answered the phone, and the intake interview was conducted with him. Mr. B. described Cindy, age 4, as an extremely difficult child to manage at home. He reported that Cindy was overly active; required "constant" supervision to prevent her from hurting herself; had frequent, intense, and lengthy temper tantrums whenever she did not get her way; and did not mind her parents. Cindy lived in an intact home with a 12-year-old sister, Margaret. Mr. B. (age 38) was employed as a research scientist, and Mrs. B. (age 36) was an elementary school librarian. These problems had been present for at least 2 years, and Cindy had been a demanding infant who required little sleep. Cindy attended a preschool, where she did not present any unusual behavior problems, according to the teachers' reports to the parents. When asked why they had decided to seek help at this particular time, Mr. B. stated that "we had just reached the end of our rope." He added that he believed their constant struggle with Cindy was affecting their older daughter who complained that her parents took out their frustration on her and didn't pay any attention to her. Mr. B. that admitted he and his wife became so exhausted with managing Cindy's behavior that they did not pay much attention to Margaret. However, Margaret was doing well in school, spent lots of time with her friends, and was a member of the school tennis team.

When asked about previous attempts to solve the problem, Mr. B. said they had tried time out, bribery, spanking, and ignoring. He stated that his wife believed he gave in too easily, but he did not know what to do when Cindy threw one of these fits. He expressed high levels of frustration and guilt because he and his wife could not handle the problem on their own.

The initial problem formulation was that Cindy had a difficult temperament, characterized by high emotional intensity, a high activity level, a tendency to overreact to stimuli, poor adaptation, high persistence, and a negative mood. Cindy might meet the diagnostic criteria for oppositional defiant disorder or attention-deficit hyperactivity disorder. The parents had a repertoire of parenting skills that would be adequate for most children. However, Cindy's behavioral problems had overtaxed the parents' skills. Consequently, the parents had become inconsistent in their parenting approach and lacking in self-confidence. They had begun to disagree with each other's approach, which weakened parental control and strengthened Cindy's control over the family.

Based on this initial problem formulation, the therapist decided to have Cindy and her parents come to the initial interview. Although most of the questions would be addressed to the parents, and Cindy would be provided with age-appropriate toys to play with during the interview, Cindy's presence was considered important for the following reasons:

1. Having Cindy present would provide an opportunity to observe her and to note any unusual physical factors (e.g., gross and fine motor control) that would warrant further child assessment.

2. Cindy's presence would also provide the opportunity to directly observe Cindy's activity level, attention span, and reaction to the therapist. Although a child's behavior in the interview may not be representative of the child's behavior in other settings, young children are less capable of inhibiting behavior impulses and of conforming their behavior to environmental conditions than are older children.

3. A parent–child interview would furnish an opportunity to observe interactions between Cindy and her parents, including the parents' use of limit setting, enforcement of limits, and use of praise, criticism, and instruction, as well as Cindy's attempts to control her parents and her parents' responses to these attempts.

4. Finally, such an interview would help to clarify aspects of family interactions, such as the parents' degree of support for each other in their discipline efforts and the function that Cindy's behavior might serve in the marital relationship.

Mark

The telephone intake for Mark H., age 12, was completed with Mrs. H. who presented the problem as Mark's lack of motivation. He was making mostly C's in seventh grade, although she knew he could do better, and she had to "stand over him" for up to 4 hours each night to get him to complete his homework. He was also overweight and refused to follow his diet. Moreover, Mark and his 9-year-old sister, Clara, fought "continuously." She acknowledged that Clara provoked Mark by calling him "fat" or by going into his room, but she thought Mark's reaction, to hit, was too extreme.

Questions about the family revealed that Mr. H., age 39, was a successful owner of a printing company and worked long hours. According to Mrs. H., he did not understand why she could not control the children and thought she let them walk all over her. Mrs. H., age 39, was a certified teacher who had not taught or worked outside the home since Mark was born.

Their previous attempts to deal with the problem had included paying for grades, grounding, loss of privileges, spanking, and having Mark tested to determine whether he had a learning disability. The test results found Mark to have above- average intelligence and no learning problems.

When asked what had prompted her to seek treatment at this time, Mrs. H. stated that Mark had received a notice of a failing grade at the midpoint of the grading period. Mr. H. had spanked Mark for the failing grade and then felt guilty over having been so hard on him. He felt Mark was too old to spank, but he could not just "stand by and let

Mark fail school and ruin his life." Mrs. H. spoke with a sad affect and expressed feelings of hopelessness ("Nothing works"), low self-esteem ("I'm probably the problem), fatigue, and guilt ("I know it's wrong, but I feel irritated just being with Mark").

Based on the telephone interview, Mark's poor school performance and failure to take responsibility for his school work were hypothesized to be a result of family problems in the areas of family structure, problem solving, and belief systems. In addition, it was hypothesized that Mrs. H. was experiencing symptoms of depression. Regarding the family's structure, it was hypothesized that the father was disengaged and that the marital relationship was distressed. Mark had learned to get his father's attention through misbehavior (e.g., fighting and failing classes). Mrs. H. was overly involved, overcontrolling, and overly critical with her children. She assumed responsibility for their behavior, which contributed to Mark's sense of incompetence and his lack of pride in achievement. Ironically, the mother's attempts to control Mark had given Mark considerable power in the family, as the mother reacted to his problems and behaviors. The fact that Mr. H. was openly critical of his wife's parenting suggested a weak parental coalition. Problem-solving deficiencies were suggested in their attempts to solve the homework problems and the sibling fighting. Irrational beliefs were evidenced in the statement that if Mark did not do well in school now his life would be ruined, and in the statement that the parents had to make Mark succeed.

Because the problem formulation implicated problems in family interactions, problem-solving, and belief systems, and parental adjustment, the therapist decided to conduct the first interview with the entire family. A family interview would provide an opportunity to confirm or to disconfirm the initial hypotheses. Because the initial formulation emphasized family interactions, it was deemed likely that the assessment would be followed by family therapy. Beginning the assessment by obtaining each family member's perceptions of the problems would make it easier to move from assessment to family intervention.

CONCLUSION

These three cases illustrate the importance of developing an initial problem formulation during the first contact with a family. This formulation, however, is both incomplete and tentative. A complete behavior assessment of the problem includes a variety of methods in addition to interviewing and results in a complete behavior formulation of the problem. The resulting behavior formulation should be inclusive, explaining the interrelationships among the presenting problems, accounting for the etiology of the problems, identifying symptoms that will be the initial focus of treatment, and predicting how the problems will respond to changes in contextual variables (Meyer & Turkat, 1979). One of the most important functions of the initial formulation is the direction it offers for planning the initial interview. Some considerations in conducting three different types of interviews—parent, family, and child interviews—are discussed in the following chapter.

6

Behavioral Interviewing: Practical Applications

THE PARENT INTERVIEW

General Considerations

It is almost always necessary to obtain information from parents about their perceptions of the nature of the child's difficulties (frequency, intensity, duration); relevant developmental history (medical, educational, social); and possible factors that may be maintaining or eliciting the problem behavior. This information is usually obtained in an interview with the parents, or with the parents and child together. Some behavior assessors prefer to obtain much of this information, especially developmental history and family demographic data, with questionnaires that the parents complete prior to the initial interview. It is usually advisable to have both parents attend the parent interview. This practice provides an opportunity to assess the degree of consistency in the parents' perceptions about the problem and ways to handle it, as well as to observe the parents' interactions. Insisting on the father's attendance and eliciting his perceptions are likely to result in greater cooperation from the father in subsequent treatment.

A number of standardized formats have been published for interviewing parents (Holland, 1970; Kanfer & Grimm, 1977; Wahler & Cormier, 1970). These formats tend to be quite general and focus almost exclusively on information about the child. However, research on the relationship between parental characteristics and adjustment on the one hand, and children's functioning in the home and at school on the other (e.g., Forehand, Long, Brody, & Fauber, 1986), indicates that

127

it is important to expand the scope of the parent interview to include information about the parents and about family interactions. In addition, because different controlling variables are important to different disorders, the general nature of these parent interviews does not address those variables most important to assess with a specific problem.

> The nature of an interview with the parent of a depressed child should be different from that conducted with the parent of a socially aggressive child. It is believed that an understanding of the parameters associated [with a specific disorder] *in coordination with* the general principles of behavioral interviewing (e.g., Turkat, 1986), will serve to generate more specialized and ultimately more useful assessment in each of these areas. (Mash & Terdal, 1988, p. 16, italics in original)

It is possible to identify interview content that is relevant to a wide range of disorders. The specific questions within content areas, however, will depend on those behavior constellations, situations, and con-

TABLE 6.1. Content of Parental Interview

Family Composition and Demographics
Parental perceptions of the problem
   Nature of the problem (frequency, onset, intensity)
   Cause of the problem
Parental expectations and goals for the child
Parental feelings about the problems
Possible factors (antecedent and consequent stimuli) that may maintain or elicit the problem behaviors (i.e., situational and temporal variations in the problem).
Parents' usual response to the problem behavior, and child's subsequent response
Historical information related to the manifestation of the problem (onset, changes in manifestation of the problem)
Past treatment efforts
Relevant Developmental and medical history
Educational performance Child's social relationships
Parents' motivation and resources for particpating in a behavior change program
Recent psychosocial stressors experienced by family members
Marital relationship and satisfaction
Parents' health
Parents' level of stress
Factors prompting referral now

---

trolling variables common to a particular disorder and on the purpose of the interview. For example, in interviewing parents of a child suspected of autism, the interviewer would ask questions about the child's language development, sensory experiences, and reaction to people. In interviewing parents of a child suspected of having attention-deficit hyperactivity disorder (ADHD), information about impulsivity, attention, peer relationships, activity, and compliance would be sought.

The list of content areas to be covered in the parent interview, included in Table 6.1, is based on the work of Mash and Terdal (1988), Haynes and Jensen (1979), and Barkley (1988). In addition to addressing these content areas, the interviewer establishes an agreement with the parents concerning the goals and methods of treatment and elicits parental cooperation for ensuing treatment.

Problem-Specific Interviews

Several researchers have published problem-specific parent interviews (Barkley, 1988; Taylor, 1988; Wolfe, 1988). It is instructive to compare these interviews to discover their commonalities and differences.

Barkley's Interview Format for Parents of ADHD Children

Barkley (1988) believes that parental reports, whether accurate or not, "provide an ecologically valid and important source of information concerning the children's difficulties" (p. 79). He states that the reliability and accuracy of the interview are enhanced by using specific questions that focus on specific complaints and the functional parameters of the problem. The interview outline in Table 6.2 is adapted from Barkley (1988).

The last part of the interview yields highly specific information about the parent–child interactions across settings. Table 6.3 presents nine questions that are asked in response to each situation in which the parent reports compliance to be a problem. The interview ends with asking parents to report on the child's positive behavior.

Barkley's interview format is very similar to the interviews recommended by Forehand and McMahon (1981) and Wahler and Cormier (1970) for conduct-disordered children. These similarities are not surprising, considering the fact that ADHD and conduct disorders represent undercontrolled or externalized psychopathology. Common to all interviews for these disorders are specification of the problem behaviors and settings in which behaviors occur, followed by a series of questions to determine consequences of parent–child interactions. Basically, the interviewer asks, "What happens next?" until he or she has a clear understanding of the sequence of parent–child interactions in problem situations. The following interview excerpt provided by McMahon and Forehand (1988, p. 118) illustrates this interviewing technique.

> THERAPIST: Do you have any problems with Mark at bedtime?
> PARENT: Oh my gosh, yes. It takes forever for him to go to sleep. He gets out of bed again and again.

TABLE 6.2. Interview Guide for Parents of ADHD Children

1. Demographic data concerning child and family
2. Major referral concern on part of parent and/or other referral agents, if appropriate.
3. Details of each major concern, to incude specific problem behaviors and their frequency, age of onset, chronicity, and situational and temporal variation in the behaviors and the consequences of behaviors.
4. Reason for seeking services at this time.
5. Potential rewards and punishers.
6. Preferred alternative behaviors (i.e., what do the parents want the child to do in the situation in which the problem behavior occurs?)
7. Developmental history related to:
   Motor development
   Language development
   Intellectual development
   Academic development
   Emotional development
   Social functioning
8. If other disorders are suspected, symptoms of these (inappropriate thinking, affect, social relationships, or motor abnormalities)
9. Presence or history of tics in child or in child's immediate biological family members
10. Child's medical history
11. Child's educational history
12. Family History—psychiatric difficulties in parents and siblings, marital difficulties, stressors (medical, employment, etc.) on family
13. Prior treatments for the identified child and family problems
14. Level of insularity of family (social support available to family)
15. Child's ability to appropriately carry out parental directives in a variety of settings, to exhibit self-control, and to follow rules for behavior.

Note. Adapted from "Attention Deficit Disorder with Hyperactivity" by R. A. Barkley, 1988, in E. J. Mash & T. G. Terdal (Eds.), *Behavioral Assessment of Childhood Disorders* (2nd ed., pp. 69–104), New York: The Guilford Press. Copyright 1988 by The Guilford Press. Adapted by permission.

TABLE 6.3. Parental Interview Format: Parent–Child Interactions across Settings

Situations to be discussed with parents	Follow-up questions for each problematic situation
General—overall interactions Playing alone Playing with other children Mealtimes Getting dressed in morning During washing and bathing While parent is on telephone While watching television While visitors are at home While visiting others' homes In public places (supermarkets, shopping centers, etc.) While mother is occupied with chores or activities When father is at home When child is asked to do a chore At bedtime Other situations (in car, in church, etc.)	1. Is this a problem area? If so, then proceed with questions 2 through 9. 2. What does the child do in this situation that bothers you? 3. What is your response? 4. What will the child do next? 5. If the problem continues, what will you do next? 6. What is usually the outcome of this interaction? 7. How often do these problems occur in this situation? 8. How do you feel about these problems? 9. On a scale of 0 to 10 (0 = severe problem), how severe is the problem to you?

Note. From: *Hyperactive Children: A Handbook for Diagnosis and Treatment* by R. A. Barkley, 1981, New York: Guilford Press. Copyright 1981 by The Guilford Press. Reprinted by permission. Adapted by Barkley from interview used by C. Hanf, 1976, University of Oregon Health Sciences Center.

THERAPIST: Tell me about your family's routine during the half-hour before Mark's bedtime.

PARENT: At 7:30 I help Mark with his bath. After he brushes his teeth and goes to the bathroom, I read him a story. Then Bob and I kiss him goodnight.

THERAPIST: O.K., then what happens?

PARENT: Well, things are quiet for about 10–15 minutes. Then Mark is up. He gets out of bed and comes into the den where Bob and I are watching TV.

THERAPIST: What does Mark do when he gets up?

PARENT: He usually comes in and climbs in either Bob's or my lap and complains that he can't sleep.

THERAPIST: What do you do then?

PARENT: Sometimes we let him sit with us for a while, but usually I take him back to bed and tell him goodnight again.

THERAPIST: What happens then?

PARENT: Mark stays there for a while, but he's soon out again.

THERAPIST: And then what do you do?

PARENT: I may tell him he's being a bad boy. Then I take him back to bed. Usually I read him another story, hoping he'll get sleepy this time.

THERAPIST: Does that work?

PARENT: No, he's up again before I have time to get settled in my chair.

THERAPIST: What happens then?

PARENT: The whole thing repeats itself. I put him in bed, read him another story, and he gets up again.

THERAPIST: How long does this go on?

PARENT: For about 2 or 3 hours—until Bob and I go to bed.

THERAPIST: What happens when you and your husband go to bed?

PARENT: Mark still gets up, but we let him get in bed with us and he goes to sleep then.

THERAPIST: How many nights a week does this happen?

PARENT: Every night! I can't think of a night's peace in the last few months.

THERAPIST: How long has Mark been doing this?

PARENT: Oh, I would guess for about a year.

THERAPIST: Have you or your husband tried any other ways of handling Mark at bedtime?

PARENT: Sometimes I get angry and yell at him. Sometimes Bob tries spanking him, but then Mark just ends up crying all evening. At least my way, we have a little peace and quiet. (McMahon & Forehand, 1988, p. 118)

Taylor's Interview Format for Parents of Children with Learning Disabilities

Taylor (1988) recommends a parent interview in assessing learning disabilities in order to "collect information on the child, assess family functioning, and build rapport with parents" (p. 430). Given the wide range of child and family factors associated with learning disabilities, assessment procedures must include broad-based procedures. The wide scope of the interview permits screening of a large number of factors potentially important to the etiology of learning problems and to their treatment. Taylor recommends using parent-completed questionnaires to obtain background information, rather than collecting this information in the interview. He also recommends having parents and teachers complete behavior checklists, and obtaining samples of schoolwork and scores on any previously administered standardized tests of achievement or cognition prior to the initial parent interview. Recognizing the importance of a comprehensive assessment, Taylor believes, that "the interview itself constitutes the most important single source of information about the child" (p. 430). Taylor's guideline for conducting the parent interview is reproduced in Table 6.4.

TABLE 6.4. Taylor's Guidelines for Initial Interview with Parents of Children with Learning Disabilities

Topics Covered and Typical Order

1. Reasons for referral
2. Nature of problem(s)
   a. Description(s)
   b. Examples
   c. History
   d. Attempted solutions and how parents are currently helping the child to cope (e.g., homework assistance, tutoring, discussions with teachers or the child)
   e. Parents' perceptions of reasons for problem(s)
   f. Other opinions (e.g., teachers, physicians, psychologists, or other professionals)
   g. Parents' expectations of child in problem areas
   h. Why parents decided to have child assessed at this time
3. Survey of other areas
   a. Review as necessary of educational history: schools attended, problems noted by teachers, special programs, grades retained
   b. Review as necessary of developmental history (see Table 1): perceived lags in earlier development; past and present status relative to siblings or peers in areas not covered above, including attention, memory, comprehension, reasoning, speech and language, coordination, academic abilities, peer relationships, temperament or personality traits
   c. Review as necessary of medical history (see Table 1): current medical or somatic complaints, current medical care, histories of serious illness or injuries, hospitalizations, previous medical diagnoses
   d. Review as necessary of family history and family stresses (see Table 1): history of learning problems in parents, siblings, or other relatives; impact on family of child's problems; supports available to the family; family functioning and stress on family, including conflict within family, pressure from relatives, financial problems, illnesses, and mental health problems
   e. Behavioral adjustment: compliance, self-control, independent functioning and self-initiative, attitude toward self and school, relationships with family members
   f. Disciplinary strategies of parents and other caregivers: general approach to management of child, expectations regarding child's behavior, parental reactions to misbehavior, consistency
   g. Strengths (special characteristics or skills valued by parents, others, or child)
   h. Parents' future aspirations for the child
4. Parents' summarization of questions they would like answered and of their expectations regarding possible outcomes of having the child assessed

Note: From "Learning disabilities" by H. G. Taylor, 1988, in E. J. Mach & L. G. Terdal (Eds.), *Behavioral assessment of Childhood Disorders* (2nd ed., p. 430), New York: Guilford Press. Copyright 1988 by The Guilford Press. Reprinted by permission.

Wolfe's Guideline for Interviewing Maltreating Parents

Child abuse is implicated as a contributing factor in a wide range of developmental deviations. Because child maltreatment interacts with other child and family variables, a search for a linear relationship between child maltreatment and adjustment disorders is misfocused. Abuse occurs in the context of inappropriate and abnormal parenting, including social isolation, emotional rejection, lack of responsiveness and sensitivity to the child's needs, insufficient sensory stimuli, inadequate prenatal and child medical care, and harsh treatment (Wolfe, 1988). In addition, child characteristics (e.g., minor handicaps, difficult temperament) place a child at risk for maltreatment (Wolfe, 1988). Thus, it is necessary to assess not only the nature of the physical abuse, per se, but the parent–child relationship, parent and family characteristics, child characteristics, environmental stressors, and available support to the family.

Contemporary models of child abuse stress the dynamic interplay among parent, child, family, and social factors. Abuse is viewed as a result of both distant events (e.g., exposure to parental violence during childhood) and present contextual events (e.g., a crying child) that affect parent–child interactions (Burgess, 1979, Wolfe, 1988). Factors relevant to the behavior assessment of abuse include individual, family, and societal factors, and both distant and proximate events.

Behavior assessment of child abuse concerns "the interplay of a constellation of factors involving the entire family. This constellation is known to include the parents' childhood and early adult history, child-rearing skills, recent stressful events, social relationships, and features of the child, among others" (Wolfe, 1988, pp. 646–647). To assess this broad range of contextual variables that influence parent–child interactions, a variety of assessment methods is necessary. The particular methods employed will depend on the purpose and specific situation. For example, an assessment conducted for the purpose of determining dangerousness and risks to the child would differ from an assessment to determine parental strengths and weaknesses in relationship to child-rearing demands, or from an assessment to determine the child's emotional adjustment and coping abilities. When the child is expected to remain at home or to return home, and the purpose of the interview is to identify parental needs in the area of child rearing, in order to plan a behavioral intervention, the interview would address the content in Table 6.5.

Table 6.5 provides a guide for the parent interview. The guide is general, denoting areas to be assessed rather than specifying a questioning strategy or the specific content. Thus, it serves as a screening for

TABLE 6.5. Wolfe's Parent Interview and Assessment Guide: Abuse and Neglect

The following is a selected summary of the major factors associated with child abuse and neglect, requiring further interviewing and assessment of the parent, as indicated. The framing and emphasis of each question are left up to the discretion of the interviewer.

I. Identifying general problem areas
   A. Family background
      1. Early rejection or abuse during own childhood; relationship with biological and/or psychological parents
      2. Methods of punishment and reward received during own childhood
      3. Family planning and effect of children on the marital relationship
      4. Preparedness for and sense of competence in child rearing
      5. Early physical, emotional, behavioral problems of child (i.e., illnesses, trauma, temperament)
   B. Marital relationship
      1. Length, stability, and quality of present relationship
      2. Examples of conflict or physical violence
      3. Support from partner in family responsibilities
      4. Substance abuse
   C. Areas of perceived stress and supports
      1. Employment history and satisfaction
      2. Family income and expenses, chronic economic problems
      3. Stability of occupation, income, and living arrangements
      4. Perceived support from within or outside of the family
      5. Daily/weekly contacts with others (e.g., neighbors, social workers)
      6. Quality of social contacts and major life events (i.e., positive vs. negative influence on the parent)
   D. Symptomatology
      1. Recent or chronic health problems; treatment; drug and alcohol use
      2. Identifiable mood and affect changes; anxiety; social dysfunction
      3. Previous psychiatric evaluations or treatment

II. Assessing parental responses to child-rearing demands
   A. Emotional reactivity
      1. Perception of how particular child differs from siblings or other children known to the parent
      2. Feelings of anger and "loss of control" when interacting with child (describe circumstances, how the parent felt, how the parent reacted)
      3. Typical ways of coping with arousal during/following stressful episodes
   B. Child-rearing methods
      1. Parental expectations of child (i.e., accuracy of expectations for child behavior and development, in reference to child's actual developmental status)
      2. Examples of recent efforts to teach new or desirable behavior to child
      3. "Preferred" and "typical" manner of controlling/ disciplining child
      4. Attitudes toward learning "different" or unfamiliar child-rearing methods
      5. Perceived effectiveness of parent's teaching and discipline approach
      6. Pattern of child behavior in response to typical discipline methods (i.e., accelerating, decelerating, manipulative, responsive)

Note. From "Child Abuse and Neglect" by D. A. Wolfe, 1988, in E. J. Mash & L. G. Terdal (Eds.), *Behavioral Assessment of Childhood Disorders* (2nd ed., p. 652). New York: Guilford Press. Copyright 1988 by The Guilford Press. Reprinted by permission.

other, more specific assessment procedures. For example, if marital discord is suggested, the clinician might administer the Dyadic Adjustment Scale (DAS; Spanier, 1976); if a lack of positiveness in parent–child interactions is suspected, the clinician might observe the parent–child interaction, using a structured behavior observation system (Burgess & Conger, 1978).

THE FAMILY INTERVIEW

Behavior assessors are increasingly recognizing family contributors to child disorders and incorporating family assessment into comprehensive child assessments. Family assessment is based on the assumption that the family context influences a child's behavior and that changes in that context will produce changes in the child. Because the child's symptoms are viewed as adaptive responses to the social systems of which the child is a part, it is believed that symptoms are best understood and treated within the context of these systems.

Increasingly, behavior assessors combine family assessment practices such as those described by Minuchin (1974) and Forman and Hagan (1984) with more traditional behavioral assessment approaches, such as direct observation and self-report questionnaires. Robin and Foster's (1989) intervention with families experiencing adolescent–parent conflict combines skill training and structural family therapy, and is based on an "understanding of family structure and the functional characteristics of family interaction sequences" (p. 5). In their model, the family interview is the primary tool for assessing family structure and family interactions. Before their approach to family interviewing is described, the basic tenets of structural family therapy are briefly summarized.

Basic Family Structure Concepts

The structural school of family therapy (Minuchin, 1974) posits that the family's structure is evident in repeated patterns of interaction. These patterns of interaction are manifestations of invisible relationship rules that govern the role and behavior of family members. The most noteworthy elements of family structure are boundaries, alignments, and power (Aponte & VanDeusen, 1981).

"Boundaries" refer to relationship rules that can be characterized on a continuum from "enmeshed" to "disengaged." Optimally, boundaries or roles within a family are clearly defined, such that family members experience sufficient autonomy and independence, yet there is a free exchange of nurturance and opinion. In enmeshed relationships, boundaries between two members are diffuse, members are closely involved in the affairs of other members, privacy is minimal, independence is thwarted, and there is pressure to conform to family norms. Family members overreact to changes in other members' behaviors and affect. Members frequently interrupt each other because they feel they can read each other's thoughts. When relationships are disengaged, boundaries are rigid, family members have infrequent interactions with each other and are distant and uninvolved in each other's affairs. Members are independent and maintain private lives with little sharing and interpersonal involvement. Both extremes place a child at risk for adjustment difficulties: enmeshed boundaries are associated with internalizing disorders (Minuchin et al., 1978), and disengaged boundaries are associated with delinquency and substance abuse (Hoffman, 1981).

"Alignment" refers to joining or opposing someone who is carrying out an operation (Aponte & VanDeusen, 1981). Within a family, members form alignments or alliances with other family members to accomplish or to thwart certain goals. "Coalitions" and "triangulations" are two common types of alignments. In dysfunctional families, alignments are rigid and cross generational boundaries. Problem coalitions include (1) parents who fail to work together (weak parental coalition); (2) alliances between a child and the more lenient parent, such that the parental relationship is weakened and rules of the stricter parent are overruled; (3) parents who detour conflict by scapegoating a "bad" child; and (4) parents who avoid conflict by overprotecting a "sick" child. A special type of alignment is triangulation, in which parents compete with each other to enlist the support of the child against the other parent. The child alternatively shifts alignments, preventing parents from imposing behavioral limits. Overly rigid parental alignment, in which the child's attempts to express an opinion or to seek freedoms are consistently punished, is also dysfunctional and interferes with the child's development of autonomy.

"Power" refers to the relative influence of persons or subsystems to affect family rules and interactions. Typically, parents have greater power and control over decision making. Dysfunctional power relationships, in which children have more power than parents, are thought to be associated with externalizing disorders (Haley, 1978).

Additional aspects of family structure are the family's adaptation to changing circumstances, including developmental change. Adaptive families change relationship rules (boundaries, alignments, power) in response to changes within the family, such as the birth of a child, a child's entering school, the teen years, and extra family pressures (e.g., the mother's entering the labor force). Robin and Foster (1989) address intrafamily changes associated with adolescence, and stress the need for families to renegotiate relationship rules to accommodate adolescents' capacity and need for independence and autonomy.

Family Behavioral Interviewing

Robin and Foster (1989) state that a family's ability to respond adaptively to the developmental changes that occur during adolescence depends on the family's problem-solving skills, communication skills, existing family structure, and family beliefs or cognitions. The purpose of the behavioral family interview is to assess family processes related to these constructs.

Problem Solving and Communication

Problem solving involves the application of specific skills at different stages. Spivack, Platt, and Shure (1976) have delineated the following steps as important in effective problem solving:

1. *Problem finding*: recognizing the presence of an interpersonal problem.
2. *Problem definition*: formulating the problem in clear-cut terms, collecting information relevant to the formulation of the problem, and communicating the formulation to others.
3. *Generation of solutions*: generating a variety of creative alternatives for resolving the problem through the use of brainstorming or related techniques.
4. *Evaluation*: projecting the benefits and costs of implementing the solutions, viewing them from a variety of perspectives.
5. *Decision-making*: choosing and negotiating a solution that maximizes the benefits and minimizes the costs for everyone involved in the problem.
6. *Implementation planning*: specifying the details required to implement a chosen solution effectively.
7. *Verification*: evaluating the effectiveness of the solution in resolving the problem and recycling through the earlier steps if the solution fails to solve the original problem.

Problem-solving and communication skills are assessed in an interactional context—that is, the family interview:

Applying problem solving within an interactional context requires skills in expressive and receptive communication. Family members need to express their feelings and opinions assertively yet unoffensively, to listen to each other's statements attentively, and to decode messages accurately. Accusations, denials, threats, commands, poor eye contact, and so forth, impede effective communication by provoking anger and reciprocated negative statements. Reflections, paraphrases, brief acknowledgements, empathetic remarks, and appropriate eye contact and posture facilitate effective communication. Deficits in any problem-solving and communication skills may result in increased conflict and argument. For instance, not defining a problem in clear-cut terms may lead different family members to address different problems and be confused as to what topic is indeed being considered. Families who cannot brainstorm a variety of solutions may become bogged down in their original positions, unable to perceive alternatives for overcoming their conflict, while families who prematurely evaluate the first new ideas they suggest are likely to inhibit novel ideas. Inability to project the consequences of solutions can result in impulsive adoption of an impractical, implausible course of action doomed to failure. Difficulty in negotiating compromises can result in the breakdown of an entire discussion. (Robin & Foster, 1989, p. 12)

An assessment of family problem solving also includes assessing the family's decision-making processes, which exist on a continuum ranging from authoritarian or autocratic to permissive or *laissez faire*. Robin and Foster (1989) believe that children need to have greater decision-making power as they grow older and that parents who continue to rely on authoritarian decision making when their children are teenagers are likely to experience high levels of conflict.

Cognitions

Parents' beliefs, expectancies, and attributions regarding parenting and child rearing affect parent–child interactions and the family's ability to resolve problems. The interviewer directs his or her attention to communication within the family that is indicative of certain cognitive errors or distortions. These cognitive distortions, as described by Beck (1967, 1976), affect parents' perceptions of problems and their behaviors. For example, the father who states, in response to his son's forgetting to bring home a book needed to complete homework, that his son is always irresponsible and doesn't care about school is committing a cognitive error referred to as "selective abstraction." Selective abstraction is focusing on a detail out of context, ignoring evidence contrary to the conclusion reached. Another cognitive error, "arbitrary inference," refers to drawing a specific conclusion in the absence of supporting evidence, or even in a case when the evidence is contrary to the conclusion. "Ruination," a special example of arbitrary inference, refers to parents' believing that if their child engages in certain undesirable behaviors,

TABLE 6.6. Types of Questions Asked in Family Interview

Content-focused questions

What do you like [dislike] about your family [mother, father, son, daughter]?

If you could choose three things never to discuss [argue about] again, what would they be?

When you have arguments with your parents [son, daughter], what are they most often about?

Think about the last time you had a good talk [an argument]. What did you talk [argue] about?

If you wanted to make your parents [child] really mad, what would you do? Do you ever do that?

Do you ever feel like you are "nagging"? What are the things you find yourself reminding others about?

Process-focused questions

Think of the last time your family had an argument. Describe what I would have seen if I'd been there. Is this typical?

How do you let your child [parents] know when you are angry with him [her, them]? (When you are happy with him [her, them])? How does he [does she, do they] react?

What do you do when your mother [father, child] gets angry? How do you feel? What do you think about?

Do you ever try to talk problems over calmly? If so, what happens? How are the times you resolve things different from the times you argue?

(To parents) How often do you find yourself yelling at your child? When are you most likely to yell? What is the effect?

I'd like to get a general picture of what your family life is like. Could you describe for me a typical day? Start from the time you get up, and tell me about when you see each other, the kinds of things you do, and so forth.

What would you most like to change about the way you and _____ get along?

What is it about the way _____ acts that makes you say that? What is it about that behavior that particularly bothers you?

What things about yourself could you change to help improve the way you get along with _____?

How do arguments in the family end?

What would the ideal family be like for you? How is your family like and not like this? What specific things about your family make you say that?

What is it about _____'s behavior that makes you say he [she] is [trait label]?

If you wanted to get _____ to change something about her [his] behavior, how would you go about it? How do you think she [he] would react? How would you feel [think] about that?

How can you keep from getting into arguments? What happens when you do that?

To parents) How often do you agree on decisions involving your son [daughter]?

How do you handle disagreements? How does this influence the way each of you gets along with your son [daughter]?

(To adolescent) Which of your parents do you get along with better? What are the differences between your mom and dad that make you say that? Who is stricter? More lenient?

(To adolescent) When you want something (a privilege, a favor, etc.) from your parents, how do you try to get it?

Do you have any family rules or routines? What are they? Do people stick to them? If not, what happens? Do you see this as a problem?

Note. From *Negotiating Parent–Adolescent Conflict* (p. 50) by A. L. Robin and S. L. Foster, 1989, New York: Guilford Press. Copyright 1989 by the Guilford Press. Reprinted by permission.

catastrophic results will occur. "If he fails seventh grade, he'll amount to nothing" and "If she has sex at 16, her life is ruined" are examples of this cognitive error.

Detailed guidance for conducting the family behavior interview is provided in Chapter 4 of Robin and Foster (1989). Although their 2- to 3-hr interview is designed for parents and adolescent children experiencing conflict, it is adaptable to parent–child conflict with younger children. The interview proceeds in four stages:

1. Greeting and overview of session
2. Information gathering
3. Providing feedback to family and deciding relevant treatment approaches
4. Setting goals and establishing treatment contract

In the information-gathering stage, two types of information are needed: the content of family discord, and the process by which disagreements are resolved or left unsettled. Table 6.6 gives examples of the content-focused and process-focused questions

The therapist's role is both directive and warm. Robin and Foster (1989) report research on the characteristics of effective family therapists, which documents the importance of warmth and direction. Directive skills include sticking to specific topics, providing structure and guidance to the interview, allowing each family member to speak, and preventing excessive arguing. Involving all family members and remaining unaligned are important rapport-building skills.

THE CHILD INTERVIEW

The child interview was given little emphasis in earlier work in behavior assessment. As discussed in Chapter 5, the purpose of the behavior assessment was completion of a functional analysis of behaviors of concern. Children, especially those under 10 years old, were considered unreliable reporters of their behaviors, the conditions under which behaviors occurred, and the consequences that maintained those behaviors. Child interviewing consisted of an opportunity to observe a child directly and to ask the child about potential reinforcers that might be used in a contingency management plan (Cautela, 1977).

As behavior therapists began to focus on modifying internal mediating events to affect desired behavior changes, child behavior assessment practices began to change also. During the past few years, a number of child self-report questionnaires have appeared in the behavioral assessment literature (for reviews, see Hughes, 1988; Witt et al., 1988). Information obtained from child interviews and self-report questionnaires complements rather than displaces other behavior assessment procedures. Rather than asking children to report on their behavior and controlling variables, behavior assessors ask children to report on that which they are most capable of reporting on—their thoughts, beliefs, perceptions, and thinking processes.Interview strategies for assessing children's cognitions, problem solving, and affect are discussed in this section.

Assessing Children's Cognitions

Because the content of the child interview depends on the parameters of the specific problem, no general interview guide is suggested. For example, in interviewing a socially anxious girl, the interviewer asks the child to report on her expectations for social interaction. The interviewer can do this by presenting the girl with a situation involving joining in with peers, such as two girls jumping rope. "Pretend you want to jump rope, too. What do you think would happen if you asked them if you could jump, too? How sure are you that you could go up to them and ask them if you could jump rope? What might make it easier (or harder) for you to ask?" Socially anxious children are less confident of their ability to initiate social interaction and have less positive expectation for performance (LaGreca, Dandes, Wick, Shaw, & Stone, 1988).

Thought bubbles assist children in reporting on their self- talk. With the socially anxious girl, the interviewer might draw a picture of two girls jumping rope and a third girl standing off to the side. "Pretend this is you and you want to jump rope, too. You're thinking about asking them if you can jump rope. Tell me what you are thinking, and I'll write it in here in this bubble, like in the cartoon strips." Anxious and depressed children endorse self-statements indicative of certain cognitive errors. If these self-statements, or self-talk, can be elicited, the interviewer can assess the child's tendency to make these cognitive errors.

For example, one of us (Jan Hughes) interviewed a 9-year-old girl, Pat, who became very tense and anxious in testing situations. Hughes asked her to draw a picture of herself at school, and she did so. The interview proceeded as follows:

JH: You look scared.

PAT: I feel that way sometimes.

JH: Tell me what your picture tells about.

PAT: I'm taking a spelling test and it's Friday. The Big One! Mrs. Franke just said "get our your paper and pencil and number 1 to 20.

Jᴴ: I want to draw a thought bubble on your picture—like in the cartoon strips. Would that be okay with you?

Pᴀᴛ: Yea. Are you going to show it to somebody?

Jᴴ: No. It's just for us to talk about. If you want to keep the picture, that's okay. But I'd like to make a copy to keep too, so I can remember how you felt and what you were thinking. I will not show it to anyone else.

Pᴀᴛ: Okay.

Jᴴ: (*Draws the bubble.*) There. Now I want you to pretend you are in this picture right now. You are getting ready to take a spelling test right now. If you close your eyes you will find it easier to pretend. Good. Do you feel like you are there? Can you feel the desk and hear the teacher say "count to 20"?

Pᴀᴛ: Yes.

Jᴴ: Okay. Now tell me what you are thinking. Just talk out loud.

Pᴀᴛ: I hate spelling tests. I'll probably miss a bunch and everyone will think I'm dumb. I'll have the baddest grade in the class. I wish I were home. I feel scared. I can't do this—I can't spell.

Jᴴ: Wow! You do a lot of thinking, and a lot of that thinking probably makes you feel real nervous.

Pat's report of her self-talk revealed that her thoughts during testing situations included off-task thoughts ("I wish I were home"), negative self-evaluations ("I can't do this"), and cognitive errors and distortions ("Everyone will think I am dumb"). Highly test-anxious children do report more off-task thoughts, more coping statements, more negative evaluations, and fewer positive evaluations than do children low in test anxiety (Zatz & Chassin, 1983, 1985). Cognitive errors (self-referencing, overgeneralization, and dichotomous thinking) also characterize anxious (and depressed) children (Leitenberg, Yost, & Carroll-Wilson, 1986). The interview helped to assess maladaptive cognitions that needed to be altered in therapy.

Important cognitions to assess are a child's "attributions," or causal explanations, for events. As discussed further in Chapter 8, depressed children, like depressed adults, attribute success to external, unstable, specific causes and failure to internal, stable, and global causes (Kaslow, Rehm, & Siegel, 1984). One method of assessing children's attributions is to question the child about the reasons for the child's successful and unsuccessful experiences. If the child does not provide personal experiences, the interviewer can present hypothetical situations that are likely to be relevant to the child. The interviewer might refer to the Children's Attributional Style Questionnaire (CASQ; Fielstein, et al., 1985) for examples of success and failure experiences. The CASQ is a self-report questionnaire, and the child is asked to select a statement that describes what she or he would think in the situation depicted in the item. Because an open-ended response format elicits more accurate attributions (Palmer & Rholes, 1989), an interview adaption of the CASQ might elicit more accurate information about the child's spontaneous attributions. Of course, the existing psychometric data on the CASQ would not apply to such an adaption. Two items from the CASQ, one depicting athletic success and one depicting social failure, illustrate this approach to assessing attributions:

(Athletic Success)

You and some friends are playing soccer. You get the ball, dribble past someone on the other team, and score a goal. Which of the following reasons best explains why this happened?

    (a) I'm good at soccer (skill).
    (b) I tried my best (effort).
    (c) I got lucky (luck).
    (d) It was an easy game (task ease).

(Social Failure)

You have two friends whom you like to walk to school with. One day you see them walking to school together and they didn't come to get you. Which of the following reasons best explains why this happened?

    (a) People never like me as much as they like their other friends (lack of skill).
    (b) They were not in a friendly mood that day (bad luck).
    (c) It's hard to be friendly with more than one person at the same time (task difficulty).
    (d) I didn't let them know how much I wanted to walk with them (lack of effort). (Fielstein, et al., 1985, pp. 386–387)

Ellis (1977; Ellis & Harper, 1975) has identified a number of important irrational beliefs that create emotional and behavioral difficulties for adults. Most of these beliefs can be grouped into one of four types of irrational beliefs (Walen, DiGuiseppe, & Wessler, 1980):

1. Should statements, reflecting the belief that there are universal musts.
2. Awfulizing statements, reflecting the belief that there are terrible and catastrophic things in the world
3. Need statements, reflecting the belief that the client must have things to be happy.

4. Human worth statements, reflecting the belief that people can be rated (pp. 115-116).

Specific irrational beliefs common in children are discussed in Chapter 8, when strategies for interviewing children with internalizing symptoms are offered.

Bernard and Joyce (1984) recommend direct questioning to elicit the child's irrational beliefs:

"What were you thinking when_____happened?"
"What sorts of things were you saying to yourself when_____?"
" What name did you call your brother when he_____?"
"Tell me the first things which come into your mind when you think about_____?"
"Picture yourself back in class, what did you think when_____?" (Bernard & Joyce, 1984, p. 195)

Assessing Problem Solving

Deficits in problem-solving skills are associated with adjustment problems in childhood (Asarnow & Callan, 1985; Ford, 1982; Spivack et al., 1976; Richard & Dodge, 1982). Within the past 10 years, considerable research has supported the view that specific social problem-solving deficits are characteristic of aggressive children. For example, aggressive children generate fewer solutions to social problems (Richard & Dodge, 1982; Asarnow & Callan, 1985), and their solutions are less effective and more aggressive than are those of nonaggressive children (Asarnow & Callan, 1985; Deluty, 1981; Lochman & Lampron, 1986; Richard & Dodge, 1982). Aggressive boys are less accurate in interpreting social situations. For example, they demonstrate a systematic bias to infer hostile intent in social situations in which a peer's intention is ambiguous (Dodge, Murphy, & Buchsbaum, 1984; Steinberg & Dodge, 1983), and they selectively attend to and remember aggressive cues in a social situation (Dodge & Frame, 1982). These social problem-solving deficits and distortions are causally related to their aggressive responses (Dodge et al., 1984).

Problem-solving deficits and distortions can be assessed in a semi-structured interview (Dodge, 1986; Asarnow & Callan, 1985; Hughes & Hall, 1987). These interviews employ the hypothetical—reflective interview method. In brief, the psychologist presents a series of social problem situations by means of stories representing different social problem-solving contexts. The child is asked a number of questions about each story. These questions are designed to obtain information on children's problem-solving processes. For example, a child who has difficulty responding to peer provocations can be told a story about a child who is walking home from school one rainy day when a classmate rides by on his bike. When the boy rides by, mud is splashed on the child's pants. The interviewer then asks the child being interviewed a series of questions to assess the child's ability to accurately interpret the situation, generate and evaluate solutions to the problem, and apply the solutions generated (Hughes & Hall, 1987):

  I. Read
   a. What is the story about?
   b. What happened?
   c. Why did that happen?
   d. Does the child have a problem? What is the problem?
   e. What is the child thinking and feeling?

  II. Generate
   a. What could the child do to solve the problem?
   b. What might happen next if the child did that?
   c. What else could the child do?
     • What might happen if the child did that?
     • What would be the best thing to do? Why?

  III. Apply
   a. Is that what you would do?
   b. How good are you at doing that?
   c. Show me how you would do that.

The use of actual situations rather than hypothetical situations may permit a more accurate assessment of the child's reasoning about important social experiences in his or her child's life. Use of the child's actual experiences also enables the interviewer to maintain a conversational style of communication that may facilitate subsequent counseling.

The following is an excerpt from an interview with Ben, a 10-year-old boy referred for counseling by his teacher because of low motivation and difficulty getting along with classmates (Hughes, 1988). The interview began with general questions about friendship concepts and then proceeded to an assessment of Ben's social problem-solving skills in the context of a recent conflict Ben had experienced with a peer:

I[NTERVIEWER]: Sometimes best friends stop being best friends. What could happen to cause best friends to break up?

B[EN]: You can accidentally run and fall and trip and then they fall over you and think you tripped them and that's why you can lose a friend.

I: So, you have misunderstandings about why you did something. Has that happened to you?

B: Last weekend I had a new double wing boat and I told my friend Chris not to throw it because I said the missiles and bombs would come off. He goes, "O.K. I'll just take them off." I told him not to but he went ahead. It was already in mid-air by then. It hit the concrete because I couldn't catch it. It scattered all over the place. He won't buy me a new one so...(*pause*)

I: It was your boat with missiles on it. He got ready to throw it. You said not to and he threw it anyway.

B: Unhuh [i.e., yes]. So I told him how he threw it. He said he threw it underhanded so I could catch it. He didn't. He threw it overhanded as hard as he could.

I: Why do you think he did that?

B: I don't know. So while I was showing him how he did it, I used one of his guys this time because he had tore that boat up and it wasn't even mine. It was my friend Jeff's and he [Jeff] told me I could use it and now he's [Chris] broken it. There are two things missing on it, and I think the reason he threw it was just to be mean. And he stole a little G.I. Joe man and gun and if he doesn't give it...He left over the G.I. Joe backpack and it holds three boomerangs and if he doesn't give me my gun and man back, I won't give him the backpack. That's what my Dad says.

I: So you think he threw the boat overhand like that against the wall [be]cause he just wanted to be mean?

B: Yea[h].

I: What makes you think he did it to be mean?

B: When he gets with other kids he gets mean like some friends do. They think—you see these other kids he plays with are mean and they don't like me and they tell him and he might not like me then.

I: What did you want to happen when you threw his guy— what outcome did you hope for?

B: I wanted to punish him so he wouldn't do that again.

I: What could you do when something like that happens— like his throwing your boat against the wall?

B: Nothing really. I showed him how to do it. I used his guy and when it hit the concrete it broke and I said, "O.K., now we're even," and he said, "O.K., we're even."

I: So you each broke something and were even. That's one thing you can do when a friend breaks something. What else could you do?

B: Tell them not to do it and if he does make him buy you another one or tell their parents.

I: Anything else?

B: No.

I: What do you think is the best thing to do if someone breaks one of your toys?

B: Don't let them play with your toys. Like he always wants me to get out all my toys and once I got them all out—I set up all my G.I. Joe[s] and he says "Let's go play hide and seek" or something. Then I'll say "O.K. Now you made me bring it out now help me put it up," and he says "O.K." and puts one thing up and then runs off and won't help me and makes me put it up. (Hughes, 1988, pp. 255–256)

The interview continued, with the interviewer asking about probable consequences of alternative solutions, and Ben's evaluation of solutions. Ben demonstrated tendencies to attribute hostile intent to peers' provocations, to attend selectively to negative interactions and behaviors, to detect aggressive goals, and to generate and apply aggressive solutions in conflict situations.

Assessing Affect

It is often important to assess a child's degree of emotional arousal. Because children's feelings tend to be polarized (e.g., something is all good or all bad), and because they tend to deny negative feelings, it is sometimes difficult to assess children's affect. Emotional feeling scales help children report on their affective experiences. Children are given a 10-point scale such as the "feeling thermometer" and are asked to describe how much of a particular emotion they experience in a specific situation. In addition to helping children report on the intensity of their feelings, the scale teaches children that emotions exist on a gradient rather than on an all-or-none basis. This method is especially useful in assessing children's fears. Chapter 8 discusses the use of emotional feeling scales with fearful and anxious children.

CONCLUSION

Throughout this chapter and the preceding one, the importance of disorder-specific interviews has been stressed. In the remaining two chapters, interviewing procedures and interview content specific to two major classifications of child behavior disorders, externalizing disorders and internalizing disorders—are discussed. These two classifications represent two dimensions of childhood behavior disorders that have consistently emerged across studies using multivariate statistical procedures to identify symptoms that tend to go together (Quay, 1986b). Children's externalizing disorders include disruptive, aggressive, overly active, restless, impulsive, noncompliant, and oppositional behaviors. Internalizing disorders include anxious and depressed symptoms. Although specific disorders within these two major classifications require differences in interviewing content, the similarities among the disorders within these classifications indicate that interviews for each of the two types will be more similar than different. For example, an interview to obtain a functional analysis of problem situations and behaviors is conducted similarly in interviewing parents of ADHD children and parents of children with conduct disorders. In interviewing anxious and depressed children, information about family structure, irrational beliefs, self-concept, attributions, and prevalent mood will be obtained, in addition to information necessary to complete a functional analysis of problem behaviors, such as fears or social withdrawal. The similarities and differences in interviewing children and their families presenting with problems within these two major classifications are discussed in the following two chapters.

III

PROBLEM-SPECIFIC INTERVIEWING

7

Interviewing Children with Externalizing Behavior Problems

An alternative to the classification of childhood disorders based on a clinical taxonomy such as the DSM-III-R (American Psychiatric Association, 1987) is the classification of disorders based on multivariate statistical procedures (Quay, 1986a). From multivariate procedures two broad categories of behavior problems have emerged: behaviors that are of an "internalizing" nature and those that can be categorized as "externalizing." According to Kazdin (1989), "Internalizing consists of such symptoms as depression, anxiety, and withdrawal. Externalizing consists of undercontrolled or outward directed behaviors such as aggression, delinquency, and hyperactivity" (p. 183).

This chapter discusses interviewing approaches for children with externalizing problem behaviors, particularly those children who present with aggressive and overactive behavior. Chapter 8 discusses interviewing approaches for children with internalizing behavior problems.

PURPOSES OF THE INTERVIEW

A fundamental consideration in interviewing children who are referred for externalizing problem behaviors is the determination of the degree to which these behaviors interfere with adaptive functioning. One purpose of the interview is to delineate the frequency, duration, and severity of the behavior. By doing so, the clinician is able to determine whether the behaviors are of sufficient magnitude to warrant a diagnosable disorder. In the DSM-III-R, aggressive and overactive behaviors are symptoms of a group of disorders referred to as disruptive behavior disorders. Included under this grouping are attention-deficit hyperactivity disorder (ADHD), conduct disorder, and oppositional defiant disorder.

Because ADHD and conduct disorder share many of the same features, it is often difficult to distinguish between the two. In as many as 60% of diagnosable cases, both disorders are present (August, Stewart, & Holmes, 1983; Lahey, Schaughency, Strauss, & Frame, 1984). Both ADHD and conduct-disordered children exhibit difficulty with rule-governed behavior and interpersonal relationships (Carlson & Lahey, 1988). Because the problem behaviors of ADHD and conduct-disordered children are similar, the use of parent and teacher ratings may not be useful in distinguishing between the two. The parent–child interview may yield information concerning etiological factors and parent–child interactions that is essential to discriminating these two common childhood disorders.

Numerous studies indicate that ADHD can be distinguished from conduct disorder (Loney & Milich, 1981; McGee, Williams, & Silva, 1984; Quay, 1986a). A major distinction between the two are the essential features that must be present to make a diagnosis. According to the DSM-III-R, ADHD is characterized by excessive inattention, impulsivity, and hyperactivity. The essential features of conduct disorder are behaviors that violate the rights of others and age-appropriate social norms, such as engaging in physical violence, theft outside the home, and failing to establish affective bonds with others. Oppositional defiant disorder is similar to conduct disorder, with the exception that children with oppositional defiant disorder do not violate the rights of others or age-appropriate social norms. Instead, the behavior of children with oppositional defiant disorder is characterized by disobedient and oppositional behavior in relation to authority figures.

Another means of distinguishing between ADHD and conduct disorders is the consideration of etiological factors. There is no single etiological factor that explains the occurrence of ADHD; rather, a number of potential causative influences have been advanced (for an extended discussion, see Barkley, 1988). Whereas neurological, genetic, constitutional, and environmental factors have been proposed to account for ADHD, more empirical evidence is needed to validate each of these factors. In regard to the debate over the causative factors of ADHD, Barkley (1988) notes that there are "potentially numerous etiologies, among which the biological causes appear to have the greatest support. Most likely, the causes of the disorder should be viewed much as one views those of mental retardation—multiple causes having a final common pathway inevitably affecting the development of particular abilities" (p. 78).

Environmental factors are emphasized over biological factors as contributors to the development of conduct disorders. Current thinking on the etiology of conduct-disordered behavior in children is that it is learned and follows a developmental sequence. On the basis of a substantial body of research, Patterson, DeBaryshe, and Ramsey (1989) have proposed the social-interactional model to explain the development of conduct-disordered behavior. Patterson and his colleagues maintain that family members condition the child to exhibit coercive antisocial behaviors, which lead to patterns of academic and social failure. In this model the noncontingent application of positive reinforcement and punishment contributes to the development of antisocial behavior in the young child. By the time the child enters school, a repertoire of coercive behaviors has been established, which adversely affects the child's ability to negotiate peer relations and accept direction in academic settings. Deficits in social skills leave the child vulnerable to peer rejection and increase the probability of membership in a deviant peer group, where the expression of delinquent behavior is reinforced and thus maintained. Poor internal controls and the use of coercive behaviors such as noncompliance place the conduct disordered child at odds with the demands of a structured learning environment, leading to poor academic achievement and school failure. If such a cycle continues uninterrupted, the child is most likely to be identified as delinquent by adolescence.

INTERVIEWING PARENTS

A salient feature of externalizing behavior problems is the social discord they create (Henker & Whalen, 1989). Children who are aggressive, defiant, and overactive call attention to themselves because of the social disruption their behavior creates. The parent interview is an important component in the assessment process, because parents are continually faced with management problems related to such a child's difficulty with rule-governed behavior. The overt nature of externalizing problem behaviors makes them amenable to behavioral analysis, and parents can contribute important data regarding the frequency, intensity, and duration of problem behaviors. The parent interview also provides an opportunity to investigate the nature of interactional problems that exist between the parents and the child. Parental descriptions of difficulties with compliance and management contribute to the identification of target behaviors that can serve as foci for assessment and intervention activities. In addition, the parent interview is useful in elucidating the antecedent events and consequences that maintain problem behaviors.

Because the disruptive behaviors of children with externalizing disorders are easily identified and observed, the parent interview lends itself well to a behavioral approach. Barkley (1988) recommends that the parent interview for children suspected of having ADHD begin with an inquiry regarding the referral question, followed by a standard intake during which developmental, medical, school, and family histories are obtained (see Chapter 6 for a description of Barkley's interview).

The next phase of the interview involves a structured discussion of the child's ability to follow rules. This phase includes reviewing the child's ability to exhibit self-control and respond to directives across a variety of settings. In order to accomplish this task, Barkley recommends the use of a semistructured format that addresses the child's behavior and the parents' response to the behavior across a number of settings involving interactions between the parents and the child (e.g., getting dressed, taking a bath, mealtime, homework). Table 6.3 (Chapter 6) provides the format for this part of the interview. The information gained through this process will aid the interviewer in understanding the type of noncompliance the child exhibits as well as the management style of the parents.

The following excerpt is taken from an interview one of us (Jan Hughes) conducted with the parents of a 4-year-old girl referred for hyperactivity and oppositional behaviors.

Jн: Does Cindy have difficulty playing alone?

Mr. B.: Yes. She wants our constant attention. Her best trick is to lose something. Then she has a fit until we find it for her.

Jн: How often does this happen?

Mr. B.: Nearly every day.

Jн: Remember a recent time it happened and tell me what Cindy did.

Mrs. B.: It was just last night. I was cooking dinner and Cindy was playing in her room when she shouted, "Where is my mermaid?"

Jн: Is that the mermaid Cindy was looking for [Mr. B. was holding a little mermaid doll with long hair]?

Mrs. B.: Yes. She has a fit whenever she can't find it, so we try to keep up with it.

Jн: (*To Mrs. B*) What did you do when Cindy shouted, "Where is my mermaid?"

Mrs. B.: I told her it was somewhere in the house and to look for it.

J<small>H</small>: What did Cindy do next?

M<small>RS.</small>B.: She ran out of her room and started screaming, "I have to have it."

J<small>H</small>: What happened next?

M<small>RS.</small>B.: I kept cooking. Cindy came into the kitchen and started yelling at me to find it.

J<small>H</small>: And then what happened?

M<small>R.</small>B.: I was building a fire in the living room. I knew Cindy would get completely out of control unless we found it. So I told her I'd look for it.

J<small>H</small>: What did Cindy do next?

M<small>R.</small>B.: She calmed down and followed me while I looked for it.

J<small>H</small>: (*To Mrs. B.*) What did you do next?

M<small>RS.</small>B.: I kept cooking. I think Cindy has to learn how to cope with not being able to find something. I think she is being manipulative.

M<small>R.</small>B.: I know she is, but you wouldn't believe how upset she can get. It can last for 2 hours if we don't try to find it.

J<small>H</small>: After you looked for the mermaid, what happened next?

M<small>R.</small>B.: I looked for about 15 to 20 minutes. I couldn't find it, but Cindy started playing with her dollhouse and forgot about the mermaid.

M<small>RS.</small>B.: For a while. Remember after supper she wanted her mermaid to take a bath with. She cried again and I sent her to her room, and she kicked the door.

J<small>H</small>: What did you do next?

M<small>RS.</small>B.: I went in and told her she needed to calm down, and I promised to let her put some of my bubble bath in her tub if she would stop crying.

J<small>H</small>: What did she do next?

M<small>RS.</small>B.: She took her bath and was pretty good until bedtime.

During this same interview, the parents indicated that mealtime was another problem situation for them.

J<small>H</small>:What does Cindy do at mealtimes that is a problem?

M<small>RS.</small>B.: She won't stay at the table. She gets up 5 to 6 times during the meal, unless we have the television on, which I don't like. So we are all finished and she has hardly begun to eat.

J$_H$: What do you do when she leaves the table?

M$_R$. B.: We tell her to come back.

J$_H$: What does she do then?

M$_R$. B.: She turns the TV on.

J$_H$: What do you do?

M$_R$. B.: I turn the TV off. We tell her we'll take her plate away unless she sits at the table.

J$_H$: What does she do next?

M$_R$. B.: She comes back for a while and then gets up and turns on the TV.

J$_H$: What do you do then?

M$_R$. B.: Well, sometimes by that point we're so exhausted we just let her watch it. Or we take her food away. Sometimes I spank her, but I don't like to spank.

M$_{RS}$. B.: If we take her food away, in an hour she says she is starving and starts to have a fit. I want her to go to sleep, but she won't if she is complaining about being hungry. So I usually let her have a glass of milk or some cereal.

This interview yielded specific information about the problematic parent–child interactions. Cindy's misbehaviors were maintained by the positive consequences that followed misbehavior. Furthermore, the parents' lack of agreement concerning how to respond to Cindy's misbehavior weakened the parental coalition, thereby strengthening Cindy's power.

A growing body of research indicates that parents of ADHD children experience a variety of stressors that affect family functioning. For example, Befera and Barkley (1985) found that parents of ADHD children report more marital discord than parents of normal children and that mothers of ADHD children are frequently more depressed than mothers of normal children. Compared to parents of clinic-referred non-ADHD children and normal children, parents of ADHD children report higher levels of family stress and lowered parenting self-esteem (Mash & Johnston, 1983). In addition, mothers of ADHD children have been found to engage in more negative and controlling behavior with their children than mothers of non-ADHD children; this contributes to a perpetual cycle of negative interactions (Barkley, 1981; Mash & Johnston, 1982).

For the interviewer, these findings would suggest that during the parent interview efforts should be made to help the parents identify the ways in which the behavior of the ADHD child has affected marital and family relations. The identification of such stressors is an important part of assessing what types of interventions may be most appropriate for treatment planning.

Given the fact that managing the behavior of the ADHD child can be frustrating and time-consuming to parents, it is important to find time in the parent interview to discuss the child's positive characteristics. Barkley (1988) recommends that the end of the parent interview be used to discuss positive qualities of the child and to identify reinforcers that are desirable to the child. Such a discussion can facilitate the beginning of a parent training process that attends to and reinforces the child's ability to engage in rule-governed behavior.

Forehand and McMahon (1981) recommend that the interviewer make every effort to interview both parents together. The rationale behind this recommendation is that it provides the interviewer with the opportunity to identify patterns of interactions among the child and the parents. The joint interview also allows the interviewer to elicit the degree of concordance between the parents in regard to child management beliefs and behaviors.

Interactions between child and parents as well as parental attitudes toward child rearing, are key components in the identification of conduct problems in children. The problem guidesheet developed by Forehand and McMahon (1981) serves as a means for helping the interviewer and the parents structure the interview so that specific events can be analyzed to determine the exact nature of parent–child interactions that are problematic. In addition to understanding the nature of interactional problems, Forehand and McMahon recommend using the parent interview as a vehicle for obtaining information on potential reinforcers and punishments that may be useful in treatment planning and evaluation.

Patterson and his colleagues (Patterson, 1980, 1982; Patterson, Dishion, & Bank, 1984; Patterson & Bank, 1986) have described a model of family interaction in families with antisocial children. The model is based on extensive research on family determinants of aggressive behavior and on treatment of antisocial youths and their parents. The model emphasizes the central role parental skills play in the development of antisocial child behaviors. This research supports the importance of parental *discipline* and *monitoring*. Interviews with parents and with children are essential to the assessment of these two constructs. Regarding discipline, parents of antisocial boys tend to scold, threaten, and nag in response to child behavior problems. Furthermore, they respond similarly both to trivial and to major behavioral infractions, and they often fail to back up their threats. When they do carry out punishment, they tend to use extreme forms of physical punishment, such as hitting and grabbing or beating with an object. In summary, "inept parental disciplinarians meddled in trivial incidents, threatened without delivering consequences, and also periodically were physically assaultive" (Patterson & Bank, 1986, p. 57).

Parents of aggressive boys also demonstrated deficits in monitoring. They typically did not take note of or believe reports of misbehavior from outside the home. Because they did not monitor infractions outside the home, they did not respond with punishment to their children's misbehavior outside the home, which the children tended to interpret as permission to misbehave. Furthermore, they did not monitor their children's whereabouts, especially when their children were 10 years old or older. In contrast, parents of nondeviant boys knew what was going on at home, at school, and in the community. Because they monitored their children's activities, they knew what was trivial and what was not, and responded consistently to major infractions.

In the parental interview, it is important to determine whether the parents distinguish between major and trivial misbehaviors and whether they respond differently to misbehaviors differing in severity. One way to obtain this information is to ask the parents to report the number of behavior infractions occurring during the past 3 days. To refresh their memory, the interviewer should ask them questions about infractions that occurred during different parts of the day (such as in the morning before school or right after school), and should also ask questions about any reports of misbehavior from other persons. Next, the interviewer should ask the parents how they responded to each misbehavior. In separate interviews, the parents and the child should be asked to report on the amount of time the child spends in unsupervised activity (Patterson & Bank, 1986). For example, the child might be asked, "Where do you go after school? How long after you have been home from school do you have contact with one of your parents or some other adult?" "When you leave the house in the evening, do you need to tell somebody where you are going? How often do you need to check in with somebody?" "Do you tell your parents where you are going or when you'll be home when you go out?" "Do you talk to your parents about your daily plans?"

THE CHILD INTERVIEW

The interview with the child presenting with externalizing behavior problems should begin in the same way as any other unstructured initial interview. Some may expect that the child referred for problems related to difficulty in self-control and compliance will be difficult to manage in an initial interview. This assumption is unwarranted. The child with externalizing problem behaviors is similar to any other child referred for mental health services, in that he or she is experiencing distress. Although the child may not personally acknowledge distress, it is likely that important adults in the child's life have become distressed with the child's behavior and have communicated their distress and frustration to the child. By the time child arrives at the interview, it is likely that he or she concerned about being evaluated and judged. An accepting and nonjudgmental attitude on the part of the interviewer can help foster cooperation by minimizing the likelihood that the child will feel devalued or punished.

Although it is unfair to expect the child with externalizing problems to be difficult to manage in the interview, it is equally erroneous to dismiss the concerns of parents and teachers when the referred child is pleasant and cooperative during the interview. It is generally agreed that the behaviors associated with ADHD are often situation-specific (Barkley, 1981; Zentall, 1984). Given the novelty of the interview setting and the interviewer's interest in establishing rapport with the child, it is reasonable to expect that the child may find the experience reinforcing and interesting, and may therefore refrain from exhibiting the problem behaviors that prompted the referral.

A good place to begin the interview is to inquire as to the reasons why the child believes he or she is being seen. Such an inquiry implies that the interviewer is concerned with understanding the child's particular situation. It also provides the opportunity to evaluate the child's perceptions and misperceptions as to the reason and purpose of the interview. When the child has indicated the reasons why he or she is being seen, the interviewer can take the opportunity to clarify the purpose of the interview. If the child has an accurate perception of the reasons for the referral, the interviewer can validate the child's perceptions and expand on the child's responses if necessary. However, if the child has misperceptions of the reasons for the referral, the interviewer can explain his or her own understanding of the reasons for the visit.

Consider the following excerpt from an interview with an 8-year-old boy referred for counseling because of aggressive behavior toward peers at home and school.

INTERVIEWER: Why do you think you are coming here to visit with me?

DAVID: I'm not sure. It was my mom's idea.

INTERVIEWER: What did she tell you?

DAVID: She said you were nice and we would do exercises and learn things.

INTERVIEWER: Why would she want you to come here?

DAVID: I don't know, maybe 'cause I have trouble writing.

INTERVIEWER: I want to know about how school is going, but I also want to talk to you about some other things that your mom talked to me about. Your mom is worried about how you get along with other kids. She said that you seem mad at kids at school and around your house and that sometimes you get into fights with them.

DAVID: They pick on me and always start things.

INTERVIEWER: So other kids pick on you and start things that you get mad about?

After the interviewer has reached an understanding with the child as to the purpose of the interview, a number of alternatives are available as to the structure and content of the remainder of the interview. A generic and unstructured approach would involve discussing the child's perceptions about a variety of content areas, such as school, friends, activities, interests, and family life. Some children with externalizing behavior problems may be able to participate meaningfully in an unstructured interview, but others may be able to provide more meaningful information in an interview that is more structured.

There are a number of structured interview formats available for use with children who exhibit externalizing behavior problems. Patterson and Bank (1986) have developed a structured interview that assesses a number of dimensions related to the expression of conduct-disordered behavior. The interview contains structured questions that provide self-report data related to the child's relationship with family members and peers, the expression of problem behaviors, and reinforcement contingencies.

The psychometrically based diagnostic interviews reviewed in Chapter 3 are also a good source of information regarding externalizing problem behaviors. Most structured diagnostic interviews for children utilize an identical interview forms for the parent and the child. This format allows the clinician to identify the degree of concordance between the parent and the child in regard to the presence or absence of externalizing problem behaviors. Moderate to high parent–child agreement has been reported for both the Diagnostic Interview Schedule for Children (DISC) and the Diagnostic Interview for Children and Adolescents (DICA) for the DSM-III diagnoses of attention deficit disorder and conduct disorder (Edelbrock 1986; Welner 1987).

Several researchers have suggested interview formats for aggressive or conduct-disordered children that assess the child's social-cognitive processes (Asarnow & Callan, 1985; Feldman & Dodge, 1987; Hughes & Hall, 1987). These child interview formats are based on research documenting deficits in social problem solving among aggressive or rejected children. For example, aggressive or rejected children, compared to nondeviant children, tend to select competitive rather than cooperative goals in social situations (Renshaw & Asher, 1982); selectively attend to and recall social cues consistent with hostile versus nonhostile intentionality (Dodge & Frame, 1982; Dodge & Newman, 1981); collect fewer pieces of information prior to making an attribution of a peer's intent in a situation resulting in a negative outcome (Dodge & Newman, 1981; Milich & Dodge, 1984); overattribute hostility to a peer's behavior that results in some frustration to the child (Dodge et al. 1984); underattribute prosocial intent to peers' positive behaviors (Robinson, 1990); generate fewer solutions to interpersonal problems (Richard & Dodge, 1982; Asarnow & Callan, 1985); generate more aggressive solutions to interpersonal problems (Asarnow & Callan, 1985; Richard & Dodge, 1982); value assertive solutions more negatively and aggressive solutions more positively (Asarnow & Callan, 1985), and are more confident that aggression will produce tangible rewards and will reduce aversive treatment by others (Perry, Perry, & Rasmussen, 1986). Furthermore, these cognitive processing errors and distortions are directly related to their aggressive behavior (Dodge et al. 1984).

Both structured and unstructured interviews can yield information about children's social information processing. The following excerpt taken from an interview Jan Hughes conducted with a 9-year-old boy is representative of a low-structure interview.

Jₕ: Do you have any problems with the other kids at school?

Rₐₙdy: They're all right. Except four or five of the kids. They bother, me but I'm taking karate and they better not mess with me anymore.

Jₕ: What do boys do that bothers you?

Rₐₙdy: They tease me or tell Mrs. Cooper that I did something and I get in trouble for it. If I just barely push them, they cry like babies and I get in trouble.

Jₕ: Did something like that happen today, or this week?

Rₐₙdy: Well, there is this guy Mark. He sits in front of me and he started making lots of noise—humming and doing his pencil like this (*demonstrates drumming a pencil*).

Jₕ: How was that a problem for you?

RANDY: I couldn't think. I was trying to do my times [i.e., multiplication tables] and I couldn't with that racket.

Jh: Why do you think he was doing that?

RANDY: To bother me. He doesn't want me to make a good grade.

Jh: What did you do when he was making noise?

RANDY: I knocked him on the head like this (*Demonstrates by thumping his middle finger on the table*).

Jh: What happened next?

RANDY: He screamed and told the teacher I hit him. She didn't even let me tell her why. I had to stay after school for 10 minutes. But I'll get him back for that.

Jh: Why did you hit him?

RANDY: To teach him a lesson not to mess with me.

Jh: Did you want him to stop making noises?

RANDY: Sure.

Jh: What else could you have done to get him to stop?

RANDY: I could tell the teacher, but she probably wouldn't care.

Jh: What else could you have done?

RANDY: I don't know. Maybe fight him after school, 'cause then he couldn't tell the teacher.

Hughes asked Randy about several other disagreements he had with children. Each time, Randy was asked what was happening, what Randy thought the problem was, why he thought the other person did what he or she did, what Randy did, and what other strategies Randy could think of for solving the problem. Randy was likely to misperceive minor provocations as resulting from other children's intent to be mean to him, and many of his solutions involved retaliation for the perceived wrongdoing. When asked about events, such as a soccer game the previous Saturday, Randy selectively remembered the negative and hostile events, indicating that he was cognitively "primed" to attend to and to encode hostile cues. When asked why it is important to have a best friend, he responded, "If you have a best friend, people don't pick on you so much." Significantly, he did not mention the prosocial benefits of a best friend, such as companionship, loyalty, and reciprocity of positives.

There are several published interview formats for obtaining information about a child's social-cognitive processing. These interviews are semistructured or highly structured and have been developed for research purposes. An advantage of these interviews is the availability of evidence of reliability and validity. Disadvantages include lack of flexibility and dependence on hypothetical situations rather than on situations the child has experienced.

An example of a published interview is found in Renshaw and Asher (1983), who assessed children's goals and strategies for social situations by presenting the children with four hypothetical social situations and asking questions about what they would do and why they would do that. The purpose of the interview was to determine the kinds of goals children construe in social interactions:

> In their play with one another, children continuously face the task of construing goals and coordinating or reconciling potentially contradictory goals. Consider, for example, two children who are playing a board game. What might their goals be here?: To win the game? To maintain or enhance the relationship? To get better at the game? If one child was excessively preoccupied with the first goal he or she might cheat, dominate the game, or in other ways undermine the relationship between the children. The child might know how to play cooperatively but fail to do so because of certain goal commitments in the situation. (Renshaw & Asher, 1983, p. 355)

The four social situations each involved the establishment or maintenance of positive peer relationships. Each situation began with setting information, which consisted of descriptions of the social, temporal, or physical context. Next an initiating event was provided, which described an occurrence likely to cause some response from the protagonist. Children were asked to imagine that the situation was happening to them and to tell what they would say or do in that situation. Next, in order to assess children's goals for social situations, children were asked why they would choose that strategy. Responses were rated as to the level of friendliness and assertiveness they represented. The four situations were as follows:

Contact
Your parents have moved to a new town. This is your first day at a new school. (setting information)
As recess begins, the children go out to play. (initiating event)
Entry
One free period you have nothing to do. Then you see two children getting out a game of Monopoly. (setting information)
You go over to them to play and they say "Hey, we didn't ask you." (initiating event)

Friendship
You play with your friend at recess most of the time. (setting information)
One day at recess you see your friend playing with a child that you dislike. (initiating event)
Conflict
You ask a child who is new to the neighborhood to watch cartoons one Saturday morning. (setting information)
After about ten minutes, the child changes the channel without asking. (initiating event) (Renshaw & Asher, 1983, p. 358)

Renshaw and Asher found that well-accepted children's responses suggested more positive-outgoing goals than the responses given by less well-accepted children.

One final example is the interview offered by Asarnow and Callan (1985). They investigated five social-cognitive skills in fourth- to sixth-grade boys with positive and negative (rejected) peer status: (1) ability to generate a number of alternative solutions to social problems; (2) ability to generate nonaggressive, positive solutions to problems; (3) ability to evaluate possible solutions; (4) ability to plan adaptively; and (5) ability to make accurate attributions. After being presented with four social vignettes representing both aggressive and friendship situations, children were asked to generate solutions to the problem. Next, children were asked to evaluate solutions to the vignette problems. After children's responses to the situations and evaluations of responses to the four vignettes were obtained, the same situations were presented again, and each child was asked to describe what he would "feel and think" in each situation. Finally, each child was presented with six possible self-statements that the "child in the story might be thinking and feeling" and asked to rate each one is terms of how likely the story child would be to feel and think that way. Compared with popular boys, rejected boys generated fewer solutions to the hypothetical problems; generated less mature, prosocial, and assertive solutions; generated more aggressive solutions; evaluated aggressive strategies more positively and prosocial strategies more negatively; and showed less adaptive and more maladaptive planning. Specifically, rejected children were less likely to give a response indicating consequential thinking (e.g., "If I hit him, I'd get in trouble"), anticipation of obstacles to a solution, reference to social rules, or goal setting.

OTHER SOURCES OF DATA

Observing the degree of parent–child agreement on structured diagnostic interviews is one example of the way in which other sources of data in combination with the child interview can be used to obtain information regarding the presence of externalizing problem behaviors.

The rapid development of behavior checklists and behavior rating scales has contributed greatly to the identification and diagnosis of behavior problems in children. Behavior rating scales have the advantage of sampling a broad range of behaviors; in addition to identifying problem behaviors, they are also useful in evaluating treatment outcome (Atkeson & Forehand, 1978). The behavior rating scales described below are representative of scales that possess adequate psychometric properties and have been demonstrated to be effective in identifying children with externalizing behavior problems.

The Child Behavior Checklist (CBCL; Achenbach & Edelbrock, 1983) is a popular behavior checklist for use with children 2 to 16 years of age. Four profiles are available, according to a child's age and sex. The same profile is used for boys and girls ages 2–3, while separate profiles are used for boys and girls ages 4–5, 6–11, and 12–16. An attractive feature of the CBCL is the availability of parent and teacher forms. This allows the clinician to gather data regarding a child's behavior across settings and observers. In addition, Achenbach and Edelbrock (1987) have developed a youth self-report version of the CBCL.

The parent version of the CBCL takes about 20 minutes to complete and yields scores on a Social Competence Scale and a Behavior Problem Scale. The Social Competence Scale contains 20 items that produce scores in three areas: Activities, Social Involvement, and School Performance. A profile sheet allows the clinician to determine the referred child's standing relative to the normative population. The Behavior Problem Scale contains 113 child behaviors that parents rate on a 3-point scale (0 = "not true"; 1 = "somewhat or sometimes true"; 2 = "very true or often true"). The items of the Behavior Problem Scale are represented on profile sheets that correspond to the child's age and sex. Factor-analytic studies of the behavior problem items have yielded a number of scales that vary according to the child's age and sex. For example, for boys ages 6 to 11 there are nine scales: Schizoid or Anxious, Depressed, Uncommunicative, Obsessive/Compulsive, Somatic Complaints, Social Withdrawal, Hyperactive, Aggressive, and Delinquent.

A second-order factor analysis of the Behavior Problem Scale has yielded two primary factors, which have been labeled Internalizing and Externalizing. Scores for each of these factors can be computed, yielding T-scores and percentiles.

Normative data for the CBCL for boys and girls ages 4–16 are based on 1300 randomly selected nonreferred children between 4 and 16 years of age (Achenbach & Edelbrock, 1981, 1983). For boys and girls ages 2–3 normative data are based on parent completed checklists of

398 children between the ages of two and three. The sample was equally divided between boys and girls and consisted of clinic referred and normal children (Achenbach, Edelbrock, & Howell, 1987).

Studies of the psychometric properties of the parent CBCL for children 4–16 years of age have shown it to be a reliable and valid instrument (Achenbach & Edelbrock, 1983). Test–retest reliabilities range from .89 for 1 week to .64 for over 4 months, and the CBCL has been shown to correlate highly with other behavior rating scales. Similar findings have been reported from the teacher version of the CBCL (Edelbrock & Achenbach, 1984).

The CBCL appears well suited for use in identifying children with externalizing behavior problems. Mash and Johnston (1983) found that the parent CBCL could significantly discriminate among children with attention deficit disorder, children with other psychiatric disorders, and normal children. In addition, the parent CBCL has shown to be sensitive to the treatment effects of parent training for conduct disorders (Webster-Stratton, 1984, 1985).

The Teacher Report Form of the CBCL (Edelbrock & Achenbach, 1984) is modeled after the parent version, with changes made to reflect school related behaviors. Edelbrock, Costello, and Kessler (1984) found that the Teacher Report Form could discriminate children with attention deficit disorder with and without hyperactivity from children with other psychiatric diagnoses. The teacher version has also been shown to correlate highly with various scales of the revised Conners Teacher Rating Scale that assess externalizing behavior problems (Edelbrock, Greenbaum, & Conover, 1985) and to discriminate between clinic-referred and nonreferred children (Edelbrock & Achenbach, 1984).

The Revised Behavior Problem Checklist (RBPC; Quay, 1983) is an 89-item behavior checklist that is available in parent and teacher forms. Factor analysis of the items of the RBPC have yielded six scales of behavioral problems: Conduct Disorder, Socialized Aggression, Attention Problem–Immaturity, Anxiety–Withdrawal, Psychotic Behavior, and Motor Excess. Normative data are available that allow for comparisons of a referred child's standing relative to clinical and nonclinical populations. Initial studies of the reliability and validity of the RBPC have shown it to be a psychometrically sound instrument (Quay, 1983; Quay & Peterson, 1983). Reliability of the RBPC has been demonstrated by the degree of internal consistency of the scales (average = .83), mother–father agreement (average = .73), and teacher agreement (.85 for Conduct Disorder, .75 for Socialized Aggression, and an average of .55 for the remaining scales). Test–retest reliabilities ranged from .49 to .83 over a 2-month period. Validity data indicates that the RBPC can discriminate between referred and nonreferred children, as well as between subgroups of psychiatrically diagnosed children.

Barkley (1981) has developed the Home Situations Questionnaire (HSQ) and the School Situations Questionnaire (SSQ) as means for identifying the settings where children display problem behaviors rather than the type of problem displayed. As such, the HSQ and the SSQ are useful adjuncts to measures such as the CBCL and the RBPC.

The HSQ describes 16 situations around the home and in public where parents might have a problem with their child. If they answer "yes" to an item, they are asked to rate the severity of the problem on a scale of 1 ("mild") to 9 ("severe"). The same format is used for the SSQ except that the SSQ describes 12 school situations and is completed by the referred child's teacher. Both the HSQ and the SSQ provide a score for the number of problem situations and a score for the mean severity rating of these problems. Normative data and test–retest reliabilities are available for the HSQ and the SSQ (Barkley & Edelbrock, 1987). Both measures have been found to discriminate between children with attention deficit disorder and normal children, and to be sensitive to changes in behavior in response to stimulant medication treatment (Barkley, Karlson, Pollard, & Murphy, 1985).

Behavior rating scales have much to offer the clinician. They are relatively quick and easy to administer, and can provide empirically valid data from a number of different sources. However, they should not be used in lieu of speaking directly with a referred child's teacher or visiting the child's school to conduct an observation. While direct observation techniques do not provide as much psychometric vigor as some of the available behavior checklists, there are many advances being made in the development of observational systems that are worthy of consideration (for discussion, see McMahon & Forehand. 1988, and O'Leary & Johnson, 1986).

CASE STUDY

Ted, age 11, was referred by his pediatrician for family therapy. The initial telephone interview with Ted's mother, Mary, yielded the following information. Ted lived with his mother, stepfather (Walter), 8-year-old sister (Jane), and 18-month old stepbrother (Ben). Two weeks earlier, Ted's pediatrician diagnosed Ted as having ADHD, and Ted had just begun taking psychostimulant medication (Ritalin). Ted was in regular classes in fifth grade. Mary stated the problem as Ted's not minding at home and not completing his homework. She expressed some dissatisfaction with medication therapy and said she knew she and her husband needed to learn new ways to handle the problems they had with Ted. The family had had no previous experience with therapy. The reason the parents had decided to seek treatment at this time was that Ted had recently started lying to them and had stolen some books from a book fair at school.

Prior to the first visit, the parents completed a questionnaire that asked for medical, educational, social, and developmental history data. Ted's development had been normal, and he had performed satisfactorily in the area of academics in school until this year, when his grades fell and he made an F in mathematics for the fall semester. Ted's behavior problems had begun in the second grade. Ted's parents had tried grounding him, taking away his Nintendo, spanking, and scolding. Mary indicated that she felt Ted did not want to please her. Ted's biological father lived in a city about 100 miles away, and Ted visited his father once or twice a month. Mary was not employed outside the home, and Walter was employed in a supervisory position in a retail establishment.

On the basis of the intake information, the interviewer (Jan Hughes) developed the following tentative hypothesis: Ted was a highly active child who had experienced inconsistent discipline. His mother was critical of him, and his parents relied on ineffective discipline approaches. Hughes asked that Ted's mother and stepfather and Ted attend the first interview. Because of problems in arranging child care, the parents brought 18-month-old Bennie to the first session, too.

The following transcript is taken from the first interview. Introductions had been made in the waiting room.

Jн: I am glad you could make it today. Did you have any trouble finding a parking space?

Walter: I just parked in a lot that said "Faculty and Staff Only."

Jн: That shouldn't be a problem this late in the day. If you get a ticket, just give it to the clinic secretary, and she will see that it is excused.

Walter: That is power.

Ted: Do you have any paper I can draw on?

Jн: Yes, I have some right here. Would you prefer markers or pens?

Ted: I like pencils best for the kind of drawing I do.

Jн: Okay—this one looks sharp enough.

The parents got Ben out of the stroller and placed him on the floor with some toys.

Mary: You know I told you Ted was taking Ritalin. He was getting depressed on the medicine and had tummyaches so he is off of it now.

It wasn't doing any good anyway, as you can see from what I filled out. I filled that out how I'm feeling now, and I'm not in a good frame of mind now.

Jн: I want to know what is happening now that you think is a problem. But first let me tell everyone what I know already. Mary, you called me about 2 weeks ago and said you and Walter were worried about Ted. You thought he was not minding you so well and you were worried about his school work. (*Mary and Walter nod in agreement.*) The reason I asked you all to come today is that I think when one person in a family is having problems, everyone is affected by that. I also think making things better requires everyone's help.

WALTER: I know we need help. He won't do anything I ask—like take the trash out or sweep or pick up his room. He says I'm picking on him. I don't know if I am, but if I am it's cause he won't cooperate. Maybe I'm expecting too much. I don't think I am.

Jн: You aren't getting the cooperation you want from Ted and you wonder if you are expecting too much.

WALTER: If I ask Jane to do something, she does it; if I ask Ted, he just argues about it.

Jн: Ted, do you agree with your parents that there is a lot of arguing, or do you disagree with that?

TED: There is a lot of arguing, but it isn't all my fault.

Jн: Umm. Ted, what would you like to be different at home?

TED: What do you mean?

Jн: I mean, what do you want me to help your family with?

TED: I'd like to be able to go to the woods outside, and to ride my bike to the park. I can't go to the park or to my friends. Mom says I'd get poison ivy if I go to the woods, but I don't care.

Jн: You'd like more freedom to go places, and you think Mom and Walter keep you too close to home.

TED: Yeah.

Jн: Do you want to change the amount of arguing that goes on, too?

TED: I hate arguing.

Jн: I'm sure that feels bad for all of you. Before we start discussing the problem with arguing and the conflicts you are having now, I need to know a little about your family-how you came to be a family and some of the history of this family. Let's start with the two of you (*looking at Mary and Walter*). How long have you two lived together?

MARY: Three years. I knew Walter for 4 years before I left Ted's father for the last time. We were just friends for a long time before we married.

JH: When did you marry?

MARY: January of last year.

JH: So you've been married for about a year and 6 months.

MARY: Yeah, but we started living together 3 years ago. As soon as my divorce was final, we got married.

JH: Let me see. Ted was born in December 1977. Were you living with his father then?

MARY: I married Jim when I was 18 years old. I had just left my parents and then I got pregnant right after we got married. Jim played in a band. We separated five or six times after Jane was born in 1980. After Jane was born, I lost interest in my husband. He wasn't around much—on the road a lot with his band and playing at clubs late. He just slept and drank at home and didn't help out with the kids. I started spending more time with my mom, and then I started partying with my friends. I'd go out to clubs and listen to bands, too, but I didn't go to my husband's clubs. I only went out on weekends, and my mom kept the kids. That is when I first met Walter. I knew from the first time I met him that I loved him, but we were just friends for a long time. I stayed with my husband for the kids. I was scared too, being so young with two children and never having worked in my life.

JH: When did you leave Jim for the last time?

MARY: Three years ago. That is when I started living with Walter.

JH: (*to Walter*) So you've been a member of this family for 3 years. What was it like to join this family, with two children?

WALTER: I was working 2 jobs, and I had to drive two hours to one of my jobs, so I didn't get much chance to be with the kids. Ted had already moved schools three times, and we didn't want to move them again, so I commuted 2 hours each day.

JH: Ted, do you remember when Walter started living with your family permanently?

TED: I was in first grade, I think.

MARY: No. That was when you met Walter. Remember when we all moved into Chadwick Apartments, where Chris lived? That was the first time Walter stayed with us permanently. You were in third grade.

JH: How did the two of you get along at first?

TED: Walter worked a lot, but he was all right when he was there.

JH: I want to ask how Ted was as a baby.

MARY: He was always on the go—very active. It was hard to get him to take naps and to go to sleep. He cried a lot. If I left, he'd cry. He was very clingy.

JH: Can you describe to me his activity level and mood as a toddler?

MARY: He never was afraid of anything. I had to watch him constantly. He'd climb up on the refrigerator! He was usually happy, I guess, unless he was punished.

JH: What types of things did he get punished for as a toddler and preschooler?

MARY: He wouldn't take no—if I told him no, he'd keep doing it, like teasing the kitten or emptying out the trash.

JH: What kind of punishment did you use?

MARY: I'd spank him. I know I spanked him too much. But I was spanked a lot as a child and I didn't know any better. Now that I know Ted may have some problem, I am sorry I spanked him. It didn't do any good anyway, so I have just about given up on spanking now.

JH: Did you work when Ted was little?

MARY: No. I was at home always. I started working part time when Jane started first grade, but I've always been home when Ted came home from school. They kept me busy. Ted and I had a good relationship until recently. As he gets older, our relationship gets worse.

JH: When did the problems you are having now with minding and arguing begin?

MARY: When he was in second grade, notes started coming home. He was able to do the work but he was disrupting class. The teacher said he was a class clown. He didn't get his work done and was bothering other kids with his moving around and talking out. So at home I tried to help him. I sat with him and did his homework. He did well with me, so he didn't fail. I decided to ignore what the teacher said because my friends told me they want kids to be put on medicine so they would behave.

(During the past 5 or 10 minutes, Ted had been entertaining and taking care of Bennie. He pulled some electrical cords out of Bennie's reach, retrieved his toys, moved his mother's purse so that Bennie couldn't get into it, and so on.)

Jʜ: Ted, you really are helpful with Bennie. (*To Mary*) So you cared a lot about Ted and did not want him to take medicine unless he really needed it. Was his recent trial on Ritalin the first time Ted took any medication for his school problems?

Mᴀʀʏ: I finally took him to the doctor and he put him on Ritalin—that was in third grade. The teachers had a meeting and said he was hyperactive. He was nervous and shaky and depressed, so I stopped the medicine. He said he didn't want to have it, but I was having problems with my ex-husband and we fought a lot—we had a lot of bad arguments—and I thought maybe that was affecting Ted, too.

Jʜ: Were your arguments verbal or did they become physical, too?

Mᴀʀʏ: He hit me, and Ted saw it, and it affected him, too.

Jʜ: Did Jim physically abuse Ted, too?

Tᴇᴅ: No. But when he'd hit Mom I'd hold Jane 'cause she'd be scared.

Jʜ: You held her when your parents fought?

Tᴇᴅ: I held her all the time.

Jʜ: It is good for a girl to have a big brother to look out for her.

Mᴀʀʏ: Ted was always an active child, but the problem began in second grade.

Jʜ: When did your and Jim's fights become violent? How old was Ted?

Mᴀʀʏ: It started when Ted was in first grade. That's when I first left Jim.

Jʜ: Ted, what was kindergarten like for you?

Tᴇᴅ: It was okay. Mom made brownies and was always, coming up to school. It was cool. In first grade we moved. I remember jumping off the desk and I didn't do the work. We moved during the year, but I don't remember much about the second school—we were only there for a month or two.

Jʜ: What do you remember about second grade?

Tᴇᴅ: We moved again, to Klute. I met Chris and he is still my best friend. When I visit my dad he comes over, and he is coming up to spend a week with me this summer.

JH: Chris sounds like a good friend. What do you remember about school in second grade?

TED: It was okay. I was always getting in trouble. The teachers said I was a clown, but I was just trying to make friends. I'm so short, it is hard to make friends when everyone calls you a midget.

JH: When did your family move to College Station?

WALTER: We moved just after we got married—January 1988. I had a new job—the job I have now. I don't have to work two jobs or commute, so I can help more with Ted and get more involved with his problems.

JH: *(to Ted)* How did you feel about moving to College Station?

TED: I missed my friends. But I made friends here, too. I met Brian the first day of school. I just went up and started talking to him and we've been best friends.

JH: You're not the type of kid who stays in the background, but you join into things right off.

TED: I was embarrassed, but I wanted a friend.

JH: *(to Mary)* How did you feel about moving to College Station?

MARY: I was lonely at first. I still am some. I didn't know anybody here and with the baby I haven't been able to get out and meet people. But Walter is around more, and that is good.

JH: I'd like to ask you about how things are now. You said the Ritalin didn't help. What changes did you notice on the Ritalin?

MARY: We got along better, but he had tummyaches and was depressed.

JH: How did you get along better?

MARY: He was concerned about me and now he is more against me. He thinks I am a horrible person cause I yell a lot. I read that it is hereditary—the ADHD—and I think I had it. No one knew of it then. I had worse behavior problems than he. I see a lot of me in him or him in me. So it makes me feel guilty 'cause it is my fault.

JH: How do you figure it is your fault?

MARY: If I wasn't this uptight person, maybe he wouldn't be this type. I have a bad temper and lose control easy. I don't put up with it. Sometimes I'm real good, but lately he is really getting on my nerves.

JH: I wouldn't be too quick to take the blame. You are real interested in helping this family to get along better, and you have a lot of care for Ted and are eager to find ways of getting along better.

TED: I'm the same on and off medicine, but you are harder on me.

JH: How is Mom hard on you?

TED: She treats me like I'm evil. She doesn't give me a chance. She says she don't care.

MARY: I don't say I don't care. Okay. It is like this. When I say, "Go put that back," he says, "I didn't do it." I get very tired at his saying he didn't do it and not doing what I tell him to do.

JH: You're worn out by the struggle. Walter, when you get home in the evening, tell me how the evening goes.

WALTER: Everyone is uptight. Especially at mealtime. There is lots of anger between me and Ted. When me and Ted argue, Mary goes to the bedroom and eats later. She is tired of our fighting. She doesn't want to see us.

JH: Let me see if I understand. When you come home in the evening, you and Ted start arguing. What starts the argument?

WALTER: Mary tells me that Ted won't pick up his stuff, or that he didn't turn in some schoolwork—we get notes from his teacher.

JH: Then what happens?

WALTER: Well, if it's the dishwasher, he might start doing it and then go start playing, or he might tell me it isn't fair that he has to do it.

JH: What happens next?

WALTER: I tell him he is lazy, and we start arguing. He'll say he did his homework, or that the teacher is unfair, and I tell him he has to do it anyway, that sort of thing.

JH: Then what happens?

MARY: I get tired of it, so I just go back to my bedroom. I need to get away from it.

WALTER: Ted says nothing we do is fair, like his not being able to ride his bike around. (*To Ted*) Didn't you tell us you crossed Highway 21?

TED: I didn't.

WALTER: You told me you passed the bridge. You have to go across Highway 21 to get to the bridge.

TED: I don't remember telling you that.

JH: So when Walter comes home in the evenings, things are pretty tense, and Mary takes some time out to herself. Do you take over?

WALTER: I take the baby. We sit down to eat. I say, "Pass the pepper," and he says, "Get it yourself." We start arguing like that and then Mary leaves.

MARY: I try hard. I say I've handled myself all day. Then Walter comes home and they start in at each other. Either Walter or I am off the edge almost every night.

WALTER: If Ted and I argue, we get over it. With Mary, it doesn't get over. It blows over for us. With Mary it stays—just hangs in the air.

JH: What does "over the edge" mean? What happens when you get over the edge?

MARY: I'm not proud. I'm not happy about moving here, and I drink. We used to drink when we'd go out. Now, I drink most nights, to relax.

JH: So, in a sense, you self-medicate by drinking—so you won't feel so uptight.

WALTER: Yeah. I do too, but not so much any more. But I worry about Mary.

TED: I worry about her too.

JH: (*to Mary*) What happens when you start drinking in the evening?

MARY: I get mellow, usually. I just go inside myself. Sometimes I'll go walk it off, especially if Walter starts nagging me about it.

JH: Okay. I think what we're talking about now is important, and I'd like us to talk about it some more later, because I can see that each of you are unhappy about what happens in the evening, and want to make some changes. We want to find some ways for Mary to to deal with the tension without drinking, and we want to find ways to reduce the arguing and to build more cooperation. One last thing I'd like to talk about today, is the ways you have tried to handle these problems in the past. Let me take the chores. What are Ted's chores?

MARY: I have a chart on the refrigerator. Ted is supposed to pick up his room, clear the table and sweep the kitchen and dining room each evening, feed the dog, and take out the trash. But he doesn't do them most of the time—or he does them halfway.

JH: So these chores are listed on a chart. How do you keep track of what Ted does?

WALTER: At the end of the week, we just look at the chart and see if he has done them. But usually he hasn't, so we stopped checking.

J_H: Are there any consequences for Ted of doing the chores or not doing them?

M_{ARY}: He is supposed to get an allowance—$5.00 a week. But he don't do them, so he hasn't gotten that in a long time. I give him $1.00 or $2.00 some weeks, so he'll have a little spending money.

J_H: What if he gets some of them done—say half?

M_{ARY}: I'd probably give him a little allowance.

J_H: Ted, what sort of things do you spend allowance on?

T_{ED}: I hardly ever get it, even if I do the stuff.

M_{ARY}: That's not right. Sometimes I give you allowance anyway, hoping you'll do better the next week. I know that isn't right, but I don't know what to do.

J_H: What sorts of things is Ted expected to spend allowance on?

W_{ALTER}: Just extra things, like comic books—he has a hundred comic books, I think. Or video games or skating. Stuff like that.

J_H: Ted, when did you last buy a comic book?

T_{ED}: Weeks ago, at least.

M_{ARY}: I bought you one last week, 'cause you got that social studies project done.

J_H: It seems you have some plans for helping Ted learn to be more responsible, but the plans don't get carried out consistently. What else have you tried?

W_{ALTER}: We put him on restrictions and take away Nintendo. But then he will be on restriction for 3 weeks, and that isn't good, either. He needs to be outside playing with friends and stuff.

J_H: What sorts of things warrant restriction?

M_{ARY}: Well, I told you about the book fair.

J_H: Yes, and I wanted to find out more about that.

M_{ARY}: Well, I know a lot of kids took the books, but that doesn't mean it was okay. They had this book fair at school, and some of the boys took books home. They sent a note home from school, asking parents to check to see if their children had these books. I found one in Ted's bookbag. He says he thought it was free. So he returned it and the school didn't punish anybody.

T_{ED}: I thought the books were free. They were just all on a table.

J<small>H</small>: Was Ted punished at home for that?

M<small>ARY</small>: He was put on restriction for a month.

J<small>H</small>: When was that?

M<small>ARY</small>: About 3 weeks ago.

J<small>H</small>: Is Ted still on restriction?

M<small>ARY</small>: Yes. He has to come home right after school, and he can't play outside or play Nintendo.

W<small>ALTER</small>: But we let him play outside for a little while. A kid needs a break right after school.

J<small>H</small>: We've talked about problems you and Ted have. What pleases you about Ted?

W<small>ALTER</small>: He takes good care of the baby and Jane. He watches out for the kids.

J<small>H</small>: That's unusual and important, especially with a baby as active as Bennie is. I've noticed how much help you've been in our session, Ted, keeping him out of trouble and happy.

T<small>ED</small>: I like to play with Bennie, but Mom says I don't help out.

J<small>H</small>: What else pleases you?

W<small>ALTER</small>: Ted is good-hearted. What he does that is wrong isn't immoral. He is curious. He doesn't throw cats into trees or stuff like that.

M<small>ARY</small>: He takes risks and cares about me—sometimes.

J<small>H</small>: Ted is good-hearted and caring. I can help you with the problems in your relationship with Ted. It is correctable. But an uncaring heart is harder. I can't do a heart transplant, but I can help you change the ways you interact with each other.

M<small>ARY</small>: I find it hard now. I see things as all bad. Its easy to get upset.

J<small>H</small>: It is hard to see the good when you're feeling down. It will be important to help you respond to Ted's positive behavior and characteristics. You want to, but the tension is in the way, and we need to change that. You deserve to enjoy Ted more and to have more pleasant times together as a family.

M<small>ARY</small>: Yes, like we went on a bike ride and I turned around and Ted had a big smile on his face.

T<small>ED</small>: We only spent 5 minutes, and you went home.

M<small>ARY</small>: Should I put him back on the medicine?

Jₕ: Let's not now. You've tried it two times and it has not had the success you had hoped for. I'd like to complete my assessment of your problems before I make any recommendations. I would like to meet next with Ted. (to Ted) I'd like to learn more about your thoughts and feelings about your family, school, friends, and things that are important to you. After our session, I'd like to meet with your parents alone. Then I'll be ready to offer you a plan for how I will help. Is that okay with each of you?

All: Okay. Sure.

The session ended with the family's giving permission for Hughes to obtain records from the pediatrician, which included the teacher and parent forms of the CBCL; there was also a discussion of confidentiality, including Ted's privacy.

The following transcript is taken from Hughes's interview with Ted the following week. During part of the session, Ted completed a self-concept questionnaire and drawings of a person and of his family.

Jₕ: What have you been up to today?

TₑD: I've been outside.

Jₕ: You look like the outside type of boy.

TₑD: I've been doing pull-ups. I'm trying to get muscles.

Jₕ: Oh. How many pull-ups can you do?

TₑD: Eight.

Jₕ: That sounds pretty good. You're kinda lean, and that is good for pull-ups.

TₑD: What does "lean" mean?

Jₕ: Not fat.

TₑD: Everyone calls me bones.

TₑD: Are you just the size you want to be?

TₑD: I'm short. I'm two heads shorter than everyone else.

Jₕ: Than everyone?

TₑD: Well, except for two boys.

Jₕ: Well, that makes you one of the shorter ones.

TₑD: But I'm special.

J<small>H</small>: Yes, you are special. What about you is special?

T<small>ED</small>: About me? Well...Gee. I don't know. I can draw well. I do a great Dukakis. I did this picture of Dukakis in a manhole. [This interview took place during the 1988 presidential election.]

J<small>H</small>: Sounds like one of those cartoons in the newspaper—the kind that makes fun of things that are happening in politics.

T<small>ED</small>: I'll bring you one.

J<small>H</small>: I'd like that. I wanted to talk just with you today because when I talk with parents, they do most of the talking.

T<small>ED</small>: Maybe the kids are embarrassed.

J<small>H</small>: Maybe so. Did you feel embarrassed when we were talking?

T<small>ED</small>: Not really.

J<small>H</small>: I want to tell you a couple of things about our talking together. When we talk, it is private. I won't be talking to your teachers, sister, parents, or anyone about what we talk about. But you may tell me something that I think your parents or somebody needs to know. If that happens, I will ask your permission to tell your parents. If you don't want me to, I won't tell it. But there is an exception to that rule. If I think you are in some danger of being hurt or of hurting someone, I would have to tell someone who could help.

T<small>ED</small>: Like child abuse?

J<small>H</small>: Child abuse is one of the things I would need to tell someone about. Do you know who I'd have to tell child abuse to?

T<small>ED</small>: We learned about it in health.

J<small>H</small>: I would tell it to people whose job it is to protect children from being hurt by their parents.

T<small>ED</small>: My parents yell at me a lot, but that is all.

J<small>H</small>: Yelling feels bad.

T<small>ED</small>: Can I draw?

J<small>H</small>: Yes. I thought we'd draw some today. I have a couple of drawings I'd like for you to do, and you may have something you'd like to draw, too.

At this point in the interview, Ted drew a picture of Batman. Next, Hughes asked him to draw a person and his family. Ted concentrated on his drawings, taking great pains to draw well. The drawings had little material of projective significance, because he focused so much on the execution of the drawings.

Jн: I'd like to ask you some questions about things about school, friends, and your family. You're in fifth grade at Lamar School this year, right?

Ted: Yes.

Jн: What do you like most about school this year?

Ted: Art.

Jн: I can understand that. What do your teachers say about your drawings?

Ted: My art teacher likes them. She entered one in a contest. My math teacher—I don't like her, she won't let me draw in class. She says she'll send me to the office if I draw in her room. She is always putting me down.

Jн: What sort of things does she put you down about?

Ted: I don't know. She said I was never going to make it. She told me one day I had to stay after school. I called Mom to tell her. When Mom called her she said she hadn't said it. She always is putting me down in front of the other kids. She is only nice to the good kids in class—not to me.

Jн: You don't think you are one of the good kids.

Ted: I sorta am. I made an F once.

Jн: Can a good kid make an F?

Ted: Yes.

Jн: I should hope so.

Jн: What else do you like about school?

Ted: I like my friends. Brian and Chris are my best friends.

Jн: What do you and Brian and Chris do?

Ted: Well, Chris is my best friend for a long time. He lives in Klute. We used to play together every day. Now I see him when I visit my dad.

Jн: How often is that?

Ted: About once or twice a month. He would like to visit more, but it takes 2 hours to get there, and he can't always drive. Mom and Walter will take me one way, but Dad has to drive the other way.

Jₕ: So Chris lives in Klute, and Brian lives here. Does he go to Lamar, too?

Tₑ𝒹: Yes. He is my best friend here. We met the first day I came to school, last year.

Jₕ: I remember your telling me that. Is there a difference between a best friend and a regular friend:

Tₑ𝒹: I like Chris best of all. He gave me stuff.

Jₕ: He is generous.

Tₑ𝒹: Yes, but that is not why I like him. He is fun to talk to. He likes the things I like. He likes me teaching him to draw.

Jₕ: So a best friends likes things you do. That is important to best friends. What else makes a best friend?

Tₑ𝒹: That's about it.

Jₕ: So what do you and Brian like to do?

Tₑ𝒹: We draw in class. We play baseball, basketball, and Nintendo at my house, when I'm not on restriction.

Jₕ: Do you play on any teams, like baseball?

Tₑ𝒹: No. I missed the sign-up. Mom was supposed to sign me up but she missed the date.

Jₕ: Do you belong to any clubs or groups that meet after school?

Tₑ𝒹: Cub Scouts.

Jₕ: You're in scouts?

Tₑ𝒹: Not this year—in Angleton. I got a lot of awards.

Jₕ: What sorts of awards did you get?

Tₑ𝒹: Hiking, camping, and stuff.

Jₕ: Sounds like fun. Anything else you enjoy about school?

Tₑ𝒹: I have this one teacher who likes me. She is my art teacher, Miss Finfeather.

Jₕ: What sorts of things do you dislike about school this year?

Tₑ𝒹: Everyone else hated me when I started school. They still make fun of me and say they hate me.

Jₕ: That makes me feel sad.

TED: Me too.

JH: What sort of things do they say to you?

TED: "You're stupid." "You can't do anything but draw." "Short." "Midget." They hit me on the head.

JH: I'm glad you have those two best friends, 'cause some of the kids have been mean to you.

TED: Everybody but Brian, and one other guy, Phil. He is cool, too. The girls like me, too.

JH: It is hard to feel good about school when you're not getting along with the kids.

TED: I want to learn karate so they won't hit me on the head.

JH: What happens just before someone hits you on the head?

TED: What do you mean?

JH: I mean, what might cause someone to hit you on the head, or does it happen out of the blue?

TED: Out of the blue. Like I'm getting my books out of the locker, and somebody slams the door on my hand.

JH: What happens next?

TED: I tell them to stop. But they don't. If I tell the teacher, she doesn't do anything. Sometimes I fight.

JH: What happens when you fight?

TED: I usually lose. But that is better than everyone thinking I am chicken. That is why I want to take karate.

JH: What do you do when you get mad?

TED: I feel like going and beating someone up. I turn red in the face and make my muscles big, or I exercise.

JH: You've told me some of the things that make you feel mad at school. What sorts of things make you feel mad at home?

TED: When Walter gives me lots of work to do.

JH: What happens?

TED: I gripe. He says he'll give me allowance, but he doesn't.

JH: Do you get an allowance?

TED: Sometimes. He says he will give it to me every week, but I only get it sometimes.

J_H: Why do you think you only get it sometimes?

T_{ED}: He says I don't do my chores, but I do, most of the time. Mom says I don't care about anything and I hate everything, and I care about everything. It makes me feel bad.

J_H: Are there some of things you care about a whole bunch that Mom would be surprised about if she knew?

T_{ED}: Oh, Yeah! Like she says I live to make her life miserable, and I worry about her a lot. I try to help. She says I hate everyone. She doesn't understand. She says I don't try, and I try as hard as I can.

J_H: Maybe one thing we can do is help you find ways to let Mom know how much you care.

T_{ED}: Mom says I'm hyperactive. She says she might need the medicine too.

J_H: What do you think?

T_{ED}: I don't think I'm hyperactive. I'm just not interested in school. I like to draw. Mom says she will just run away. She says stuff like "I don't care if you love me."

J_H: That would feel bad. It is hard to feel good about yourself.

T_{ED}: She always says, "Shut up and go to your room."

J_H: You are having a hard time at home.

T_{ED}: That is why they call me a smart mouth.

J_H: Who calls you a smart mouth?

T_{ED}: My parents and teachers, except Miss Finfeather.

J_H: That is the teacher who appreciates your drawing. I'm glad you have her this year. You needed a bright spot this year.

T_{ED}: The other teachers put me down.

J_H: You seem to me to be a kind-hearted and caring boy and it is going to be important to find ways for other people to know that part of you, too.

T_{ED}: Very true. Mom says the only time I show appreciation is when they buy something.

J_H: What are your ways of showing appreciation?

T_{ED}: I do it all the time. I tell her I love her and I thank her for stuff. She says I never do.

JH: So you try to be caring, but you aren't getting that caring message across. You check yourself and say, "Am I caring?", and you say "Yes." Mom checks you and says "You're not caring." What are some of the good times with your mom?

TED: She helps me a lot. I go to her when I feel bad. She teaches good. Sometimes.

JH: What does it seem to depend on—how helpful your mom is?

TED: I don't know. Sometimes she is happy and sometimes mad. She usually is happy unless there is not enough money or if I do something wrong—get a cookie out of the cookie jar—and then she is mad all day. Maybe it is my fault. I'm not sure. She says if I cared I wouldn't smart-mouth her. If I hated her I wouldn't care if a big monster came up and got her.

JH: You are very sure about how you feel. You love your mom and care about her. You get mad sometimes, but you still love her. She may not be sure, but you are.

TED: She never knows except when she drinks. When she drinks she is nice. But I don't want her to drink.

JH: Sometimes when parents drink, their behavior changes, too.

TED: But she doesn't drink that much. Mostly on the weekends.

JH: Do you worry about her?

TED: Yes.

JH: When she drinks, what changes?

TED: She is more calm and nothing else. But the next morning she throws up and is sick and says, "Leave me alone." I hate it when she drinks. I worry when she walks out of the house. It's a bad neighborhood. And all the time they fight.

JH: Walter and Mom?

TED: And I worry they will break up, and one time police came 'cause they were yelling.

JH: Sometimes parents fight with words and sometimes they hit. How is it with Walter and your mom?

TED: Words. My real dad, he got her on the floor and beat her in the face. Mom has a scar from that.

JH: That scares me.

TED: I'm afraid it'll happen again.

JH: Has it ever happened between Walter and Mom?

TED: No. Nothing like that has happened.

JH: Do you worry about your safety?

TED: No.

JH: Do you worry about your mom?

TED: I'd give my life for my mom.

JH: It is clear you worry about Mom a lot and care about her. Ted, you said you didn't like the Ritalin. What about it did you not like?

TED: It gave me headaches and I fell asleep in class.

JH: Do you think it helped with your concentration—with getting your work done in class, or did it not make a difference, or make things worse?

TED: Worse, 'cause I'd go to sleep.

JH: When you visit with your dad, how does that go?

TED: Okay. I miss my father. When I talk with him on the phone he cries. He sees me just every month, and sometimes not that often. He misses me.

JH: What do you and your father do when you visit?

TED: Jane comes too. We go fishing sometimes. Sometimes he has to work—he plays in a band and we stay with my grandmother. She is nice.

JH: How do you and Jane get along?

TED: We fight some, but she is a pretty neat kid. She makes good grades.

JH: Ted, I have enjoyed talking with you today. I appreciate your being so honest with me. What I want to do next is talk with your parents alone. But I won't be telling them what you said. I do want to tell your mom how much you care about her and tell her that you worry about her. Is that okay?

TED: I think that is our whole problem. She doesn't believe that I care.

JH: Would it be all right with you if I kept this drawing and put it up on the wall outside-where some other drawings are?

TED: Sure. I can bring lots more, too.

Jₕ: The next time you come, I'd like you to bring some of your artwork, just for me to see. You can take it back home.

SUMMARY

Children who exhibit externalizing problem behaviors are easily identified as a result of the social disruption they create. The overt and observable nature of their behavior makes adults who interact with these children an important source of information regarding the frequency, intensity and duration of problem behaviors.

In some cases problem behaviors will have a negative impact on a child's family and social functioning, while in other cases family functioning will contribute to the development and maintenance of externalizing problem behaviors. The parent interview plays a major role in the interview process as it supplies important data on family variables that contribute to the manifestation of externalizing problem behaviors.

Advances in behavioral assessment via behavior rating scales and checklists allow the clinician to determine the types of problem behaviors exhibited as well as the settings in which they occur. Such data contribute not only to the identification of deviant behavior, but also to treatment planning and evaluation. Behavioral checklists and rating scales are also desirable because they can be utilized by other informants, such as teachers.

When interviewing a child with externalizing problem behaviors the clinician needs to be sensitive to the child's ability to participate in the interview process. Frequently, the child who is exhibiting disruptive behaviors has been subject to coercive management techniques and may expect adults to be critical and punitive. By approaching the child in an interested and accepting manner, the clinician is likely to facilitate a relationship with the child in which problem solving can occur.

Some children may be able to engage in meaningful dialogue related to their behavior problems, while others may not. In accordance with the child's ability to negotiate the interview process the clinician can utilize a nonstructured interview approach or rely on a more structured format.

In short, the interview process should serve as an opportunity to identify and define the antecedents and consequences that contribute to the expression of disruptive problem behaviors, and to offer means by which maladaptive behaviors can be modified.

8

Interviewing Children with Internalizing Behavior Problems

As noted in Chapter 7, multivariate approaches to the classification of childhood disorders have produced strong support for a category of behavior problems that various researchers have labeled "internalizing" (Achenbach, 1966; Kazdin, 1989; Quay, 1986a).

The term "internalizing" refers to behaviors that are indicative of depression, anxiety, and social withdrawal (Kazdin, 1989; Quay, 1986). Based on multivariate procedures applied to 61 studies appearing over a 40-year span, Quay (Quay & LaGreca, 1986) has identified a broad band of internalizing behaviors that he has labeled "anxiety–withdrawal–dysphoria." Types of behavior within this broad band include anxiety, fearfulness, shyness, depression, sadness, feelings of worthlessness, low self-confidence, frequent crying, and worrying.

Formal diagnostic systems such as the DSM-III-R subdivide internalizing disorders into specific diagnostic categories, such as those related to depressive disorders and anxiety disorders. However, the reliability and validity of such distinct diagnostic categories are questionable (Achenbach, 1979; Quay & LaGreca, 1986).

In this chapter we will present information on interviewing children with internalizing behavior problems. Rather than focus on interviewing for the purpose of affixing diagnostic labels, this chapter reviews methods for conducting child interviews that aid in the identification and amelioration of internalizing behavior problems.

PURPOSES OF THE INTERVIEW

In the assessment of internalizing disorders, the child interview is perhaps the most important element in the assessment process. The hallmark feature of internalizing problems is a subjective sense of discomfort or distress. Such subjective discomfort is not always observable by adults in the child's life, unlike symptoms reflecting externalizing disorders, such as conduct disorder or attention-deficit hyperactivity disorder. Therefore, the child's self-report becomes an important consideration in the determination of the presence and severity of internalizing behavior problems.

The reliability and accuracy of children's self-report have been topics of considerable interest to researchers and clinicians. From a clinical standpoint, the self-report of children is considered to be a valuable source of information in the assessment and treatment process. During the past two decades there has been a significant increase in research efforts to substantiate the reliability of children's self-report. As a result of these efforts, there has been a proliferation of reliable and valid child self report instruments that aid in the identification and measurement of a variety of childhood disorders (for examples of such instruments, see Witt et al. 1988).

The utility of child self-report in identifying internalizing disorders is evidenced by findings that indicate that children report more subjective symptoms, whereas parents report more behavioral symptoms (Herjanic et al., 1975; Herjanic & Reich, 1982). It is not uncommon for the clinician to encounter such reporting patterns during initial interviews with parents and children. Consider the following excerpt from an initial interview one of us (David Baker) conducted with 7-year old Todd and his mother.

Todd was brought to the mental health clinic by his mother because of her concern over his declining school performance. Six months earlier, Todd's father had left the family because of his inability to control a substance abuse problem and had not been heard from since.

Mother: Todd did fine in the first grade. His grades were good and he didn't have any problems. This year he complains a lot about school and gets in trouble for something nearly every day. I've met with his teacher and the principal, and they tell me he can do the work but chooses not to. They say he doesn't complete work and daydreams when he should be working.

Db: It seems difficult to understand what the problem is.

Mother: It sure does. I've asked him if something is wrong, but he doesn't say anything except that the teacher is mean or it's somebody else's fault. I'd like to know what the problem is and what I can do about it.

DB: (*To Todd*): "Your mom says your having problems at school, and thinks I might be able to help. Is there a problem I could help you with?

TODD: I don't know. I don't have any problems.

DB: Well, maybe "problems" isn't a good word. Sometimes kids worry about things, and sometimes the things kids worry about make them feel bad. Is there anything that you worry about or that makes you feel bad?

TODD: I worry about my dad.

DB: I can understand that. What kinds of things do you worry about, about your dad?

TODD: He takes drugs and stuff, and you know they can kill you if you take them.

DB: That's pretty scary. Are you worried that your dad might die from taking drugs?

TODD: Yeah, and I worry 'cause we never see him and he might be hurt or have to go to jail or something.

APPROACHES TO INTERVIEWING

There are a variety of ways in which an interviewer can elicit information from children regarding subjective feelings of distress. In this section, we discuss a number of methods that can be used to help children communicate their internal distress and to guide the clinician in planning effective treatment for the child with internalizing behavior problems.

Cognitive–Behavioral Approaches

Theory

As we have noted, symptoms of internalizing disorders such as sadness, anxiety, and social apprehension reflect subjective experiences that cannot always be observed in behavior. One means of identifying the internal and subjective experiences of children is to inquire about their thought processes and self-talk. Cognitive–behavioral models of internalizing disorders stress the role that cognitions play in the development of emotional distress, with particular attention given to an individual's belief systems and attributions regarding events and behaviors (Abramson, Seligman, & Teasdale, 1978; Beck, 1976; Ellis, 1984).

According to Beck (1976), negative cognitions or beliefs about oneself, the world, and the future contribute to the development of depression. Seligman's (1975) model of learned helplessness views depressive symptomatology as an individual's reaction to repeated failures at trying to influence events in his or her life. After repeated failures, the individual incorporates negative attributions and expectations regarding his or her ability to influence events which leads to a variety of behaviors associated with depression (e.g., withdrawal, passivity, etc.).

Rational–emotive therapy (RET) has been developed as a theory of personality and system of psychotherapy, based on the premise that emotional problems are the result of an individual's irrational beliefs (Ellis, 1984). Ellis (1962) has proposed the A-B-C model to explain the development of emotional disorders. According to the model, the emotional consequences (C) of an activating event (A) are mediated by the beliefs an individual has about the event (B). Emotional problems result from irrational and negative beliefs utilized in the appraisal of activating events.

For example, Travis was a fourth-grader who had recently moved to a new school district. Within a week of his being in the new school, there was an exam in social studies. The teacher, recognizing that Travis had not been exposed to the material, excused him from the class during the exam. When Travis returned home from school that day he was sullen and withdrawn. Noting that something was wrong, Travis's mother tried to find out what was upsetting him. After numerous inquiries, Travis finally admitted to his mother that he was stupid and unable to do schoolwork as well as the other children.

Irrational beliefs involve distortions of reality that are unconditional and absolute. DiGiuseppe and Bernard (1983) identify three categories of irrational beliefs: demands (e.g., "My needs must be satisfied"), awfulizing (e.g., "This is the worst thing that could ever happen"), and self-downing (e.g., "I am stupid, I am bad, etc."). Common irrational beliefs of children include the following (DiGiuseppe & Bernard, 1982, p. 53):

1. It's awful if others don't like me.
2. I'm bad if I make a mistake.
3. Everything should go my way, and I should always get what I want.
4. Things should come easily to me.
5. The world should be fair and bad people should be punished.
6. I shouldn't show my feelings.
7. Adults should be perfect.
8. There's only one right answer.

9. I must win.
10. I shouldn't have to wait for anything.

The practice of RET strives to identify the irrational beliefs of the individual and then attempts to dispute these beliefs and replace them with more rational and realistic ways of thinking.

As we have noted, cognitive–behavioral approaches to internalizing disorders emphasize the internal cognitive events that mediate experience. Various researchers have attempted to examine the relationship between cognitive variables and internalizing disorders. An especially popular area of research has been the study of attributional style and its impact on behavior. For example, socially anxious children have been found to attribute their success in social situations to external causes such as luck, while they view their social failure in terms of internal causes—namely, their belief in themselves as being socially incompetent (Ames, Ames, & Garrison, 1977; Goetz & Dweck, 1980). In comparing the cognitive performance of children high and low in test anxiety, Zatz and Chassin (1983) found that high-anxiety children make fewer positive evaluations of their ability, compare themselves negatively to others, and have more off-task thoughts than low-anxiety children. Similarly, depressed and helpless children have been found to attribute success to external, unstable, and specific factors while failures are viewed as the result of internal, stable, and global factors (Dweck, 1975; Fielstein et al., 1985; Meyer, Dyck, & Petrinack 1989; Seligman et al., 1984).

For example, Jordon, a depressed and withdrawn 10-year-old was concerned about his upcoming report card.

JORDON: We get our report cards on Friday.

DB: Do you know what your grades will be?

JORDON: Kinda. I know I did Okay in science 'cause I had a project in the science fair and anybody who did one got extra credit for it. Math I'm not sure about. I'm not good in math and I never do good in language arts.

DB: What about your other classes?

JORDON: Like band and art?

DB: Well, aren't those classes?

JORDON: Yeah, but they don't really count.

DB: Why not?"

JORDON: They're easy. I always get good grades, but so does everybody. You'd have to be really dumb to fail them."

Assessing Children's Cognitions and Attributions

There are a number of ways in which a clinician can elicit a child's beliefs, expectations, and attributions. Unstructured approaches rely on following the child's lead and use spontaneously generated comments from the child as a means for more in-depth exploration of the child's internal thought processes. The excerpt above from the conversation with Jordon is an example of such an approach.

Sentence Completion.   Increasing the degree of structure involves providing children with a stimulus to which they can respond in a way that is reflective of their subjective thoughts and feelings. One method that is often used in the assessment of children's psychosocial functioning is the sentence completion test (Goh & Fuller, 1983; Vukovich, 1983).

Sentence completion techniques can be classified as a semistructured form of self-report. In sentence completion techniques, the sentence stems provide structure by restricting the content area to which the child can respond, while the nature of the responses is defined according to the child's subjective experience. This provides more opportunity to evaluate the child's perceptions, beliefs, expectations, and attributions than is available through the use of yes–no answers or scale ratings employed in structured interviews and other self-report measures.

While there are numerous versions of sentence completion techniques available for use with children, research on their reliability and validity is limited. Typically, sentence completion tasks are designed and evaluated on the basis of clinical judgment (Baker, 1988).

Consider the responses of two 6-year-old boys, Jason and Brent, to sentence stems regarding self-evaluation and attitudes toward task performance and achievement. Both boys had been referred to a school psychologist because of their teachers' concerns about their behavior and school performance.

Jason's teacher noted that Jason often hung back from activities and rarely initiated interactions with others. She felt that his reserved nature interfered with his ability to learn up to his potential, and wanted to know whether there were any emotional factors that would explain his shy behavior. When Jason met with the school psychologist, he seemed to enjoy the attention and did not appear nervous. Jason mentioned that he liked school and had a few good friends. He had just received a "Great Job!" sticker on his math homework and was pleased to show it to the examiner. He denied having any trouble with academic subjects, and results of a readiness screening administered earlier in the year did not identify any areas of weakness. Jason willingly drew pictures with the examiner and responded to the sentence completion exercise with interest and enjoyment. Some of Jason's responses are listed below (in italics):

Most grown people are *fun to be with*.
The people in my class think I am *nice*.
My mother thinks I am *nice*.
My teacher thinks I am *neat*.
My father thinks I am *neat*.
My mother makes me feel *happy*.
My friends think I am *neat*.
When my father gives me lots of work, I *do it*.
When I see somebody do really good in school, I *say that's good*.
When no one can help me but myself I *help myself*.
When my teacher tells me to do something, I *do it*.
When my teacher corrects me, I *correct my paper*.
When I don't know what the book says, I *get help*.
When there is hard schoolwork to do, I *do it*.

It was encouraging to note that Jason perceived himself to be liked by others; similarly, he appears to enjoy his contact with others. His attitude toward task demands appeared adaptive. He gave the impression of accepting authority and direction, and showed a desire to persevere even when tasks are difficult and demanding.

Data gathered from the parents did not indicate any developmental or behavioral problems. The parents reported that they had moved to the district during the summer. Jason's father was self-employed as a construction worker, and the family had moved an average of three times a year since Jason's birth. In the preceding year, Jason had attended three different kindergartens. A classroom observation showed Jason to be quiet and cooperative. He was attentive to teaching activities and appeared relaxed with the tempo of the classroom. During a free-activity period, Jason chose to look at a picture book of animals and showed some interest in joining a group of children who were busy making bread dough. When Jason approached the group, his teacher called attention to his presence and continued to implore him to join the group. After a few minutes Jason returned to his seat and continued to look at the picture book.

The data that were collected gave no indications that Jason was exhibiting behaviors associated with an emotional disturbance. In one-to-one contact with an adult, Jason seemed very comfortable and at ease. While he reported having friends and feeling liked, his class behavior indicated that he might be reluctant to join activities or initiate interactions. However, this did not appear to be excessive or extreme. Given his history of frequent moves, Jason might not have had many opportunities to develop relationships over time. It was recommended that Jason's teacher gently encourage his participation in activities and respect his need to "warm up slowly." The situation was discussed with the parents, and it was recommended that Jason have the opportunity to remain in one school setting for longer periods of time than just a few months. The potential academic and social difficulties that could result from frequent moves were discussed, and the parents agreed that they would like to find stable employment and remain in one place while their children were in school.

Brent had been a source of concern to his teacher since the beginning of the school year. He frequently came to school tired and would easily fall asleep in class. He did not have any friends at school and was unpopular. On two occasions Brent had urinated in his pants during school. There had been a number of conferences with Brent's foster parents, which had resulted in a referral to the school psychologist.

Brent had lived a chaotic life. His mother was a single parent at the time of his birth, and she was frequently unable to keep a job or find stable housing. After an investigation of child abuse and neglect, Brent was placed in the care of the state when he was 5 years old. He had been living with his foster parents for the past 8 months and they desired to adopt him, although they reported that Brent insisted that he would go back to live with his mother.

During the evaluation, Brent was unresponsive and his affect was blunted. He passively complied with the requests of the examiner and offered no spontaneous speech except to ask how much more he would have to do. When asked about activities and interests, all Brent reported was that he liked to sleep. He denied having any friends at home or at school and reported no pleasure or interest in any type of play activity. When asked how long he had felt like this, he responded "always." Brent provided the following responses (in italics) to the sentence completion stems:

Most grown people are *smart but I'm smarter.*
The people in my class think I am *mean and bad.*
My foster mother thinks I am *cute.*
My teacher thinks I am *dumb.*
My foster father thinks I am *nice (Brent yelled this.)*
My foster mother makes me feel *mad.*
My friends think I am *bad and dumb in class.*
I am *dumb.*
When my foster father gives me lots of work, I say *thanks.*

When I see somebody do really good in school, I *throw something at them.*

When no one can help me but myself, I *growl and get mad.*

When my teacher tells me to do something, I *get mad.*

When my teacher corrects me, I *cheer.*

When I don't know what the book says, I *say "you're dumb."*

When there is hard schoolwork to do, I *go "yuk."*

Brent's responses indicated that he saw himself as "dumb" and believed that others saw him the same way. He viewed his foster parents as having positive feelings toward him, but said that his foster mother made him mad. Brent expressed negative and hostile attitudes toward task completion and school achievement. His responses reflected a lack of strategies for dealing with performance demands. Compared to the responses given by Jason, it is clear that Brent was experiencing emotional distress. In particular, he appeared to feel negative about himself and often felt angry. This seemed to be expressed in lethargic and passive behavior.

Results of intellectual testing revealed that Brent was functioning in the low average range of intelligence. His achievement was commensurate with his intellectual ability. It was recommended that Brent receive special education services as an emotionally disturbed student because of his dysphoric mood and poor peer relations. It was also recommended that Brent receive individual psychotherapy as a means of allowing him to express and gain some mastery over his internal turmoil.

Structures Self-Report Measure. A number of structured self-report measures have been developed to assess the cognitive distortions that may contribute to children's internalizing disorders. The Children's Attributional Style Questionnaire (CASQ; Fielstein et al., 1985) which has been discussed in Chapter 6, is designed to assess children's success or failure attributions to 12 vignettes depicting social, athletic, and academic situations. For each situation presented, the child is asked to select one of the following causal attributions as an explanation for success or failure: skill or lack of skill, effort or lack of effort, good or bad luck, and task ease or difficulty. Sample items from the CASQ are given in Chapter 6.

One-month test–retest reliability for a sample of 99 fourth- through sixth-graders ranged from .62 to .96 for success scenes and .52 to .85 percent for failure scenes. In comparing children with high and low self-esteem, Fielstein et al (1985) found that children with high self-esteem attributed success in all three content areas as the result of skill more often than the children with low self-esteem. Children low in self-esteem were more likely than children with high self-esteem to cite good luck as an explanation for success in all content areas. In addition, in every situation children with low self-esteem were more likely than high self-esteem children to attribute failure to a lack of skill.

The Children's Negative Cognitive Error Questionnaire (CNCEQ: Leitenberg et al., 1986) presents children with 24 hypothetical situations in a variety of social, academic, and athletic settings. Each vignette is followed by a statement reflective of one of the common cognitive errors that Beck and his colleagues (Beck, Rush, Shaw, & Emery, 1979) believe to be central to depressive symptomatology (catastrophizing, overgeneralizing, personalizing, and selective abstraction). The following is an example of a social situation:

> You call one of the kids in your class to talk about your math homework. He/she says, "I can't talk now, my father needs to use the phone." You think, "He/she didn't want to talk to me." (Leitenberg et al., 1986, p. 529)

After the situation and statement are read, the child uses a 5-point scale to rate the item in terms of its similarity to his or her own thinking (with a 1 indicating "not at all like I think," and 5 being "almost exactly like I think"). Adding up the ratings to all the items provides a total cognitive error score; in addition, scores can be obtained for each content area.

One-month test–retest reliabilities were .65 for the total score and ranged from .44 to .58 for error types in a sample of 143 children in fifth through eighth grades. Normative data were obtained on 637 public school children in the fourth, sixth, and eighth grades. It was found that older children had lower total scores than younger children, and that more cognitive errors were made in relation to the social vignettes than were made in relation to athletic or academic vignettes. This result may be reflective of the ambiguous criteria for success in social situations. In examining the relationship of depressive symptoms and cognitive errors, Leitenberg et al. (1986) found that cognitive error scores were associated with self-reported depression, low self-esteem, and evaluation anxiety.

Other Techniques. DiGiuseppe and Bernard (1983) offer a number of strategies that can be used to elicit children's thoughts and feelings. The use of "feeling scales" can be helpful in understanding the intensity of children's affective responses to a variety of situations. Using a 10-point scale, children rate the amount of affect they experience in a given situation. Such an activity can help children better understand gradients in the intensity of emotions and can help the clinician identify situations and feelings that can serve as targets for intervention. Based on clinical experience, DiGiuseppe and Bernard claim that ratings of 8 or higher are often indicative of emotional overreactions that can lead to behavioral problems.

The use of "thought bubbles" is a means of helping children see how thoughts can create feelings. This technique involves having a child fill in the bubbles that appear over the heads of characters in a cartoon strip. The clinician can draw a cartoon that depicts a child in a problem situation. The characters in the cartoon can be drawn displaying various emotional responses to the situation and the child can fill in the thought bubbles with statements that reflect what the characters in the story might be thinking.

Waters (1982) suggests activities that increase children's emotional awareness. The use of "emotional flashcards" is similar to an adult game of charades. The clinician and the child take turns drawing cards that have the names of various emotions printed on them. The person who draws the card acts the emotion out, and the other one tries to guess what emotion it is. Emotional vocabulary building involves asking a child to identify all the emotions he or she can. After this, each feeling the child identified is reviewed and the child is asked to describe a situation where they experienced the feeling, including a description of what the child was thinking.

The techniques we have described are all designed to provide access to children's thoughts and feelings. The benefits of such practices are twofold. First, they allow an opportunity to understand and evaluate a child's internal experience; second, they allow the child to verbalize and expand awareness of his or her thoughts and feelings. There are other advantages to the use of these types of techniques that we have not discussed. One is the utility of these methods with children who are reluctant to discuss their thoughts and feelings. The game-like quality of the procedures we have described can make self revelation less threatening to a child and may reinforce the expression of thoughts and feelings. Also, these techniques can be altered and "customized" to meet the needs of the individual child. There is certainly no limit to the number of activities that can be devised to assess a child's thoughts and feelings. The case of 8-year-old Patrick illustrates how techniques can be devised by the clinician to facilitate communication and information gathering during the interview process.

Case Example

Patrick's parents brought him to the psychologist because he frequently complained of aches and pains for which there was no medical basis. He often asked to stay home from school and his parents were eager to find out what might be upsetting their son. Patrick presented as an anxious child who refused to discuss any but the most trivial types of things. During the second interview, the psychologist (David Baker) attempted to find out more about Patrick's thoughts and feelings and how they related to his psychosomatic complaints.

D<small>B</small>: I am wondering if there are things that make you worry?

P<small>ATRICK</small>: Nope, I ain't worried.

D<small>B</small>: Well, are there things that happen at home or at school that you don't like, or maybe things that make you mad?

P<small>ATRICK</small>: No, not really.

D<small>B</small>: Not really? Does that mean that some things make you mad or that there are things you don't like at home or school?

P<small>ATRICK</small>: Nobody likes homework.

D<small>B</small>: Yeah, I guess most kids don't like homework. Is that a problem for you...homework?

P<small>ATRICK</small>: No, I don't have much and I get it done or else I can't watch TV.

D<small>B</small>: You like to watch TV?

P<small>ATRICK</small>: Pretty much.

D<small>B</small>: What else do you like to do?

P<small>ATRICK</small>: Nintendo.

D<small>B</small>: What's your favorite Nintendo game?

P<small>ATRICK</small>: Super Mario Brothers.

D<small>B</small>: Do you play it with other kids?

P<small>ATRICK</small>: No.

D<small>B</small>: Do you have friends that you do things with, like play Nintendo?

P<small>ATRICK</small>: Kinda.

At that point, it seemed that the interview was not moving in any direction. Patrick appeared bored, and his responses left Baker feeling that Patrick was not willing to engage in any meaningful dialogue.

D<small>B</small>: It seems like you're getting tired of all this talking.

P<small>ATRICK</small>: Kinda.

D_B: Yeah, well that's Okay. You know, there is a game I like to play sometimes and you might like it too.

P_{ATRICK}: What kinda game?

D_B: It's called Hangman. Have you ever heard of it?

P_{ATRICK}: (*Nods*) Yeah, we play it at school.

D_B: Good, so I don't have to explain it to you?

P_{ATRICK}: Nope. Who goes first?

D_B: Would you like to go first?

P_{ATRICK}: Okay. Give me the paper. I'm going to make a hard one for you. I bet you can't guess this.

D_B: You want this to be hard for me." (*After guessing several letters*) "I think I know what this is. I think it's my name.

P_{ATRICK}: You're right. I thought it would take you longer.

D_B: Well, I wasn't quite sure, but after I guessed the last two letters I was pretty sure. Okay, now it's my turn. I'll give you a hint...this is about a feeling.

P_{ATRICK}: I bet I know this one. Is there an A?

D_B: Yup here's an A.

P_{ATRICK}: And an M?

D_B: I bet you know this."

P_{ATRICK}: And a D. Yeah, I knew it was going to be "mad."

D_B: You did that quick. How about mad? What makes you mad?

P_{ATRICK}: My brother bugs me and I get mad.

D_B: Yeah, being bugged makes a lot of people mad.

The game proceeded in this manner through a number of feeling words, and Patrick was much more willing to be open about his feelings, particularly when it came to the word, "scared."

D_B: Right again! The word is "scared." That was a little harder to guess than the others.

P_{ATRICK}: I kept trying to figure it out.

D_B: And you did good. How about scared? What are you scared of?

P_{ATRICK}: I'm scared a plane is going to crash in my yard. A big plane like an overseas plane.

DB: Wow, that is a scary thought."

PATRICK: Look, see, I'm drawing a picture of it. "Hey, look out below, look out below!" [The] cops [are] too late, it crashed into their house and everything's on fire.

DB: Is anybody home?

PATRICK: They're lucky, the kids were supposed to be home but they went to their friends' house to play after school.

DB: The plane says Japan Airlines. Was it from Japan?

PATRICK: It was going to Miami and then to Hawaii, and from Hawaii it goes to Japan.

DB: Do you know anybody who went to any of those places?

PATRICK: No...well yes...my uncle took his family to Japan.

DB: When was that?

PATRICK: In the summer. It was right after we went to the beach together.

DB: Why did they go? Are they going to stay?"

PATRICK: My uncle, he works in the oil fields and they needed him over there so he went. I don't know for how long.

DB: How do you feel about their leaving? Do you miss them?

PATRICK: My mom misses them a lot. She cried when they left.

DB: What about you?

PATRICK: I feel kinda bad.

DB: What is it that you feel bad about?

PATRICK: I had a fight with my cousin before he left and I told him something bad.

DB: What was it?

PATRICK: I don't know. I'm tired of this. Can we play Hangman?

DB: We can play again but first I think it's real important to finish talking about your feeling bad about your cousin.

PATRICK: I don't want to.

DB: I know you don't want to, but I think it's important to talk about, because it may have something to do with how you feel sick at times. It would help if you'd tell me what you said to your cousin.

PATRICK: I told him I hoped he never came back.

DB: And that is real bad?

PATRICK: Well, it is, 'cause when Uncle Ron was leaving, he said he was getting insurance so if they crashed and died we would get a lot of money.

DB: I'm not sure I understand why that is bad.

PATRICK: Something might happen, like a crash or something.

DB: And it might be your fault 'cause you were mad at your cousin and told him you wished he wouldn't come back?

PATRICK: No. How much more time is there? Is it time to leave?

DB: We have about 10 more minutes left.

PATRICK: I'm tired.

DB: I bet it's hard to talk about things that make you feel bad. I really appreciate how willing you've been to tell me some things that are making you feel bad. I'm wondering if there is something that we could do to make you feel better.. I mean something we could do about how bad you're feeling about your cousin?

PATRICK: I'd like to call them but Dad says it costs too much.

DB: Have you heard anything from them?

PATRICK: I think my mom did.

DB: Well, it may be a good idea to talk to them. I can talk to your parents about it, and if they won't let you call you could write your cousin a letter. Does that sound like a good plan?

PATRICK: Yeah.

After this interview, Baker met with Patrick's parents and discussed the incident involving Patrick and his cousin. The parents were willing to let Patrick call his cousin in Japan and said they would do so before Patrick's next visit. The following week, Patrick said he had been able to talk to his cousin and reported in great detail all the things they discussed. Patrick appeared animated and pleased that he had spoken to his cousin. Patrick did not see any connection between his psychosomatic complaints and his fearful thoughts about airplane crashes and the well-being of his relatives. However, he reported that he had not had any headaches or stomach pains in the last week.

Patrick was seen again 2 weeks later, and his parents reported that his somatic complaints had diminished and that he had not missed any school days in the last 2 weeks. Patrick did not want to talk about any more "worries" and reported that while it was fun to visit with the psychologist, he would rather be able to go out and play soccer on Monday afternoons. It was felt that Patrick's referral problem was resolved, and the case was terminated with an understanding that Patrick and his family would call if there were any further problems.

Structured Interviewing Approaches

As discussed in Chapter 3 there are a number of structured diagnostic interviews that can be used to assess internalizing behavior problems. All of the interviews presented in Chapter 3 can be used to determine diagnoses pertaining to affective disorders.

The Schedule for Affective Disorders and Schizophrenia for School-Age Children (Kiddie-SADS or K-SADS; Puig-Antich & Chambers, 1978) and the Interview Schedule for Children (ISC; Kovacs & Beck, 1977) were designed specifically to study childhood depression, and both have demonstrated adequate reliability and validity in diagnosing depressive disorders. A limitation in the use of these instruments is that extensive training and clinical expertise are necessary for administering the interviews and arriving at a diagnosis.

The Diagnostic Interview for Children and Adolescents—Revised (DICA-R; Reich & Welner, 1989) and the Child Assessment Schedule (CAS; Hodges, 1987) can both be useful in diagnosing affective and anxiety disorders. While it is recommended that interviewers be trained in the use of these instruments, they do not require the intensive training required for the K-SADS and ISC. Diagnoses can be obtained from the DICA-R and the CAS by using computer algorithms, thereby eliminating the need for the clinical judgment required by the K-SADS and ISC for determining diagnoses. Comparisons of the K-SADS with the original DICA (Carlson, Kashani, Thomas, Vaidya, & Daniel, 1987) and the CAS (Hodges et al., 1987), found adequate agreement for affective disorders. Hodges (1990) notes that when assessing depressive disorders, researchers and clinicians may find either the K- SADS, the DICA or DICA-R, or the CAS useful.

CASE STUDY

We conclude this chapter with another case example. This case illustrates the value of unstructured interviewing in the identification and amelioration of children's internalizing disorders.

Eric was an 8-year-old boy who was referred for psychotherapy by his caseworker, Judy. Eric and his younger brother were currently living in a foster home with their foster parents, Bill and Marie. The boys had been removed from their parents 6 months earlier because of charges of child abuse and neglect. Charges of physical abuse had been confirmed, and the father was awaiting sentencing. Eric's mother had a history of substance abuse and had been on probation for a variety of offenses including child neglect. The parents were well known to Child Protective Services (CPS), and the most recent charges had led to a motion by CPS to have parental rights terminated.

Eric's caseworker and foster parents were concerned about Eric's adjustment. He was frequently wetting his bed and had recurrent nightmares. At school he was making satisfactory academic progress, but often got into fights with his peers and was manipulative. On numerous occasions, he stole other children's belongings and refused to accept responsibility for his actions.

The caseworker reported that she had spent a great deal of time with Eric and his brother, and noted that Eric was very protective of his younger brother. When Judy originally interviewed Eric regarding the charges of physical abuse against his father, Eric was able to give her the necessary information but had not spoken any more about it to her or the foster parents.

On the basis of the information provided, the psychologist (David Baker) hypothesized that Eric's behavioral problems were the result of his internalization of feelings of confusion, anger, and fear, which were expressed through bedwetting, nightmares, fighting, and stealing.

During the first 2 therapy sessions, Eric was unwilling to discuss anything about his family or his current situation. He preferred to play board games and frequently cheated in order to win. Eric's foster father reported that Eric would express reservations about coming to therapy, but appeared happy when he left the sessions.

Prior to the third session, Eric's foster father reported that he had a conflict with Eric earlier in the week that had upset both of them. Bill reported that Eric and his brother were allowed to visit their maternal uncle once a week. A problem had emerged during the last visit, and Bill indicated to Baker that he hoped it could be discussed during the therapy session. The following is an excerpt from the third session.

D<small>B</small>: Do you want to talk about what Bill said?

E<small>RIC</small>: Nope, it's between me and Bill.

D<small>B</small>: He thought it was important for us to talk about."

ERIC: It's about behavior.

DB: Behavior?

ERIC: Bad behavior, but I don't want to talk about it, it's between me and Bill. We don't want to talk about it.

DB: You kinda don't want to talk about it. Bill thinks it would be important to talk about.

ERIC: I want to play Connect Four [a board game].

DB: I want us to be able to play too, but I think we should first talk about this.

ERIC: What's to talk about?

DB: Sometimes when something happens that upsets you or worries you, you don't want to think or talk about it.

ERIC: Sometimes I don't like to talk about bad behavior.

DB: Do you think I'd get mad or not like you if I knew something bad you did?

ERIC: That's not it. I'm embarrassed to talk about it.

DB: Yeah, sometimes it's embarrassing to talk about things that happen.

ERIC: What I can say is that I may be moving out of Bill's house and moving in with my uncle, but I'd still be able to come here, maybe. I'm not sure if I'm doing it yet. Bill said it's up to me and I don't know yet.

DB: Is that because of what happened?

ERIC: No, I just want to get a change of pace. I might go for a year or two and come back.

DB: But that has nothing to do with what happened. That's totally different.

ERIC: Yup.

DB: What would it be like being there?

ERIC: I'd miss my brother, but he could go too. He does everything I do 'cause he's afraid somebody will hurt him; he stays with me a lot. There is something I want to talk about. I don't understand. We were on our bikes and some lady started chasing my brother in her car. I guess she wanted to get him and take him to her house 'cause we were doing something, but all we were doing was riding our bikes.

Dᴮ: When did this happen?

Eʀɪc: Last week.

Dᴮ: Sounds pretty scary having somebody chase you.

Eʀɪc: We gave her a chase. She had to go all the way around the block. She went way, way back down the block.

Dᴮ: Did you know who she was? Had you seen her before?

Eʀɪc: No, I never saw her before.

Dᴮ: Why do you think she was chasing you?

Eʀɪc: I don't know. We were laughing so hard we could hardly ride our bikes.

Dᴮ: You thought it was funny?

Eʀɪc: I did until I thought what if he [his brother] gets killed. She might have a knife or a gun.

Dᴮ: Did you tell somebody about it?

Eʀɪc: No, we told Bill.

Dᴮ: What did he say?

Eʀɪc: He said, "Well try to stay out of trouble." Usually when we get in trouble he stands back and watches us.

Dᴮ: Did you get in any trouble?

Eʀɪc: Not for that.

Dᴮ: But you did get in trouble for something else?

Eʀɪc: Yeah.

Dᴮ: And I'm wondering why all of a sudden you might go live with your uncle. I'm wandering what you want a change of pace from.

Eʀɪc: He's nicer.

Dᴮ: Sometimes when people get in trouble or get mad at somebody, one thing they can do is go somewhere else.

Eʀɪc: I'll say one thing, I wrapped my legs around the porch and he [Bill] pulled on me.

Dᴮ: You were trying to hang on to the porch and Bill was pulling on you?

ERIC: I was hanging on and he kept pulling and when I rested he pulled me off.

DB: Did that hurt?

ERIC: No, I was really hanging on.

DB: Wow, you really didn't want to move."

ERIC: I wanted to stay at my uncle's. I was having fun there."

DB: So you were at your uncle's and you didn't want to leave?

ERIC: We were visiting for the day and Bill came to get us, and I wasn't ready to go.

DB: So you were hanging on to the porch and not wanting to go?

ERIC: At first I didn't know I'd do that, but when he said "Let's go," I thought I'd just hang on to the porch.

DB: What did Bill say?

ERIC: "Get off the porch, it's time to go!"

DB: What did you say?

ERIC: "Leave me alone!"

DB: You wanted to stay?

ERIC: Yeah, and he made me mad, cause he wouldn't let me and I was yelling and yelling and when I calmed down he let me stay the night, but now I'm in big trouble.

DB: What kind of trouble?

ERIC: I'm on punishment.

DB: What does that mean?

ERIC: I can't go play after school for a week. When I'm off punishment I'm going to decide what I'll do.

DB: I feel bad that you and Bill had such a struggle.

ERIC: It didn't make me feel bad, it kinda scared me.

DB: What scared you the most about it?

ERIC: He was pulling on me.

DB: So he was angry and pulling on you, and that scared you?

ERIC: Yeah, and it made me mad.

D_B: It's pretty scary when an adult is angry and pulling on you. It also makes you mad when that happens. Has that happened to you before?

E_{RIC}: My real dad wanted me dead, he hated me.

D_B: What did he do that made you know that?

E_{RIC}: One time he was hitting my mom and he knocked her down and was on the floor trying to hit her, and I jumped on his back and he grabbed my arm and threw me across the room and screamed at me, but I wasn't going to let him hurt her.

D_B: Boy, I would be scared and mad if that happened to me. It's pretty hard to be a kid and try to protect your mom from your dad, who is an adult and a lot bigger and stronger than you.

E_{RIC}: I hate him. He told me he would kill me if I hit him, he said I was nothing but trouble, and once he tried to stab my mom with a knife and when I yelled he pointed it at me. I would have shot him with a gun, I'm a good shot and he knows it.

D_B: That is really scary. It's not right for your dad to do those things and that's one of the reasons why Judy [the social worker] took you to the shelter and your dad was arrested.

E_{RIC}: Yeah, he's crazy, and I hate him and don't want to see him.

D_B: I understand that, and you don't have to see him.

E_{RIC}: But I like seeing my uncle. I have fun at his house, and it's fun at Bill's too.

D_B: You should have fun. It's been hard having to be at home where everybody is so mad and where you get hurt and feel scared.

E_{RIC}: I'm never going back there. It was crazy.

D_B: Why do you think your dad acted like that?" Why did he do those things to you?

E_{RIC}: He was mean to everybody.

D_B: Sometimes kids think it was their fault, like they did something that made their parents hate them or want to hurt them.

E_{RIC}: It wasn't my fault. He was crazy.

D_B: Your dad has problems. Adults shouldn't treat kids like that and your dad's problems don't have anything to do with you. You did all you could do to protect yourself, your mom, and your brother, but that's too much for one boy. You should be in a home where you are safe and have fun.

Eric: I know. Bill and Judy said my mom and dad are going to get help and we could stay with Bill and have fun.

Db: What do you think about that?

Eric: I like it. I'm glad my brother's here too. I don't want to go back to our old apartment.

Db: I know, and Judy said you don't have to go back. Bill said you could stay with him and Marie for as long as you want to.

Eric: We're going fishing next week. Bill's dad has a ranch and there's a pond with lots of fish in it.

Db: That sounds like fun.

Eric: I always catch the biggest fish.

Db: That's great. You know, I'm wondering if when Bill got mad at you last week and was trying to pull you off the porch, if you thought he might hate you or hurt you like your dad did?

Eric: No, not really. Bill said he was sorry. He didn't hurt me; he put me on punishment and that makes me mad. But my dad, he would just hit us and act crazy.

Db: Bill and your dad are different in how they treat you.

Eric: I'm mad at my dad (*knocks blocks off table*).

Db: I know. It's OK to be mad at your dad.

Eric: I'm tired of this. Can we play a game now?

Db: Yeah, we have talked a lot about things that make you feel pretty angry and scared.

Eric: That's for sure. I want to play Connect Four."

Db: Okay. Thanks for telling me about what happened with Bill and all the things that happened with your dad. Sometimes you can feel less scared and angry when you talk about those things.

References

Abramson, L. Y., Seligman, M.E.P., & Teasdale, J. D. (1978). Learned helplessness in humans: Critique and reformulation. *Journal of Abnormal Psychology, 87,* 49–74.

Achenbach, T. M. (1966). The classification of children's psychiatric symptoms: A factor analytic study. *Psychological Monographs, 80,* 1–37.

Achenbach, T. M. (1979). The Child Behavior Profile: An empirically based system for assessing children behavioral problems and competences. *International Journal of Mental Health, 7,* 24–42.

Achenbach, T. M., & Edelbrock, C. S. (1981). Behavioral problems and competencies reported by parents of normal and disturbed children aged four through sixteen. *Monographs of the Society for Research in Child Development, 46* (1, Serial No. 18).

Achenbach, T. M., & Edelbrock, C. S. (1983). *Manual for the Child Behavior Checklist and Revised Child Behavior Profile.* Burlington VT: University of Vermont, Department of Psychiatry.

Achenbach, T. M., & Edelbrock, C. (1987). *Manual for the Youth Self-Report and Profile.* Burlington,VT: University of Vermont, Department of Psychiatry.

Achenbach, T. M., Edelbrock, C. S., & Howell, C. T. (1987). Empirically-based assessment of the behavioral/emotional problems of 2–3 year-old children. *Journal of Abnormal Child Psycholgoy, 15,* 629–650.

Ainsworth, M.D.S., Blehar, M., Waters, E., & Wall, S. (1978). *Patterns of attachment.* Hillsdale, NJ: Erlbaum.

American Psychiatric Association. (1968). *Diagnostic and statistical manual of mental disorders* (2nd ed.). Washington, DC: Author.

American Psychiatric Association. (1980). *Diagnostic and statistical manual of mental disorders* (3rd ed.). Washington, DC: Author.

American Psychiatric Association. (1987). *Diagnostic and statistical manual of mental disorders* (3rd ed., rev.). Washington, DC: Author.

Ames, R., Ames, C., & Garrison, W. (1977). Children's causal ascriptions for positive and negative interpersonal outcomes. *Psychological Reports, 41,* 595–602.

Aoki, S. (1981). The retest reliability of the Sand Play Technique: II. *British Journal of Projective Psychology and Personality Study, 26,* 25–33.

Aponte, H. J., & VanDeusen, J. M. (1981). Structural family therapy. In A. S. Gurman & D. P. Kniskern (Eds.), *Handbook of family therapy* (pp. 310–360). New York: Brunner/Mazel.

211

Arend, R., Gove, F., & Sroufe, L. A. (1979). Continuity of individual adaptation from infancy to kindergarten: A reductive study of ego resilience and curiosity in preschoolers. *Child Development, 50,* 950–959.

Asarnow, J. R., & Callan, J. W. (1985). Boys with peer adjustment problems: Social cognitive processes. *Journal of Consulting and Clinical Psychology, 53,* 80–87.

Atkeson, B. M., & Forehand, R. (1978). Parent behavioral training for problem children: An examination of studies using multiple outcome measures. *Journal of Abnormal Child Psychology, 6,* 449–460.

Atkeson, B. M., & Forehand, R. (1981). Conduct disorders. In E. J. Mash & L. G. Terdal (Eds.), *Behavioral assessment of childhood disorders* (pp. 185–219). New York: Guilford Press.

August, G. J., Stewart, M. A., & Holmes, C. S. (1983). A four-year follow-up of hyperactive boys with and without conduct disorder. *British Journal of Psychiatry, 143,* 192–198.

Axline, V. (1947). *Play therapy.* Boston: Houghton Mifflin.

Axline, V. (1969). *Play therapy* (rev. ed.). New York: Ballantine Books.

Baker, D. B. (1988). *Quantification of the Haak Sentence Completion.* Unpublished doctoral dissertation, Texas A & M University.

Bandura, A. (1969). *Principles of behavior modification.* New York: Holt, Rinehart & Winston.

Bandura, A. (1977). *Social learning theory.* Englewood Cliffs, NJ: Prentice-Hall.

Bandura, A. (1989). Human agency in social cognitive theory. *American Psychologist, 44,* 1175–1184.

Barenboim, C. (1977). Developmental changes in the interpersonal cognitive system from middle childhood to adolescence. *Child Development, 48,* 1467–1474.

Barenboim, C. (1978). Development of recursive and nonrecursive thinking about persons. *Developmental Psychology, 14,* 419–420.

Barkley, R. A. (1981). *Hyperactive children: A handbook for diagnosis and treatment.* New York: Guilford Press.

Barkley, R. A. (1988). Attention deficit disorder with hyperactivity. In E. J. Mash & L. G. Terdal (Eds.), *Behavioral assessment of childhood disorders* (2nd ed., pp. 69–104), New York: Guilford Press.

Barkley, R. A., & Edelbrock, C. S. (1987). Assessing situational variation in children's behavior problems: The Home and School Situations Questionnaires. In R. Prinz (Ed.), *Advances in behavioral assessment of children and families* (Vol. 3, pp. 157–176). Greenwich, CT: JAI Press.

Barkley, R. A., Karlson, J., Pollard, S., & Murphy, J. (1985). Developmental changes in the mother–child interactions of hyperactive boys: Effects of two dose levels of Ritalin. *Journal of Child Psychology and Psychiatry, 26,* 705–715.

Bateson, G. (1976). A theory of play and fantasy. In J. S. Bruner, A. Jolly, & K. Sylva (Eds.), *Play.* New York: Basic Books.

Beck, A. T. (1967). *Depression: Causes and treatment.* Philadelphia: University of Pennsylvania Press.

Beck, A. T. (1976). *Cognitive therapy and the emotional disorders.* New York: International Universities Press.

Beck, A. T., Rush, A. J., Shaw, B. F., & Emery, G. (1979). *Cognitive therapy of depression.* New York: Guilford Press.

Beer, D. W. (1989). Guidelines for interviewing children. In J. Garbarino, F. M Stott, & Faculty of the Erikson Institute (Eds.), *What children can tell us* (pp. 170–202). San Francisco: Jossey-Bass.

Befera, M., & Barkley, R. A. (1985). Hyperactive and normal girls and boys: Mother–child interactions, parent psychiatric status, and child psychopathology. *Journal of Child Psychology and Psychiatry, 26,* 439–452.

Behar, D., & Rapoport, J. L. (1983). Play observation and psychiatric diagnosis. In C. E. Schaefer & K. J. O'Connor (Eds.), *Handbook of play therapy* (pp. 193–199). New York: Wiley.

Bellak, A.S. (1979). A critical appraisal of strategies for assessing social skill. *Behavioral Assessment, 1,* 157–176.

Bellak, L. (1954). A study of limitations and "failures": Toward an ego psychology of projective techniques. *Journal of Projective Techniques, 18,* 279–292.

Bellak, L., & Bellak, S. S. (1949). *Children's Apperception Test.* New York: C.P.S.

Benjamin, A. (1969). *The helping interview.* Boston: Houghton Mifflin.

Bernard, M. E., & Joyce, M. R. (1984). *Rational–emotive therapy with children and adolescents.* New York: Wiley.

Bessell, H., & Palomares, V. H. (1967). *Methods in human development.* San Diego, CA: Human Development Training Institute.

Bierman, K. L. (1983). Cognitive development and clinical interviews with children. In B. B. Lahey & A. E. Kazdin (Eds.), *Advances in clinical child psychology* (Vol. 6, pp. 217–250). New York: Plenum.

Bierman, K. L., & Schwartz, L. A. (1986a). Clinical-child interviews: Approaches and developmental considerations. *Journal of Child and Adolescent Psychotherapy, 3,* 267–278.

Bierman, K. L., & Schwartz, L. A. (1986b, August). *Selecting social intervention techniques for aggressive rejected children.* Paper presented at the annual meeting of the American Psychological Association, Washington, DC.

Borke, H. (1975). Piaget's mountains revisited: Changes in the egocentric landscape. *Developmental Psychology, 11,* 102–108.

Bousha, D. M. (1985). *A controlled investigation of therapeutic focus in limit-setting insight-oriented psychotherapy with acting-out children.* Unpublished doctoral dissertation, University of Rochester.

Brody, G., & Forehand, R. (1986). Maternal perceptions of child maladjustment as a function of the combined influence of child behavior and maternal depression. *Journal of Consulting and Clinical Psychology, 54,* 237–240.

Buck, J. N. (1948). The H–T–P technique: A qualitative and quantitative scoring manual. *Journal of Clinical Psychology, 4,* 317–396.

Bugental, P. B., Whalen, C. K., & Henker, B. (1977). Causal attributions of hyperactive children and motivational assumptions of two behavior-change approaches: Evidences for an interactionist position. *Child Development, 48,* 874–884.

Burgess, R. L. (1979). Child abuse: A social interactional analysis. In B. B. Lahey & A. E. Kazdin (Eds.), *Advances in clinical child psychology* (Vol. 2, pp. 142–172). New York: Plenum.

Burgess, R. L., & Conger, R. (1978). Family interactions in abusive, neglectful, and normal families. *Child Development, 49,* 1163–1173.

Carlson, C. L., & Lahey, B. B. (1988). Conduct and attention deficit disorders. In J. C. Witt, S. N. Elliott, & F. M. Gresham (Eds.), *Handbook of behavior therapy in education* (pp. 653–677). New York: Plenum Press.

Carlson, G., Kashani, J., Thomas, M., Vaidya, A., & Daniel, A. (1987). Comparison of two structured interviews on a psychiatrically hospitalized population of children. *Journal of the American Academy of Child and Adolescent Psychiatry, 26,* 645–648.

Cautela, J. R. (1977). *Behavior analysis forms for clinical intervention.* Champaign, IL: Research Press.

Ceci, S. J., Toglia, M. P., & Ross, D. F. (Eds.). (1987). *Children's eyewitness memory.* New York: Springer-Verlag.

Chambers, W., Puig-Antich, J., Hersche, M., Paey, P., Ambrosini, P. J., Tabrizi, M. A., & Davies, M. (1985). The assessment of affective disorders in children and adolescents by semi-structured interview: Test–retest reliability of the K-SADS-P. *Archives of General Psychiatry, 42,* 696–702.

Cole, C. B., & Loftus, E. F. (1987). The memory of children. In S. J. Ceci, M. P. Toglia, & D. F. Ross (Eds.), *Children's eyewitness memory* (pp. 178–208). New York: Springer-Verlag.

Compas, B. E., Howell, D. C., Phares, V., Williams, R. A., & Giunta, C. T. (1989). Risk factors for emotional/behavioral problems in young adolescents: A prospective analysis of adolescent and parental stress and symptoms. *Journal of Consulting and Clinical Psychology, 57,* 732–740.

Conners, C. K. (1969). A teacher rating scale for use in drug studies with children. *American Journal of Psychiatry, 126,* 884–888.

Corsaro, W. (1979). Young children's conception of status and role. *Sociology of Education, 52,* 46–59.

Costello, A. (1989). Reliability in diagnostic interviewing. In C. G. Last & M. Hersen (Eds.), *Handbook of child psychiatric diagnosis* (pp. 28–40). New York: Wiley.

Deluty, R. H. (1981). Alternative-thinking ability of aggressive, assertive, and submissive children. *Cognitive Therapy and Research, 5,* 309–312.

Demos, V. (1983). A perspective from infancy research on affect and self-esteem. In J. E. Mack & S. L. Albon (Eds.), *The development and sustaining of self-esteem in childhood* (pp. 1–42). New York: International Universities Press.

DiGiuseppe, R. A., & Bernard, M. E. (1983). Principles of assessment and methods of treatment with children. In A. Ellis & M. E. Bernard (Eds.), *Rational–emotive approaches to the problems of childhood.* New York: Plenum.

Dodge, K. A. (1986). A social information processing model of social competence in children. In M. Perlmutter (Ed.), *Cognitive perspectives on children's social and behavioral development* (pp. 77–125). Hillsdale, NJ: Erlbaum.

Dodge, K. A., & Frame, C. L. (1982). Social cognitive biases and deficits in aggressive boys. *Child Development, 53,* 620–635.

Dodge, K. A., Murphy, R. R., & Buchsbaum, K. C. (1984). The assessment of intention-cue detection skills in children: Implications for developmental psychology. *Child Development, 55,* 163–173.

Dodge, K. A., & Newman, J. P. (1981). Biased decision-making processes in aggressive boys. *Journal of Abnormal Psychology, 90,* 375—379.

Donaldson, M. (1978). *Children's minds.* New York: W.W. Norton.

Donaldson, S. K., & Westerman, M. A. (1986). Development of children's understanding of ambivalence and causal theories of emotions. *Developmental Psychology, 22,* 655–662.

Dumas, J. E., Gibson, J. A., & Albin, J. B. (1989). Behavioral correlates of maternal depressive symptomatology in conduct-disorder children. *Journal of Consulting and Clinical Psychology, 57,* 516–521.

Dumas, J. E., & Wahler, R. G. (1983). Predictors of treatment outcome in parent training: Mother insularity and socio-economic disadvantage. *Behavioral Assessment, 5,* 301–313.

Dweck, C. S. (1975). The role of expectations and attributions in the alleviations and attributions in the alleviation of learned helplessness. *Journal of Personality and Social Psychology, 31,* 674–685.

Edelbrock, C., & Achenbach, T. M. (1984). The Teacher Version of the Child Behavior Profile: I. Boys aged 6–11. *Journal of Consulting and Clinical Psychology, 52,* 207–217.

Edelbrock, C. S., Costello, A. J., Dulcan, M. K., Conover, N. C., & Kalas, R. (1986). Parent–child agreement on child psychiatric symptoms assessed via structured interview. *Journal of Child Psychology and Psychiatry, 27,* 181–190.

Edelbrock, C., Costello, A. J., Dulcan, M. K., Kalas, R. L., & Conover, N. C. (1985). Age differences in the reliability of the psychiatric interview for the child. *Child Development, 56,* 265–275.

Edelbrock, C., Costello, A. J., & Kessler, M. D. (1984). Empirical corroboration of attention deficit disorder. *Journal of the American Academy of Child Psychiatry, 23,* 285–290.

Edelbrock, C., Greenbaum, R., & Conover, N. C. (1985). Reliability and concurrent relations between the Teacher Version of the Child Behavior Profile and the Conners Revised Teacher Rating Scale. *Journal of Abnormal Child Psychology, 13,* 295–303.

Edelstein, B. A., & Berler, E. S. (1987). Interviewing and report writing. In C. L. Frame & J. L. Matson (Eds.), *Handbook of assessment in childhood psychopathology* (pp. 163–184). New York: Plenum.

Elliott, S. N. (1986). Children's ratings of the acceptability of classroom interventions for misbehavior: Findings and methodological considerations. *Journal of School Psychology, 24,* 23–35.

Ellis, A. (1962). *Reason and emotion in psychotherapy.* New York: Lyle Stuart.

Ellis, A.(1977). Rational–emotive therapy: Research data that supports the clinical and personality hypothesis of RET and other modes of cognitive–behavior therapy. *Counseling Psychologist, 7,* 2–42.

Ellis, A. (1984). Rational emotive therapy. In R. J. Corsini (Ed.), *Current psychotherapies* (pp. 196–238). Itasca, Illinois: F. E. Peacock.

Endicott, J., & Spitzer, R. L. (1978). A diagnostic interview: The schedule for affective disorders and schizophrenia. *Archives of General Psychiatry, 35,* 837–844.

Erikson, E. (1950). *Childhood and society.* New York: W.W. Norton.

Evers-Pasquale, W. L. (1978). The Peer Preference Test, a measure of reward value: Item analysis, cross-validation, and replication. *Journal of Abnormal Child Psychology, 6,* 175–188.

Evers-Pasquale, W. L., & Sherman, M. (1975). The reward value of peers: A variable influencing the efficacy of film modeling in modifying social isolation in preschoolers. *Journal of Abnormal Child Psychology, 3,* 179–189.

Fein, G. G. (1979). Play and the acquisition of symbols. In L. Katz (Ed.), *Current topics in early childhood education* (pp. 195–225). Norwood, NJ: Ablex.

Feldman, E., & Dodge, K. A. (1987). Social information processing and sociometric status: Sex, age, and situational effects. *Journal of Abnormal Child Psychology, 15,* 211–227.

Field, T., De Stefano, L., & Koewler, J. H., III. (1982). Fantasy play of toddlers and pre-schoolers. *Developmental Psychology, 18,* 503–508.

Fielstein, E., Klein, M. S., Fischer, M., Hanon, C., Kobuger, P., Schneider, M. J., & Leitenberg, H. (1985). Self-esteem and causal attributions for success and failure in children. *Cognitive Therapy and Research, 9,* 381–398.

Flavell, J. H. (1985). *Cognitive development* (2nd ed.). Englewood Cliffs, NJ: Prentice-Hall.

Flavell, J. H. (1986). The development of children's knowledge about the appearance–reality distinction. *American Psychologist, 41,* 418–425.

Flavell, J. H., Green, F. L., & Flavell, E. R. (1986). Development of knowledge about the appearance–reality distinction. *Monographs of the Society for Research in Child Development, 51,* (1, Serial No. 212).

Ford, M. E. (1982). Social cognition and social competence in adolescence. *Developmental Psychology, 18,* 323–340.

Forehand, R. L., Long, N., Brody, G. H., & Fauber, R. (1986). Home predictors of young adolescents' school behavior and academic performance. *Child Development, 57,* 1528–1533.

Forehand, R., & McMahon, R. J. (1981). *Helping the noncompliant child: A clinician's guide to parent training.* New York: Guilford Press.

Foreyt, J. P., & Goodrick, G. K. (1988). Childhood obesity. In E. J. Mash & L. G. Terdal (Eds.), *Behavioral assessment of childhood disorders* (2nd ed., pp. 528–551). New York: Guilford Press.

Forman, B. D., & Hagan, B. J. (1984). Measures for evaluating total family functioning. *Family Therapy, 11,* 1–36.

Freud, A. (1974). The role of transference in the analysis of children. In *Introduction to psychoanalysis*. London: Hogarth Press. (Original work published 1926)

Freud, A. (1937). *The ego and the mechanisms of defense.* London: Hogarth Press.

Freud, S. (1955). Analysis of a phobia in a five-year-old boy. In J. Strachey (Ed. and Trans.), *The standard edition of the complete works of Sigmund Freud* (Vol. 10, pp. 5–147). London: Hogarth Press. (Original work published 1909)

Freud, S. (1955). Beyond the pleasure principle. In J. Strachey (Ed. and Trans.), *The Standard Edition of the Complete Works of Sigmund Freud* (Vol. 18, pp. 3–64). London: Hogarth Press. (Original work published 1920)

Freud, S. (1955). Postscript to analysis of a phobia in a five-year-old boy. In J. Strachey (Ed. and Trans.), *The standard edition of the complete works of Sigmund Freud* (Vol. 10, pp. 148–149). London: Hogarth Press. (Original work published 1922)

Furman, W., & Buhrmester, D. (1985). Children's perceptions of the personal relationships in their social networks. *Developmental Psychology, 21,* 1016–1024.

Garbarino, J., Stott, F. M., & Faculty of the Erikson Institute. (Eds.). (1989). *What children can tell us.* San Francisco: Jossey-Bass.

Garber, J. (1984). Classification of childhood psychopathology: A developmental perspective. *Child Development, 55,* 30–48.

Gardner, R. A. (1979). Helping children cooperate in therapy. In T. Noshpitz (Ed.), *Basic handbook of child psychiatry* (Vol. 3, pp. 414–433). New York: Basic Books.

Gardner, R. A. (1983). The Talking, Feeling, and Doing Game. In C. E. Schaefer & K. J. O'Conner (Eds.), *Handbook of play therapy* (pp. 259–273). New York: Wiley.

Glucksberg, S., Krauss, R. M., & Higgins, E. T. (1975). The development of communication skills in children, In F. Horowitz (Ed.), *Review of child development research* (Vol. 4). Chicago: University of Chicago Press.

Goetz, T. E., & Dweck, C. S. (1980). Learned helplessness in social situations. *Journal of Personality and Social Psychology, 39,* 246–255.

Goh, D. S., & Fuller, G. B. (1983). Current practices in the assessment of personality and behavior. *School Psychology Review, 12,* 240–243.

Goldfried, M. (1979). Behavioral assessment: Where do we go from here? *Behavioral Assessment, 1,* 19–22.

Goldfried, M., & Davison, G. C. (1976). *Clinical behavior therapy.* New York: Holt, Rinehart & Winston.

Goldman, J., Stein, C., & Guerry, S. (1983). *Psychological methods of child assessment.* New York: Brunner/Mazel.

Gollin, E. S. (1958). Organizational characteristics of social judgments: A developmental investigation. *Journal of Personality, 26,* 139–154.

Goodman, G. S. (1984). The child witness: Conclusions and future directions. *Journal of Social Issues, 40,* 157–175.

Goodman, G. S., & Reed, R. S. (1986). Age differences in eyewitness testimony. *Law and Human Behavior, 10*(4), 317–331.

Gottman, J. M., Gonso, J., & Rasmussen, B. (1975). Social interaction, social competence, and friendship in children. *Child Development, 46,* 709–718.

Green, K. P., Forehand, R., Beck, S. J., & Vosk, B. (1980). An assessment of the relationship among measures of children's social competence and children's academic achievement. *Child Development, 51,* 1149–1156.

Greenspan, S. I. (1981). *The clinical interview of the child.* New York: McGraw-Hill.

Gresham, G. M., & Davis, C. J. (1988). Behavioral interviews with teachers and parents. In E. S. Shapiro & R. R. Kratochwill (Eds.), *Behavioral assessment in schools: Conceptual foundations and practical applications* (pp. 455–493). New York: Guilford Press.

Gross, A. M. (1984). Behavioral interviewing. In T. H. Ollendick & M. Hersen (Eds.), *Child behavioral assessment: Principles and procedures* (pp. 61–79). New York: Pergamon Press.

Gurucharri, C., Phelps, E., & Selman, R. (1984). Development of interpersonal understanding: A longitudinal and comparative study of normal and disturbed youths. *Journal of Consulting and Clinical Psychology, 52,* 26–36.

Haley, J. (1978). *Problem-solving therapy.* San Francisco: Jossey-Bass.

Hammer, E. F. (1980). Expressive aspects of projective drawings. In E. F. Hammer (Eds.), *The clinical application of projective drawings* (pp. 57–79). Springfield, IL: Charles C. Thomas.

Harter, S. (1982). A cognitive-developmental approach to children's understanding affect and trait labels. In F. Serafica (Ed.), *Social-cognitive development in context* (pp. 27–61). New York: Guilford Press.

Harter, S. (1983). Developmental perspectives on the self-system. In E. M. Hetherington (Vol. Ed.), *Handbook of child psychology (4th ed.): Vol. 4. Socialization, personality, and social development.* (pp. 275–385) New York: Wiley.

Harter, S., & Buddin, B. J. (1983, April). *Children's understanding of the simultaneity of two emotions: A developmental acquisition sequence.* Paper presented at the biennial meeting of the Society for Research in Child Development, Detroit.

Haworth, M. R. (1966). *The CAT: Facts about fantasy.* New York: Grune & Stratton.

Hay, W. M., Hay, L. R., Angle, H. V., & Nelson, R. O. (1979). The reliability of problem identification in the behavioral interview. *Behavioral Assessment, 1,* 107–118.

Hayes, S. C., Nelson, R. O., & Jarrett, R. B. (1987) The treatment utility of assessment: A functional approach to evaluating assessment quality. *American Psychologist, 42,* 963–974.

Haynes, S. N., & Jensen, B. J. (1979). The interview as a behavioral assessment instrument. *Behavioral Assessment, 1,* 97–106.

Henker, B., & Whalen, C. K. (1989). Hyperactivity and attention deficits. *American Psychologist, 44,* 216–223.

Herjanic, B., Herjanic, M., Brown, F., & Wheatt, T. (1975). Are children reliable reporters? *Journal of Abnormal Child Psychology, 3,* 4–48.

Herjanic, B., & Reich, W. (1982). Development of a structured psychiatric interview for children: Agreement between child and parent on individual symptoms. *Journal of Abnormal Child Psychology, 10,* 307–324.

Hess, T. M., & Baker-Ward, L. E. (1987, April). *Children's knowledge and recall of a simple game: Familiarity and centrality effects.* Paper presented at the biennial meeting of the Society for Research in Child Development, Baltimore.

Hodges, K. (1987). Assessing children with a clinical research interview: The child assessment schedule. In R. J. Prinz (Ed.), *Advances in behavioral assessment of children and families* (Vol. 3, pp. 203–233). Greenwich, CT: JAI Press.

Hodges, K. (1990). Structured diagnostic interviews. In A. La Greca (Ed.), *Through the eyes of the child: Obtaining self-reports from children and adolescents* (pp. 109–149). Boston: Allyn and Bacon.

Hodges, K., Cools, J., & McKnew, D. (1989). Test–retest reliability of a clinical research interview for children: The Child Assessment Schedule. *Psychological Assessment: A Journal of Consulting and Clinical Psychology, 1,* 317–322.

Hodges, K., Kline, J., Barbero, G., & Flonery, R. (1985). Depressive symptoms in children with recurrent abdominal pain and in their families. *Journal of Pediatrics, 107,* 622–626.

Hodges, K., Kline, J., Barbero, G., & Woodruff, C. (1985). Anxiety in children with recurrent abdominal pain and their parents. *Psychosomatics, 26,* 859–866.

Hodges, K., Kline, J., Stern, L., Cytryn, L., & McKnew, D. (1982). The development of a child assessment interview for research and clinical use. *Journal of Abnormal Child Psychology, 10,* 173–189.

Hodges, K., McKnew, D., Burbach, D. J., & Roebuck, L. (1987). Diagnostic concordance between the child assessment schedule (CAS) and the Schedule for Affective Disorders and Schizophrenia for school-age children (K-SADS) in an outpatient sample using lay interviewers. *Journal of the American Academy of Child and Adolescent Psychiatry, 26,* 654–661.

Hoffman, L. (1981). *Foundations of family therapy: A conceptual foundation for system change.* New York: Basic Books.

Holland, C. J. (1970). An interview guide for behavioral counseling with parents. *Behavior Therapy, 1,* 70–79.

Hug-Hellmuth, H. (1921). On the technique of child analysis. *International Journal of Psychoanalysis, 2,* 287–305.

Hughes, J. N. (1987). Children's lying. In A. Thomas & J. Grimes (Eds.), *Children's needs* (pp. 336–343). Kent, OH: National Association of School Psychologists.

Hughes, J. N. (1988). Interviewing children. In J. Dillard & R. Reilley (Eds.), *Systematic interviewing: Communication skills for professional effectiveness* (pp. 90–113). Columbus, OH: Charles E. Merrill.

Hughes, J. N. (1988). *Cognitive behavior therapy with children in schools.* New York: Pergamon Press.

Hughes, J. N. (1989). Child interviewing. *School Psychology Review, 18,* 247–259.

Hughes, J. N., & Hall, R. J. (1987). A proposed model for the assessment of children's social competence. *Professional School Psychology, 2,* 247–260.

Hughes, J. N., & Hall, R. J. (Eds.) (1989). *Cognitive–behavioral psychology in the schools.* New York: Guilford Press.

Irwin, E. C. (1983). The diagnostic and therapeutic use of pretend play. In C. Schaefer & K. O'Connor (Eds.), *Handbook of play therapy* (pp. 148–173). New York: Wiley.

Iwanaga, M. (1973). Development of interpersonal play structure in three-, four-, and five-year old children. *Journal of Research and Development Education, 6,* 71–82.

Johnson, M. K., & Foley, M. A. (1984). Differentiating fact from fantasy: The reliability of children's memory. *Journal of Social Issues, 40*(2), 33–50.

Kagan, J. (1966). Reflection–impulsivity: The generality and dynamics of conceptual tempo. *Journal of Abnormal Psychology, 71,* 17–24.

Kail, R. (1984). *The development of memory in children* (2nd ed.). San Francisco: W. H. Freeman.

Kanfer, F. H., & Grimm, L. G. (1977). Behavioral analysis: Selecting target behavior in the interview. *Behavior Modification, 1,* 7–28.

Kanfer, F. H., & Saslow, G. (1969). Behavioral diagnosis. In C. M. Franks (Ed.), *Behavior therapy: Appraisal and status.* New York: McGraw-Hill.

Kaslow, N. J., Rehm, L. P., & Siegel, A. W. (1984). Social-cognitive and cognitive correlates of depression in children. *Journal of Abnormal Child Psychology, 12,* 605–620.

Kazdin, A. E. (1987). Assessment of childhood depression: Current issues and strategies. *Behavioral Assessment, 9,* 291–319.

Kazdin, A. E. (1988). Childhood depression. In E. J. Mash & L. G. Terdal (Eds.), *Behavioral assessment of childhood disorders* (2nd ed., pp. 157–195). New York: Guilford Press.

Kazdin, A. E. (1989). Developmental psychopathology: Current research, issues, and directions. *American Psychologist, 44,* 180–187.

References

219

Kazdin, A. E., Esveldt-Dawson, K., Sherick, R. B., & Colbus, D. (1985). Assessment of overt behavior and childhood depression among psychiatrically disturbed children. *Journal of Consulting and Clinical Psychology, 53*, 201–210.

King, M. A., & Yuille, J. C. (1987). Suggestibility and the child witness. In S. J. Ceci, M. P. Toglia, & D. F. Ross (Eds.), *Children's eyewitness memory* (pp. 24–35). New York: Springer-Verlag.

Kirigin, K. A., Braukmann, C. J., Atwater, J. D., & Wolf, M. M. (1982). An evaluation of teaching-family (Achievement Place) group homes for juvenile offenders. *Journal of Applied Behavior Analysis, 15*, 1–16.

Kistner, J. A., & Torgesen, J. K. (1987). Motivational and cognitive aspects of learning disabilities. In B. B. Lahey & A. E. Kazdin (Eds.), *Advances in clinical child psychology* (Vol. 10, pp. 289–333). New York: Plenum.

Klein, M. (1948). The psychological principles of infant analysis. In E. Jones (Ed.), *Contributions to psychoanalysis* (pp. 140–151). London: Hogarth Press. (Original work published 1926)

Korchin, S. J., & Schuldberg, D. (1981). The future of clinical assessment. *American Psychologist, 36*, 1147–1158.

Kovacs, M. (1983). *The Interview Schedule for Children.* Unpulished manuscript, University of Pittsburgh School of Medicine.

Kovacs, M. (1985). The Interview Schedule for Children (ISC). *Psychopharmacology Bulletin, 21*, 991–994.

Kovacs, M., & Beck, A. T. (1977). An empirical–clinical approach toward a definition of childhood depression. In J. G. Shulterlmondt & A. Raskin (Eds.), *Depression in childhood: Diagnosis, treatment, and conceptual models* (pp. 1–25). New York: Raven Press.

Kovacs, M., Feinberg, T. L., Crouse-Novak, M. A., Paulauskas, S. L., & Feinstein, R. (1984). Depressive disorders in childhood: I. A longitudinal prospective study of characteristics and recovery. *Archives of General Psychiatry, 41*, 229–237.

Kovacs, M., & Paulauskas, S. (1986). The traditional psychotherapies. In H. C. Quay & J. S. Werry (Eds.), *Psychopathological disorders of childhood* (pp. 496–522). New York: Wiley.

Krall, V. (1986). Projective play techniques. In A. I. Rabin (Ed.), *Projective techniques for adolescents and children* (pp. 264–278). New York: Springer.

Labov, W. (1972). Some principles of linguistic methodology. *Language in society, 1,*(1) 97–120.

Ladd, G. W., & Oden, S. (1979). The relationship between peer acceptance and children's ideas about helpfulness. *Child Development, 50*, 402–408.

Lafferty, P., Beutler, L. E., & Crago, M. (1989). Differences between more and less effective psychotherapists: A study of select therapist variables. *Journal of Consulting and Clinical Psychology, 57*, 76–80.

LaGreca, A. M., Dandes, S. K., Wick, P., Shaw, K., & Stone, W. L. (1988). Development of the Social Anxiety Scale for Children: Reliability and concurrent validity. *Journal of Clinical Child Psychology, 17*, 84–91.

Lahey, B. B., Schaughency, E. A., Strauss, C. C., & Frame, C. L. (1984). Are attention deficit disorders with and without hyperactivity similiar or dissimiliar disorders? *Journal of the American Academy of Child Psychiatry, 23*, 302–309.

Larrance, D. T., & Twentyman, C. t. (1983). Maternal attributions and child abuse. *Journal of Abnormal Psychology, 92*, 449–457.

Lazarus, A. A. (Ed.). (1976). *Multi-modal behavior therapy.* New York: Springer.

Leitenberg, H., Yost, L. W., & Carroll-Wilson, M. (1986). Negative cognitive errors in children: Questionnaire development, normative data, and comparisons between children with and without self-reported symptoms of depression, low self-esteem, and evaluation anxiety. *Journal of Consulting and Clinical Psychology, 54*, 528–536.

Lerrick, M. F. (1983). *They could not talk and so they drew.* Springfield, IL: Charles C Thomas.

Levy, S. (1980). Human figure drawing. In E. F. Hammer (Ed.), *The clinical application of projective drawings* (pp. 81–112). Springfield, IL: Charles C Thomas.

Lewis, C. (1985). *Listening to children.* New York: Jason Aronson.

Lindfors, J. W. (1987). *Children's language and learning* (2nd ed.). Englewood Cliffs, NJ: Prentice-Hall.

List, J. A. (1986). Age and schematic differences in the reliability of eyewitness testimony. *Developmental Psychology, 22*(1), 50–57.

Livesley, W. J., & Bromley, D. B. (1973). *Person perception in childhood and adolescence.* Chichester, England: Wiley.

Lochman, J. E., & Lampron, L. B. (1986). Situational social problem-solving skills and self-esteem of aggressive and nonaggressive boys. *Journal of Abnormal Child Psychology, 14*, 605–617.

Loney, J., & Milich, R. (1981). Hyperactivity, inattention, and aggression in clinical practice. In M. Wolraich & D. K. Routh (Eds.), *Advances in behavioral pediatrics* (Vol. 2). Greenwich, CT: JAI Press.

Looff, D. H. (1976). *Getting to know the troubled child.* Knoxville: University of Tennessee Press.

Lowenfeld, M. (1970). *The Lowenfeld technique.* Oxford, England: Pergamon Press.

Mahler, M. S., Pine, F., & Bergman, A. (1975). *The psychological birth of the human infant.* New York: Basic Books.

Mahoney, M. J. (1974). *Cognition and behavior modification,* Cambridge, MA: Ballinger.

Main, M., & Goldwyn, R. (1984). Predicting rejection of her infant from mother's representation of her own experience: Implications for the abused–abusing intergenerational cycle. *Child Abuse and Neglect, 8*, 203–217.

Markman, E. M. (1977). Realizing that you don't understand: A preliminary investigation. *Child Development, 48*, 986–992.

Martin, R. P. (1988). *Assessment of personality and behavior problems: Infancy through adolescence.* New York: Guilford Press.

Mash, E. J., & Johnston, C. (1982). Parental perceptions of child behavior problems, parenting self-esteem, and mothers' reported stress in younger and older hyperactive and normal children. *Journal of Consulting and Clinical Psychology, 51*, 68–99.

Mash, E. J., & Johnston, C. (1983). Sibling interactions of hyperactive and normal children and their relationships to reports of maternal stress and self-esteem. *Journal of Clinical Child Psychology, 12*, 91–99.

Mash, E. J., & Terdal, L. G. (1988). Behavioral assessment of child and family disturbance. In E. J. Mash & L. G. Terdal (Eds.), *Behavioral assessment of childhood disorders* (2nd ed., pp. 3–65). New York: Guilford Press.

Matas, L., Arend, R., & Sroufe, L. A. (1978). Continuity of adaptation in the second year: The relationship between quality of attachment and later competence. *Child Development, 49*, 547–556.

McCune-Nicolich, L. (1981). Toward symbolic functioning: Structure of early pretend games and potential parallels with language. *Child Development, 52*, 386–388.

McGarrigle, J., & Donaldson, M. (1974). Conservation accidents. *Cognitions, 3*, 341–350.

McGee, R., Williams, S., & Silva, P. A. (1984). Background characteristics of aggressive, hyperactive boys. *Journal of the American Academy of Child Psychiatry, 23*, 280–284.

McMahon, R. J., & Forehand, R. (1983). Consumer satisfaction in behavioral treatment of children: Types, issues, and recommendations. *Behavior Therapy, 14*, 209–225.

McMahon, R. J., & Forehand, R. (1988). Conduct disorders. In E. J. Mash & L. G. Terdal (Eds.), *Behavioral assessment of childhood disorders* (2nd ed., pp. 105–156). New York: Guilford Press.

McNamee, G. D. (1989). Language development. In J. Garbarino, F. M. Stott, & Faculty of the Erikson Institute (Eds.), *What children can tell us* (pp. 67–391). San Francisco: Jossey-Bass.

Melton, G., & Thompson, R. (1987). Getting out of a rut: Detours to less traveled paths in child witness research. In S. J. Ceci, M. P. Toglia, & D. F. Ross (Eds.), *Children's eyewitness memory* (pp. 209–229). New York: Springer-Verlag.

Meyer, N. E., Dyck, D. G., & Petrinack, R. J. (1989). Cognitive appraisal and attributional correlates of depressive symptoms in children. *Journal of Abnormal Child Psychology, 17*, 325–335.

Meyer, V., & Turkat, I. D. (1979). Behavioral analysis of clinical cases. *Journal of Behavioral Assessment, 1*, 259–270.

Milich, R., & Dodge, K. A. (1984). Social information processing in the child psychiatric populations. *Journal of Abnormal Child Psychology, 12*, 471—490.

Minuchin, S. (1974). *Families and family therapy*. Cambridge, MA: Harvard University Press.

Minuchin, S., Rosman, B., & Baker, L. (1978). *Psychosomatic families*. Cambridge, MA: Harvard University Press.

Morgan, C. D., & Murray, H. A. (1935). A method for investigating fantasies: The Thematic Apperception Test. *Archives of Neurology and Psychiatry, 34*, 289–306.

Mossler, D. G., Marvin, R. S., & Greenberg, M. T. (1976). Conceptual perspective taking in 2- to 6-year-old children. *Developmental Psychology, 12*, 85–86.

Murstein, B. I. (1963). *Theory and research in projective techniques*. New York: Wiley.

Nelson, R. O., & Hayes, S. C. (1981). Nature of behavioral assessment. In M. Hersen & A. Bellack (Eds.), *Behavioral assessment: A practical handbook* (2nd ed., pp. 3–37). New York: Pergamon Press.

Nordquist, V. M. (1971). The modification of a child's enuresis: Some response–response relationships. *Journal of Applied Behavior Analysis, 4*, 241–247.

O'Connor, K. J. (1983). The color-your-life technique. In C. E. Schaefer & K. J. O'Connor (Eds.), *Handbook of play therapy* (pp. 251–258). New York: Wiley.

O'Leary, K. D., & Johnson, S. B. (1986). Assessment and assessment of change. In H. C. Quay & J. S. Werry (Eds.), *Psychopathological disorders of childhood* (3rd ed. pp. 423–454). New York: Wiley.

Orvaschel, H. (1985). Psychiatric interviews suitable for use in research with children and adolescents. *Psychopharmacology Bulletin, 21*, 737–746.

Orvaschel, H. (1989). Diagnostic interviews for children and adolescents. In C. F. Last & M. Hersen (Eds.), *Handbook of child psychiatric diagnosis* (pp. 483–495). New York: Wiley.

Orvaschel, H., & Puig-Antich, J. (1987). *Schedule for Affective Disorder and Schizophrenia for School-age Children: Epidemiologic version*. Pittsburgh: Western Psychiatric Institute and Clinic.

Orvaschel, H., Puig-Antich, J., Chambers, W., Tabrizi, M. A., & Johnson, R. (1982). Retrospective assessment of prepubertal major depression with the Kiddie-SADS-E. *Journal of the American Academy of Child Psychiatry, 21*, 392–397.

Paget, K. D. (1984). The structured assessment interview: A psychometric review. *Journal of School Psychology, 23*, 415–427.

Paley, V. G. (1981). *Wallip stories*. Cambridge, MA: Harvard University Press.

Palmer, D. J., & Rholes, W. S. (1989). Conceptual and methodological issues in the assessment of children's attributions. In J. N. Hughes & R. J. Hall (Eds.), *Cognitive–behavioral psychology in the schools* (pp. 166–205). New York: Guilford Press.

Parker, W. C. (1984). Interviewing children: Problems and promise. *Journal of Negro Education, 53,* 18–28.

Patterson, G. R. (1980). Mothers: The unacknowledged victims. *Monographs of the Society for Research in Child Development, 45,* (5, Whole No. 186).

Patterson, G. R., (1982). *Coercive family process.* Eugene, OR: Castalia.

Patterson, G. R., & Bank, L. (1986). Bootstrapping your way in the nomological thicket. *Behavioral Assessment, 8,* 49–73.

Patterson, G. R., DeBaryshe, B. D., & Ramsey, E. (1989). A developmental perspective on antisocial behavior. *American Psychologist, 44,* 329–335.

Patterson, G. R., Dishion, T. J., & Bank, L. (1984). Family interaction: A process model of deviancy training. *Aggressive Behavior, 10,* 253–267.

Patterson, G. R., & Stouthamer-Loeber, M. (1984). The correlation of family management practices and delinquency, *Child Development, 55,* 1299–1307.

Pearl, R., Bryan, T., & Donahue, M. (1980). Learning disabled children's attributions for successful and failure learning. *Learning Disability Quarterly, 3*(1), 3–9.

Perlmutter, M., & Lange, G. (1978). Development of recall–recognition distinctions. In P. A. Ornstein (Ed.), *Memory development in children* (pp. 243–258). Hillsdale, NJ: Erlbaum.

Perry, P. G., Perry, L. C., & Rasmussen, P. (1986). Cognitive social learning mediators of aggression. *Child Development, 57,* 700–711.

Piaget, J. (1954). *The construction of reality in the child.* New York: Basic Books.

Piaget, J. (1962). *Play, dreams and imitation in childhood.* New York: W.W. Norton.

Piaget, J., & Inhelder, B. (1969). *The psychology of the child.* New York: Basic Books.

Piers, M. (1989). Foreword. In J. Garbarino, F. M. Stott, & Faculty of the Erikson Institute (Eds.), *What children can tell us* (pp. xi–xxi). San Francisco: Jossey-Bass.

Poznanski, E. O., Grossman, J. A., Buchsbaum, Y., Banegas, M., Freeman, L., & Gibbons, R. (1984). Preliminary studies on the reliability and validity of the Children's Depression Rating Scale. *Journal of Child Psychiatry, 23,*191–197.

Prout, H. T., & Ferber, S. M. (1988). Analogue assessment: Traditional personality assessment measures in behavioral assessment. In E. S. Shapiro & T. R. Kratochwill (Eds.), *Behavioral assessment in schools: Conceptual foundations and practical applications* (pp. 322–350). New York: Guilford Press.

Puig-Antich, J., & Chambers, W. (1978). *The Schedule for Affective Disorders and Schizophrenia for School-Age Children (Kiddie-SADS).* New York: New York State Psychiatric Association.

Puig-Antich, J., Chambers, W., Halpern, F., Hanlon, C., & Sacher, E. J. (1979). Cortisol hypersecretion in prepubertal depressive illness: A preliminary study. *Psychoneuroendocrinology, 4,* 191–197.

Quay, H. C. (1983). A dimensional approach to behavior disorder: The Revised Behavior Problem Checklist. *School Psychology Review, 12,* 244–249.

Quay, H. C. (1986a). A critical analyses of DSM-III as a taxonomy of psychopathology in children and adolescents. In T. Mullon & G. Klermon (Eds.), *Contemporary directions in psychopathology* (pp. 151–165). New York: Guilford.

Quay, H. C. (1986). Classification. In H. C. Quay & J. S. Werry (Eds.), *Psychopathological disorders of childhood* (3rd ed., pp. 1–34). New York: Wiley.

Quay, H. C., & LaGreca, A. M. (1986). Disorders of anxiety, withdrawal, and dysphoria. In H. C. Quay & J. S. Werry (Eds.), *Psychopathological disorders of childhood* (pp. 73–110). New York: Wiley.

Quay, H. C., & Peterson, D. R. (1983). *Interim manual for the Revised Behavior Problem Checklist.* Unpublished manuscript, University of Miami.

Reich, W., & Welner, Z. (1989). *Diagnostic Interview for Children and Adolescents—Revised.* St. Louis: Washington University, Division of Child Psychiatry.

Reich, W., Herjanic, B., Welner, Z., & Gandhy, P. R. (1982). Development of a structured psychiatric interview for children: Agreement on diagnosis comparing parent and child. *Journal of Abnormal Child Psychology, 10*, 325–336.

Renshaw, P., & Asher, S. R. (1982). Social competence and peer status: The distinction between goals and strategies. In K. Rubin & H. Ross (Eds.), *Peer relationships and social skills in childhood* (pp. 375—396). New York: Springer-Verlag.

Renshaw, P. D., & Asher, S. R. (1983). Children's goals and strategies for social interaction. *Merrill-Palmer Quarterly, 29*, 353–374.

Rholes, W.S., & Ruble, D. M. (1984). Children's understanding of dispositional characteristics of others. *Child Development, 55*, 550–560.

Richard, B. A., & Dodge, K. A. (1982). Social maladjustment and problem-solving in school-aged children. *Journal of Consulting and Clinical Psychology, 50*, 226–233.

Robin, A. L., & Foster, S. (1989). *Negotiating parent–adolescent conflict*. New York: Guilford Press.

Robins, L., Helzer, J. E., Croughan, J., & Radcliff, K. S. (1981). National Institute of Mental Health Diagnostic Interview Schedule: Its history, characteristics, and validity. *Archives of General Psychiatry, 38*, 381–389.

Robinson, M. S. (1990). *Aggressive/Rejected and Cooperative/Accepted Children's Attributions for prosocial behaviors*. Unpublished dissertation, Texas A&M University, College Station, Texas.

Roff, M., Sells, S. B., & Golden, M. M. (1972). *Social adjustment and personality development in children*. Minneapolis: University of Minnesota Press.

Rose, S. A., & Blank, M. (1974). The potency of context in children's cognition: An illustration through conservation. *Child Development, 45*, 499–502.

Rutter, M., & Graham, P. (1968). The reliability and validity of the psychiatric assessment of the child: Interview with the child. *British Journal of Psychiatry, 11*, 563–579.

Saltz, E., & Medow, M. L. (1971). Concept conservation in children: The dependence of belief systems on semantic representation. *Child Development, 42*, 1533–1542.

Saltz, E., Dumin-Markiewicz, A., & Rourke, D. (1975). The development of natural language concepts: II. Developmental changes in attribute structure. *Child Development, 46*, 913–921.

Sarnoff, C. (1976). *Latency*. New York: Jason Aronson.

Saywitz, K. J. (1987). Children's testimony: Age-related patterns of memory errors. In S. J. Ceci, M. P. Toglia, & D. F. Ross (Eds.), *Children's eyewitness memory* (pp. 36–52). New York: Springer-Verlag.

Schwartz, A. R., & Schwanenflugel, P. J. (1989). Eyewitness testimony of children and the school psychologist. *School Psychology Review, 18*, 235–246.

Seligman, M. E. P. (1975). *Helplessness: On depression, development and death*. San Francisco: W. H. Freeman.

Seligman, M. E. P., Kaslow, N. J., Alloy, L. B., Peterson, C., Tannenbaum, R. L., & Abramson, L. Y. (1984). Attributional style and depressive symptoms in children. *Journal of Abnormal Psychology, 93*, 235–238.

Selman, R. L. (1976). Toward a structural analysis of developing interpersonal relations concepts: Research with normal and disturbed preadolescent boys. In A. D. Dick (Ed.), *Minnesota Symposium on Child Psychology* (Vol. 10, pp. 156–200). Minneapolis: University of Minnesota.

Selman, R. L. (1980). *The growth of interpersonal understanding: Developmental and clinical analyses*. New York: Academic Press.

Selman, R. L., Jacquette, D., & Bruss-Saunders, E. (1979). *Assessing interpersonal understanding: An interview and scoring manual*. Cambridge, MA: Harvard–Judge Baker Social Reasoning Project.

Shantz, C. U. (1983). Social cognition. In J. H. Flavell & E. M. Markman (Vol. Eds.),

Handbook of child psychology (4th ed.): Vol. 3. Cognitive development (pp. 495–555). New York: Wiley.

Shatz, M., & Gelman, R. (1973). The development of communication skills: Modifications in the speech of young children as a function of listener. *Monographs of the Society for Research in Child Development, 38*,(5, Serial No. 152).

Shure, M. B., & Spivack, G. (1972). Means–ends thinking, adjustment and social class among elementary school–age children. *Journal of Consulting and Clinical Psychology, 38*, 348–353.

Sjolund, M. (1981). Play-diagnosis and therapy in Sweden: The Erica method. *Journal of Clinical Psychology, 37*, 322–325.

Spanier, G. B. (1976). Measuring dyadic adjustment: New scales for assessing marriage and similar dyads. *Journal of Marriage and the Family, 38*, 15–28.

Spiegel, S. (1989). *An interpersonal approach to child therapy.* New York: Columbia University Press.

Spivack, G., Platt, J. J., & Shure, M. B. (1976). *The problem solving approach to adjustment.* San Francisco: Jossey-Bass.

Steinberg, M. D., & Dodge, K. A. (1983). Attributional bias in aggressive adolescent boys and girls. *Journal of Social and Clinical Psychology, 1*, 312–321.

Stott, F. M. (1989). Self-esteem and coping. In J. Garbarino, F. M. Stott, & Faculty of the Erikson Institute (Eds.), *What children can tell us* (pp. 18–39). San Francisco: Jossey-Bass.

Strauss, C., Forehand, R., Frame, C., & Smith, K. (1984). Characteristics of children with extreme scores on the Children's Depression Inventory. *Journal of Clinical Child Psychology, 13*, 227–231.

Stuart, R. B. (1970). *Trick or treatment: How or when psychotherapy fails.* Champaign, IL: Research Press.

Taylor, H. G. (1988). Learning disabilities. In E. J. Mash & L. G. Terdal (Eds.), *Behavioral assessment of childhood disorders* (2nd ed., pp. 402–450). New York: Guilford Press.

Todd, C. M., & Perlmutter, M. (1980). Reality recalled by preschool children. In M. Perlmutter (Ed.), *New directions in child development: Vol. 10. Children's memory* (pp. 69–85). San Francisco: Jossey-Bass.

Trad, P. V. (1989). *The preschool child: Assessment, diagnosis, and treatment.* New York: Wiley.

Tuma, J. M., & Sobotka, K. R. (1983). Traditional therapies with children. In T. H. Ollendick & M. Hersen (Eds.), *Handbook of child psychopathology* (pp. 391–426). New York: Plenum Press.

Turco, T. L., Elliott, S. M., & Witt, J. C. (1985). Children's involvement in treatment selection: A review of theory and analogue research on treatment acceptability. In S. Braaten, R. B. Rutherfor, & W. Evans (Eds.), *Programming for adolescents with behavior disorders* (pp. 54–62). Reston, VA: Council for Exceptional Children.

Turkat, I. D. (1986). The behavioral interview. In A. R. Ciminero, K. S. Calhoun, & H. E. Adams (Eds.), *Handbook of behavioral assessment* (pp. 109–149). New York: Wiley.

Turner, S. M., Beidel, D. C., & Costello, A. (1987). Psychopathology in the offspring of anxiety disorder patients. *Journal of Consulting and Clinical Psychology, 55*, 229–235.

Verhulst, F. C., Althaus, M., & Berden, G. (1987). The Child Assessment Schedule: Parent–child agreement and validity measures. *Journal of Child Psychology and Psychiatry, 28*, 455–466.

Victor, J. B., Halverson, C. F., & Wampler, K. S. (1988). Family–school context: Parent and teacher agreement on child temperament. *Journal of Consulting and Clinical Psychology, 56*, 573–577.

Vukovich, D. H. (1983). The use of projective assessment by school psychologists. *School Psychology Review, 12*, 358–364.

Wahler, R. G., & Cormier, W. H. (1970). The ecological interview: A first step in outpatient child behavior therapy. *Journal of Behavior Therapy and Experimental Psychiatry, 1,* 279–289.

Walem, S. R., DiGuiseppe, D. R., & Wessler, R. L. (1980). *A practitioner's guide to rational–emotive therapy.* New York: Oxford University Press.

Walker, N. (1957). *A short history of psychotherapy in theory and practice.* London: Routledge & Kegan Paul.

Waters, E., Wippman, J., & Sroufe, L. A. (1979). Attachment, positive affect and competence in the peer group: Two studies in construct validation. *Child Development, 50,* 821–829.

Waters, V. (1982). Therapies for children: Rational-emotive therapy. In. C. R. Reynolds & T. B. Gutkin (Eds.), *Handbook of school psychology* (pp. 570–579). New York: Wiley.

Watlington, D. K. (1990). *Abusive and nonabusive mothers' attributions for children's provocations.* Unpublished doctoral dissertation, Texas A&M University, College Station.

Webster-Stratton, C. (1984). Randomized trial of two parent-training programs for families with conduct-disordered children. *Journal of Consulting and Clinical Psychology, 52,* 666–678.

Webster-Stratton, C. (1985). Comparisons of behavior transactions between conduct-disordered children and their mothers in the clinic and at home. *Journal of Abnormal Child Psychology, 13,* 169–184.

Wechsler, D. (1974). *Manual: Wechsler Intelligence Scale for Children–Revised.* New York: Psychological Corporation.

Welner, Z., Reich, W., Herjanic, B., Jung, K. G., & Amado, H. (1987). Reliability, validity, and parent–child agreement studies of the Diagnostic Interview for Children and Adolescents (DICA). *Journal of the American Academy of Child and Adolescent Psychiatry, 26,* 649–653.

Wiens, A. M. (1983). The assessment interview. In J. B. Weiner (Ed.), *Clinical methods in psychology* (pp. 3–57). New York: Wiley.

Winnicott, D. W. (1965). Transitional objects and transitional phenomena. In *Collected papers: Through pediatrics to psychoanalysis* (pp. 229–242). New York: Basic Books. (Original work published 1951)

Witt, J. C., Cavell, T. A., Heffer, R. W., Carey, M. P., & Martens, B. K. (1988). Child self-report: Interviewing techniques and rating scales. In E. S. Shapiro & R. R. Kratochwill (Eds.), *Behavioral assessment in schools: Conceptual foundations and practical applications* (pp. 384–454). New York: Guilford Press.

Witt, J. C., & Elliott, S. M. (1983). Assessment in behavioral consultation: The initial interview. *School Psychology Review, 12,* 42–49.

Wolfe, D. A. (1988). Child abuse and neglect. In E. J. Mash & L. G. Terdal (Eds.), *Behavioral assessment of childhood disorders* (2nd ed., pp. 627–669). New York: Guilford Press.

Wood, D. J., MacMahon, L., & Cranstoun, Y. (1980). *Working with under fives.* Ypsilanti, MI: High/Scope.

Wood, H., & Wood, D. (1983). Questioning the pre-school child. *Educational Review, 35,* 149–162.

Worchel, F., Copeland, D., & Barker, D. (1987). Control related coping strategies in pediatric oncology patients. *Journal of Pediatric Psychology, 12*(1), 25–38.

Worchel, F. F., Hughes, J. N., Hall, B. M., Stanton, S. B., Stanton, H., & Little, V. Z. (1990). Evaluation of subclinical depression in children using self-, peer-, and teacher-report measures. *Journal of Abnormal Child Psychology, 18,* 271–282.

Wursten, H. (1960). Story completions: Madeleine Thomas stories and similar methods. In A. I. Rabin & M. Haworth (Eds.), *Projective techniques with children* (pp. 192–209). New York: Grune & Stratton.

Yarrow, L. J. (1960). Interviewing children. In P. J. Mussen (Ed.), *Handbook of research methods in child development* (pp. 561–602). New York: Wiley.

Zatz, S. L., & Chassin, L. (1983). Cognitions of test anxious children. *Journal of Consulting and Clinical Psychology, 51*, 526–534.

Zata, S. L., & Chassin, L. (1985). Cognitions of test-anxious children under naturalistic test-taking conditions. *Journal of Consulting and Clinical Psychology, 53*, 393–401.

Index